Becoming Canonical in American Poetry

Becoming Canonical in American Poetry

Timothy Morris

University of Illinois Press
Urbana and Chicago

© 1995 by the Board of Trustees of the University of Illinois
Manufactured in the United States of America
1 2 3 4 5 C P 5 4 3 2 1

This book is printed on acid-free paper.

Library of Congress Cataloging-in-Publication Data

Morris, Timothy, 1959–
    Becoming canonical in American poetry / Timothy Morris.
        p.   cm.
    Includes bibliographical references and index.
    ISBN 0-252-02136-3 (alk. paper). — ISBN 0-252-06428-3 (pbk. :
alk. paper)
    1. American poetry—History and criticism—Theory, etc.
2. Criticism—United States—History. 3. Canon (Literature)
I. Title.
PS303.M65   1995
811.009—dc20   94-12411
                                                                    CIP

For
Fran

Contents

Preface: The Detection and Invention of "Unsuspected Literatures"

Literary value seems to be hopelessly out of date as a useful concept. Studies of the tendentiousness of the value judgments that have contributed to canon formation, starting with Jane Tompkins's essay on Hawthorne's reputation in *Sensational Designs* (1985), have shown how false is the old assurance that years of objective evaluation have produced a canon of the undeniably "best" literary works.[1] Value can now be seen as an artifact of the cultural and material productions that surround a work's production and reception. To think of a literary work as possessing value in any intrinsic sense is now an old-fashioned and even repressive notion. There are good practical reasons for seeing value as a repressive notion, too; as feminist, Marxist, and multicultural critics have increasingly exposed the artifactual nature of value judgments, conservative and reactionary critics have invoked the self-evident—indeed, self-referential—nature of received notions of value to shore up the traditional canon.[2] Value in conservative discourse has become an almost mystic, unanswerable quality with which to berate the inroads made by writers of every minority upon the white, male, Western legacy to culture.

But the "exile of evaluation" predates 1980s reevaluations of the American literary canon; as Barbara Herrnstein Smith shows in *Contingencies of Value* (1988), central figures in the New Criticism, like W. K. Wimsatt and Northrop Frye, worked to expunge evaluation from literary criticism—where other figures just as influential in and on New Criticism, like I. A. Richards, had given evaluation a crucial role.[3] (It is a mistake to think of the white, male, Western legacy as some kind of self-consistent dogma.) Smith, noting that "the entire problematic of value and evaluation has been evaded and explicitly exiled by the literary academy," calls for study that would "clarify the nature of literary—and, more broadly, aesthetic—value in conjunction with a more general rethinking of the concept of 'value.'"[4]

The present study is a fairly concrete part of Smith's project for reconsidering evaluation; it does not range widely into the theory or history of aesthetics, but instead seeks to understand some of the local conditions of evaluation as it has been a factor in the project of American literary nationalism and its descendant, the academic discipline of American literature. In so doing, I clarify some of the issues and potentials of evaluation in that discipline at the present moment (the mid-1990s).

It is all the more important to consider the history and dynamics of evaluation now, because the reconstructions of American literary study in the past two decades have by no means effected a complete or clear break with the received canon and the motives for its assembly. The expanded canon is an accommodating thing. Expanders of the canon have had good reason to preserve the canonical place of many writers who are part of the received tradition—often by enlisting those writers as advocates of the ideology of pluralism itself.[5] Such enlistment helps justify the revision of the canon by smoothing the rupture with the past and continuing to confirm the preferences of senior scholars. If there is an opposition between the canons and the politics of American literary studies of the 1960s and the 1980s—and institutional critics like Peter Carafiol might argue that the break is neither sharp nor substantive— we are faced in the 1990s with a curious situation in which our revisionist canons include texts and writers that the sixties had adopted, received, and preserved for opposite reasons.[6]

The process of canon formation that resulted in the consensus or "received" tradition of *American Renaissance*, Major American Writers, and the American Literature Section of the MLA (itself hardly as monolithic a process as it might appear in retrospect) made use of the concept of value at every turn. The rhetoric of literary value that critics used to employ in American literary studies may now seem like the rhetoric of congressional speeches—meant not to persuade but to confirm and advertise judgments already made for quite other reasons than the rhetorical force and the logic of the speeches themselves. Yet one should perhaps not be so quick to dismiss an ancient tradition of value judgment as purely "empty" rhetoric. Rhetoric that constitutes a justification for preferences becomes in turn constitutive of a sort of aesthetic reality. When critics make value judgments, we should take those judgments—on their own terms, at least—at face value. No other kinds of judgment, for many years, were current in the critical marketplace.

Standards of literary value do not adjust quickly to new texts or new scholarly methodologies. In fact, literary values remain remarkably stable over long periods of time in American literary studies. As I will argue in this study, many of the central reasons for valuing poetry that were in use in the 1810s continue to convince critics today. If one sees literary history—narrowly defined as the evolution of texts in the primary literary genres—as a continually changing process, one must also acknowledge that the corresponding history of literary value judgments is a remarkably stable frame for that literary history. In turn, the standards of literary judgment based on value are at least partly constitutive of literary history, since writers produce texts in preemptive response to those standards of judgment. This mutual interaction between literary history and literary criticism then dictates the subject matter of what Roman Jakobson called "literary studies," the broad academic project of interpreting, contextualizing, and theorizing texts that have essentially been pre-chosen and may now be objects for work without continuing anxiety over their suitability for that work.[7]

In such a dynamic, all positive value judgments, even those widely separated by historical and material circumstances, come to be pretty much alike. The very concept of an American poetic tradition took shape around a nucleus of critical values that drew texts and critiques to itself, values of originality, organicism, and monologic language, which I group here as the poetics of presence. "Presence" in the sense in which I use it here means the belief that a work of art conveys the living presence of the artist, and the implied value that a work is better as the artist is more present in it. The poetics of presence is a matrix for the reception of literary works and for their production as well. This poetics dominated the criticism of American literature in its earliest beginnings and continues to be a central assumption for many critics today.

The poetics of presence, by valuing those texts that most directly and immediately present the writer as a living voice, came to be a guarantee of the nationalism of canonical texts: an American writer sufficiently present in a work would automatically deliver the greatest amount of Americanism in that work. The values of the poetics of presence were forged in the first period of American literary nationalism, the early republican years at and just after the turn of the nineteenth century. But their greatest exemplar was Walt Whitman, much later in the century. Whitman inherited and internalized the values of presence and wrote texts that epitomized those values.

A thorough study of the reception of Walt Whitman would take many volumes; I confine myself here to noting some of the main themes in what I call the "prereception" of Whitman—many of which were established even before he was born—and then noting the persistence of those themes both in early Whitman criticism and in the decisive period for the canonization of Whitman early in the twentieth century. Whitman became the great standard case in the development of the American poetic canon. For most academic critics of the mid-twentieth century, Whitman—or by that time, the reading of Whitman as a fully "present" poet—was the most extreme example of the positive values of American writing. In turn, post-Whitmanic poets were valued as they embodied the Whitmanic values. Any poet to be valued would be valued for the poetics of presence, and any poet to be dismissed would be dismissed because of any number of violations of those standards.

Positive value judgments come to be monotonously alike because a text positively valued will be read as having the same features as other great texts. But negative value judgments may be made for a wide range of transgressions of those central values. Because positive reviews tend in themselves to be monologic, the dialogic contrast offered by negative criticism is often far more detailed and far more peculiarly informative than the main line of reception that promotes a writer's or a text's canonization. One can often learn more about the features and qualities of a text by reading negative opinion than one can by reading positive opinion. And given the historical persistence of the values of presence, one can also learn more about the specific local values of groups of critics from a given historical period by considering the unfocused negative characterizations those critics produced. Chronicles of reception, particularly those offered in collections of the critical heritage surrounding major authors, are geared toward describing the steps by which the major authors entered the canon (and thereby achieved a certain degree of immunity from objections). But the various alternative, rejected routes *away* from the canon that are proposed in the history of "minority reports" to that critical heritage are one of the most illuminating parts of the history of critical discourse.

The idea of minority reports recalls the fact that the assembly of the canon is almost necessarily a majority business. Those minority writers who are represented are included for the majority's reasons, often with the disclaimer that, while they are minority writers, their themes are somehow "universal."[8] In any case, minority writers are a very small part of the received canon; until the mid-1970s, most of the standard American literature anthologies included no black, Hispanic, or native writers at all. Nor, until the mid-1970s, did those anthologies include many women.[9] The few women who did achieve canonical status during the mid-twentieth century, therefore, make a particularly revealing study of the critical tendencies of the largely male group that chose them for study.

Of all American women poets, Emily Dickinson is the most indisputably canonical. But it remains an anomaly that she achieved this status at all, let alone as early and as firmly as she did. Unlike any other woman writer of the United States, her canonicity has been unassailable from the beginnings of the discipline of American literature. The very first volume of *American Literature* (1929) includes an essay by Anna Mary Wells on the early reception of Dickinson; specialized scholarship on Dickinson flourished at the start of the specialized definition of the Americanist discipline. Of the thirty-nine authors in the three great series of bibliographical essays in the discipline (*Eight American Authors, 16 Modern American Authors, 15 American Authors before 1900*), Dickinson is one of only two women represented; the other is Willa Cather, whose degree of acceptance has fluctuated quite a bit during the century.[10] Clearly, there was no attempt to include Dickinson in the developing American canon *because* she was a woman or spoke to women's concerns. In fact, male critics overcame their considerable prejudice against her gender to promote her to a status as unchallenged as Mark Twain's.

Dickinson's early critics rearranged the terms of their prejudice rather than radically revising it. Critics of the early twentieth century undoubtedly heard Dickinson's voice as feminine. But they heard it as a voyeur (an *auditeur?*) might hear it: not as the distinctive idiom of a particular Victorian woman, but as the secret, unrepressed voice of Everywoman—a voice that was largely the creation of their own fantasies. In the cultural milieu created by the reception of Walt Whitman, Dickinson was read, when she was read positively, as a sort of female Whitman, sexually unbridled and spiritually heterodox. Dickinson became the woman poet as virginal site, pried loose from Victorian prudery by publication after her death and made to submit to the critical urges of liberal males. Dickinson was female but nonthreatening; she was dead before she entered critical discourse, and she had been cloistered even during her lifetime. She was the ideal fantasy plaything for male critics.

Other women writers who gained a measure of canonicity before the 1980s were more public figures than Dickinson and less available as sites for unchecked transference of male desire. But ultimately they too were read and accepted through the terms of the Whitman paradigm and its accompanying poetics of presence. The later poets who followed her into the American canon did so by virtue of compressive readings, readings that forced their work into the ancillary category of descriptive, technically skillful work about nature or animals.

Marianne Moore is the best example, a poet whose lifelong and public engagement with morality and ethics has only recently, in readings like Margaret Holley's, displaced her use of strange animals as the center of critical commentary on her work.[11] The brilliance of Moore's initial impact on American modernism, abetted by her own strong personal critical style and considerable editorial power, gained her a following among early twentieth-century modernists. But her very brilliance was unassimilable to the Whitmanic projects conceived by poets like Williams and Pound. In turn, Williams especially developed a strategy of reading—and containing—Moore that would come to dominate later academic discourse. His strategy was to see Moore as the perfect miniaturist, to construct, in his own terms, a "porcelain garden" within which her work could exhibit technical virtuosity, and remain at the vanguard of modernist expression, without ever reaching beyond the garden walls to have a vital impact on the reader. Her work remains behind those walls to an alarming extent even today. Within them she was given, by T. S. Eliot and other critics, the task of keeping a censorious watch on the English language, so that her very themes and concerns would remain those perceived as neutral and unengaged because they are interior to language itself.

Elizabeth Bishop was initially a subset of Moore, linked with that poet, read as an exemplar of her methods, and received as a descriptive poet without Moore's moralism. The early reception of her poems relegated her to only a small part of the Whitmanic project, seeing her as a filler-in of Whitmanic catalogs. While the epic projects of American poetics were being carried out by Pound, Williams, Olson, Zukofsky, and scores of other male writers, Moore and Bishop became the support staff of the canon. Moore, busy within her garden, was read as the purifier of language, presumably so that the language could then be used for grander purposes outside the garden. Bishop, in turn, was given the even more subsidiary role of archivist. Description, a value in itself, is never allowed the larger Whitmanic functions of imaginative projection of authorial presence. Like Moore's purifying function, Bishop's description was a secondary value in the economy of the American poetic tradition, a skill but not the synthesis of skills that the poetics of presence demands.

It should be evident that my own sympathies and allegiances lay with feminist criticism; what I hope to add to a feminist reconsideration of the reception of these women writers is a critique of the very ways in which feminism reinforces the poetics of presence. The initial canonization of Dickinson, Moore, and Bishop by mostly male critics was an antifeminist business that severely constrained these poets in the roles assigned to their gendered authorial images. Much feminist recuperation of Dickinson and Bishop (the case of Moore is much more problematic and unclear) has taken over the task of providing more accurate gen-

dered authorial images for them and making their texts cohere around
these revised images in the same monologic, organic, and original terms
that the poetics of presence demands. Women poets entered the American canon in diminished or twisted gendered versions that constrained
the full textual potential of their work. They remain in the canon, increasingly, in enlarged and rectified gendered versions that raise their
value to a higher level, but constrain their texts' potential no less.

It is this very textual potential, which is open for future readers to
exploit, that Walt Whitman in *Democratic Vistas* called "unsuspected literatures": "What finally and only is to make of our Western world a nationality superior to any hitherto known, and outtopping the past, must
be vigorous, yet unsuspected Literatures, perfect personalities and sociol-
ogies, original, transcendental, and expressing (what, in the highest
sense, are not yet express'd at all) democracy and the modern."[12] Traditional routes into the canon have left many potential American literatures unsuspected. We still demand images of literary artists that will
correspond to the Whitman template. His own words express the difficulties of reading unsuspected literatures: he demands "perfect personalities," a phrase that can mean voices as individual and idiosyncratic
as the dialogic welter of America can produce; or, on the other hand,
personalities that have been perfected in the direction of the aesthetics
of presence, personalities that have ceased to become personal and have
become American with a capital A. Whitman's "unsuspected" has as well
a little of the sense of mysterious evasiveness that should inhere in all
textuality. One literally cannot suspect what a less presence-bound reading may mean for these texts, these literatures.

There is, in the study of the tendentiousness of canon formation, still
something of the nationalist desire to make American literature as a discipline into an enterprise "superior to any hitherto known, and outtopping the past." Grouping and choosing the American women writers that
I set in opposition to Walt Whitman here is an activity that challenges
the notions of an American literary tradition, but from within, from a
desire to make that tradition more accurately reflect literary history and
not to overturn the concept of such a possible literary history. That in
itself is a very American thing to do: earnest, prejudiced self-criticism of
prejudice. But readings and evaluations of literature are examples of prejudice, in the Gadamerian as well as the pejorative sense. We cannot get
outside our own prejudices, but we can see their origins and the traces
that they have left on literary study. Literary criticism, and indeed literary theory, are ineluctably historical disciplines and depend on the one
lived route that a particular past has taken to this present. We cannot
sever our relation with that past, however uneasy we may feel about it.

Yet I do hope to suggest, at least implicitly, that a conscious apprehension (in both senses) of the poetics of presence can point toward an abandonment of the project of American literary nationalism itself. When we read texts by women as texts (by women) rather than as women themselves, we begin to forge connections that recognize culturally constructed sexual difference while genuinely bridging that difference from both sides. When we read texts, possibly even texts by Walt Whitman, *as* texts rather than as embodiments of culture heroes, we begin to move in the direction of criticism and teaching that embrace both difference and crosscultural, transnational connections, rather than insisting on a project that reconfirms traditionally liberal notions of an exclusionary American character. Literatures that outtop the past need not do so merely by setting new records for American ingenuity; "a nationality superior to any hitherto known" may be one that surrenders the notion of nationality altogether.

Note on Texts

When discussing the reception of texts, an absolutely crucial question is, What text is being received? For Whitman, where I take the reception history up to the 1940s, I use the 1891–92 edition of *Leaves of Grass;* it was the one that all critics of the period knew and used. For the study of Dickinson's reception before 1955, I use the 1937 *Poems* (still in print), because it preserves the readings of the various original editions through that date. For Moore I use *Selected Poems* (1935) for poems through that date and the various individual volumes afterward. I do this with some reservations. Moore, like Whitman, revised her poems continuously; her critics noted this tendency to revise in their reviews through her career. But no variorum edition of Moore's poetry exists, and the editions of her poems from before 1935 are hard to consult and cite. Almost all Moore criticism from the canonizing period is based on the 1935 text, the first to be widely circulated and reviewed. The specific poems I quote from are by and large those that have remained textually stable; and there is very little "naïve" Moore criticism based on texts that the critic did not suspect and acknowledge to be shifting. Elizabeth Bishop, by contrast, tended to hold onto poems until they had reached a "complete" form; therefore, I have been able to quote from her *Complete Poems 1927–1979*.[13]

Acknowledgments

I would like to thank three distinct groups of people who helped me when I was writing this book.

The first group includes people who read parts of the manuscript or offered advice and encouragement as I wrote: Mary Loeffelholz, who provided key criticism at an important juncture; Robert Dale Parker, Celeste Goodridge, Margaret Morris, Ann Lowry, Rita Darlene Disroe, Johanna M. Smith, Emory Elliott, Kenneth Roemer, Joanne Dobson, Nancy Wood, and Margaret Silverton.

The second group is made up of people who had a significant impact on my thinking about the issues involved in this book, though they may not have realized it at the time: Everett Emerson, Richard M. Ludwig, Richard B. Sewall, and the late Fitzroy Pyle.

The third group consists of students. It is customary to invoke general groups of students, but in this project there were many individual students who made a difference in the way they forced me to frame and argue the problems. They include Susan Cornitius, Margaret Arafat, Steve Poulter, Lisa Rathert, Billy Smith, and Elaina Phillips. Thank you all for the arguments.

The following copyright holders are gratefully acknowledged for permission to reprint the specified poems:

"The Robin's my Criterion of tune," from *The Poems of Emily Dickinson*, edited by Thomas H. Johnson (Cambridge, Mass.: The Belknap Press of Harvard University Press). Copyright © 1951, 1955, 1979, 1983 by the President and Fellows of Harvard College. Reprinted by permission of the publishers and the Trustees of Amherst College.
A different version of "The Robin's my Criterion of tune" first appeared in *The Complete Poems of Emily Dickinson*, edited by Thomas H.

ONE

The Poetics of Presence in Literary Reception

The poetics of presence is not a systematic aesthetic theory; rather, it is a kind of seat-of-the-pants critical practice.[1] It has proved durable against New Criticism and deconstruction alike because of its very lack of philosophical rigor. Rather than express it in any simple form—there are no seminal essays entitled "The Absence Fallacy"—critics who employ the poetics of presence use a complex of values. These values include monologism, organicism, and originality, which can be employed flexibly in reading literary texts. Subscribing to one of these key values usually entails subscribing to the others, in a way that reinforces the assumption of presence without necessarily entailing a fully worked-out system.

Presence in American criticism is not synonymous with either logocentrism or intentionalism, though it can overlap with both. Logocentrism, as a tendentious position in philosophy and politics, connotes the valorizing of speech over writing, and therefore of living, present oral discourse over dead, mediate textual discourse. The inherent organicism of logocentric thought makes it ideal for use in the discourse of presence. But for most uses of the poetics of presence, the distinction is oversubtle. The poetics of presence is as willing to accept texts as the documentary legacy of a present poet as it is to refer back to a poet's voice, and it usually conflates authorial text with authorial voice. Nor is presence coterminous with the author's intention. The more scientific reaches of New Critical formalism were happy to abandon intention in the search for a surer objective sense of authorial style, where authorial presence emerges even more distinctively than simple intention. Psychological and psychoanalytic readings (we shall see them in nascent form in early Dickinson criticism) can also employ presence without reference to intention, because the author's unconscious is just as organically present as the author's intention.

If the poetics of presence has a guiding philosophy, it might be what Michel Foucault calls the "author-function." Historically, the natural unit for study in American literary scholarship was never so much the text as it was the author, constructed by various techniques of stylistics, bibliography, biography, and interpretation. That author then becomes the guarantee for the worth of studying the text and for the values that are supposedly conveyed in it. As Foucault observes:

> The author is . . . the principle of a certain unity of writing—all differences, having to be resolved, at least in part, by the principles of evolution, maturation, or influence. The author also serves to neutralize the contradictions that may emerge in a series of texts: there must be—at a certain level of his thought or desire, of his consciousness or unconscious—a point where incompatible elements are at last tied together or organized around a fundamental or originating contradiction.[2]

The basic guarantee of the poetics of presence is the unity of a set of disparate textual materials, a unity that implies the author's—and the critic's—ability to control them.

A poetics of presence entails the values of originality, organicism, and monologism, because the author who is continuously present in the text must necessarily be original (he is creating his own authentic text, not reiterating another's), organic (he is bodily, not textual), and monologic (he is a style, not a palimpsest; a speaker, not a reciter; a personality, not a mirror). Especially in nineteenth-century critical discourse, a truly present American poet would naturally be a native, in the curiously untroubled way that Anglo-Americans have until recently used that word to refer to themselves instead of American Indians. In being native, he would provide a new Adamic beginning for an autochthonous American culture, freeing it from its umbilical connection to England and from any guilt over the expropriation of the Indians. And he would be he, because the truly present poet would naturally be male, for reasons that go much further back in Western culture than the American Revolution: reasons that were felt by Anne Bradstreet at the paradoxically female founding moment of American poetry itself.

Originality and organicism may seem to be self-evident terms, and even self-evident values, to many readers; I will discuss them in their more specific local versions in chapter 2, as they are found in the preception and early reception of Whitman. It is possibly far stranger to see monologism adduced as a positive critical value, and in any event the term is anachronistic when applied to any but very recent criticism in English. *Monologic* and *dialogic* have come into American critical thought since 1980, from the work of the early Soviet theorist M. M. Bakhtin. Monologic texts tend to hew very closely to a single style or single literary standard, attempting to exclude other voices and idioms in favor of individual expression or a socially cohesive purity of language. Dialogic texts assume and give expression to many of the voices that exist in all naturally heteroglot, linguistically stratified societies. "In modern English poetry," A. C. Goodson says, "the difference might be exemplified by 'The Wreck of the *Deutschland*' on the one hand, *The Waste Land* on the other."[3] If one's students are old enough to remember the Beatles, another good example might be that *A Hard Day's Night* is monologic and the White Album is dialogic.

As Bakhtin conceives of the genres, poetry tends to be monologic and fiction dialogic. In Bakhtin's work, the terms are relatively neutral generic markers. But Bakhtin's own analysis is weighted toward the dialogic genre of fiction, giving the dichotomy a value differential at its origin. In addition, *dialogic* has seemed a natural gloss for *multicultural*, even *democratic*; *monologic* has come to connote the dead hand of authority. Joseph Natoli calls for a dialogic orientation in criticism itself, because "monologism speaks one voice with one meaning; heteroglossia speaks many voices with many meanings."[4] Today, it is sometimes fighting words to call someone else's favorite text monologic. *Dialogic* has come more and more to mean merely good and *monologic* merely bad, and in response there has been a trend in criticism to reinterpret poetry as dialogic.[5] Such criticism applies this newest synonym for good to the poetry that it studies and enlists Bakhtinian theory, which would otherwise tend to valorize the novel at the expense of poetry.

The by-product of criticism that discovers the dialogic nature of poetry in the course of a defense of poetry is, of course, that the tendentiousness of Bakhtin's own distinction is unmasked. As Lennard J. Davis points out, "No author can truly be monologic if all events are dialogic, anymore than a two-dimensional person can inhabit a three-dimensional world."[6] All texts are to some extent dialogic, because the essence of dialogic language is the fact that words have been uttered before in different contexts. All texts therefore play parodically off one another and within themselves. "The Wreck of the *Deutschland*," however uniquely Hopkins in its diction, plays against the languages of the English Bible and of Anglo-Saxon poetry. *A Hard Day's Night* implicitly realizes that Elvis Presley foreshadows its univocal utterances.

Bakhtin's central discussion of the monologic word of poetry that wants to strip its previous utterances away is therefore a sort of guiding myth for literary theory rather than an empirical finding:

In the poetic image narrowly conceived (in the image-as-trope), all activity—the dynamics of the image-as-word—is completely exhausted by
the play between the word (with all its aspects) and the object (in all its
aspects). The word plunges into the inexhaustible wealth and contradictory multiplicity of the object itself, with its "virginal," still "unuttered"
nature; therefore it presumes nothing beyond the borders of its own
context. . . . The word forgets that its object has its own history of contradictory acts of verbal recognition, as well as that heteroglossia that is
always present in such acts of recognition.[7]

In this theoretical statement by Bakhtin, the poetic word commits a fallacy by believing that it can erase its verbal contexts. Bakhtin's theory
would imply that only the novelistic word realizes the impossibility of
such erasure. In critical practice (leaving aside analysis of Bakhtin's own
fairly poetic trope of the word itself as agent), the result is not so much
that any poem can cut itself free of contexts, because critics can always
show how it has failed to do so. The result is that critics (not the same
ones, perhaps) can deliberately celebrate poetic language for apparently being engaged in the project of cutting itself off. All texts are dialogic, but in the past many critics (to some extent including Bakhtin) believed that some texts tried to be monologic, and valued them insofar
as they succeeded. The concept of monologism is perhaps a better heuristic for ordering critical practices than for reading literary texts.

Where the poetics of presence holds sway, monologism, whether
identified as such or not, serves the dual purposes of ensuring the purity
of the author's original, organic expression, untainted by other influences,
and of making that pure idiom available as a founding standard for a
national literary dialect. The critical traditions of the nineteenth and
twentieth centuries in America have celebrated monologic impulses and
monologic readings because of their evident usefulness in ensuring a
coherent authorial presence. By 1980, when terminology became available for the identification of the monologic impulse, that impulse was
widely assumed to be repressive. But much recent criticism has adopted
the equation *dialogic = good* without further critiquing the notion of authorial presence; what we have gained instead is the concept of the
present dialogic artist, the master ventriloquist.[8]

As I state at the beginning of this chapter, presence has functioned
not just as a theoretical framework for literary studies but also as an evaluative criterion. American critics have valued the writers whom they
see as most personally present in their work, and have valued Walt
Whitman most of all. Tenney Nathanson says of Whitman, in a passage ostensibly descriptive rather than evaluative, that "at its best his
work does bear on us with an immediacy not ordinarily associated with

poetry: the figure who is said to rise up and appear to us in the poet's direct addresses to his audience seems to overflow the boundaries of the very work that conveys him to us, to shuck off his status as a fictive character existing in a literary representation and impinge on us personally and directly."[9] In one sense Nathanson is simply conveying the illusion of a particular reading experience. In another, the key words of the passage are the innocuous ones "at its best," suggesting that the best poetry does and ought to maintain this illusion of presence. Nathanson's words (here taken out of the context of an exemplary deconstruction of Whitman's rhetoric of presence) suggest that presence has had and continues to have an axiological function in criticism: poems where one senses the author's presence are better than ones where one doesn't.

In this sense, the poetics of presence are a major part of the criteria of value opened up to literary study by the theoretical work of Hans Robert Jauss: "the quality and rank of a literary work result neither from the biographical and historical conditions of its origin, nor from its place in the sequence of the development of a genre alone, but rather from the criteria of influence, reception, and posthumous fame, criteria that are more difficult to grasp."[10] Thanks in turn to the reception of reception theory itself since Jauss published those words in 1970, the criteria of value that are situated in reception rather than intrinsic to the work are now far less difficult to grasp than they used to be. Still, I hope to complicate Jauss's formulation in one crucial missing direction. I will argue that the historical conditions of a work's origin are indeed one source of a work's value and in some sense of its reception. All literary works are produced in a preexisting historical context of evaluative criteria, criteria that determine features of a text and are crucial in its initial reception, which inevitably becomes the matrix for "influence, reception, and posthumous fame." This preexisting matrix of reception is the stuff of literary history.

In the evolution of the literary history of American poetry, Walt Whitman is an unavoidably salient presence. But it is well known that for its contemporary audience in 1855, the publication of the first edition of *Leaves of Grass* was a minor and decidedly unimportant event. For at least fifty years afterward, Whitman had little of the salience for American critics that he has for students in the 1990s. The progress of Whitman's literary reputation toward unavoidability was a long and uncertain one in the late nineteenth and early twentieth centuries, far longer and less certain than those of Mark Twain, Ernest Hemingway, or William Faulkner.

But Whitman's progress toward canonicity began even before he started to write poetry. Fully to appreciate the criteria that led to his canonicity means going back beyond the production of his works, into the "pre-production" phase of reception that created the critical climate both for production and reception. Without the prejudices of this "pre-production," no meaningful sense of Whitman's work, whether as central, as revolutionary, or even as monstrous, could ever have existed.

Two standard models for characterizing the progress of Whitman's literary reputation base their assumptions entirely on "post-production" data. One is the gradualist approach John Macy took in 1913: "The history of Whitman, of his poetry and the effect it has had on many kinds of men, is the history of the slow advance of democracy to meet its poets."[11] In other words, the poet wrote, and then the slow dissemination of his works, combined with the devout adherence of his cultists, changed the climate of criticism, pushing it gradually toward acceptance of Whitman and his poetics. Such a gradualist model is given theoretical formulation by Levin L. Schücking in *The Sociology of Literary Taste* (1931) as the "layman's" view of literary history:

> Somewhere, at some time, an artist follows the divine summons sent him and, true to an inner urge, responsible only to himself and answering no call from the outer world, creates the work of art that is dictated by the ideal that floats before him. The works brought into the light of day, it shows divergences from existing art, and accordingly it does not fit into the contemporary scheme of taste. But by virtue of its intrinsic propaganda power it finds friends, gains recognition, and thereafter affects the general artistic taste.[12]

The gradualist, "intrinsic propaganda" model flourished for Whitman's own earliest devotees but has been largely discarded in Whitman studies. Its emphasis on artistic production as proceeding directly from inspiration, with no thought of its audience or the institutions of literature, now appears to be plain wrong in the case of Whitman, who wrote some of the *reviews* of *Leaves of Grass* at the same time that he was creating new *poems* for the volume.[13]

An alternative model is the Kuhnian approach, in which one sees no slow geological progress of the reputation but a sudden, saltatory discovery of Whitman during the early modernist period, and then a rapid paradigm shift as literary scholars acknowledged the intrinsic centrality of Whitman's poetics.[14] Such a model has many attractions, because it implies an inherent, even transcendent value in the works themselves, which merely had to be seen afresh to claim their place as classics. In either model, the canonization of Whitman in the early twentieth century involves a real change in critical values, corresponding to the rise of modernism, the emancipation of thought from Vic-

torian constraints, and the growing respectability of American literature as a discipline. Reading Whitman, in this model, instigated that
change in critical values.

But I don't believe there *was* a change in critical values accompanying the canonization of Whitman. To borrow terms, one from evolutionary biology and one from credit-card marketing: there was a preadapta-
tion of American critical thought that existed long before 1855, having
developed with no reference whatsoever to Walt Whitman, that was to
be of great use in the positive reception of Whitman. There was, therefore, a guaranteed preapproval of Whitman's poetry; it "meets the demand I am always making," said Ralph Waldo Emerson, who indeed had
theorized a poet like Whitman long before he knew of Whitman's personal existence. I take, therefore, neither a gradualist nor a Kuhnian
approach to the poetry criticism that accompanied American modernism. One might call my thesis a Beckerian one, along the lines of Carl
L. Becker's *The Heavenly City of the Eighteenth Century Philosophers*
(1932): I present the Victorian city of the twentieth-century critics.[15]

Studies of reception have suffered in the past from several different
weaknesses, practical and theoretical. Various implied readers in theory, such as those of Wolfgang Iser or Michael Riffaterre, are open to the
objection that they screen the theorist himself—that they are simply a
projection that allows an individual's reading to be presented as normative.[16] I object not to the screening but to the implied normative quality of the "informed" reader. When seen in the light of the entire social
significance of literature, such superreadings are aberrant. Literary texts
produce, in any social setting, in any community or conflict of communities, a nonnormative set of responses. The center of an interpretive
community may be formed for a long time by tendentious, flawed, stub-
born, wishful, interested, ignorant, or simply dull interpretation of a text.
Criticism in practice does not produce normative readings. That is not
the nature of hermeneutic activity even in theory, as the productive
quality of the "prejudice" theorized by Hans-Georg Gadamer would tend
to show. Abstract "reader responses" suggest that reading proceeds nor-
matively when it proceeds in ideal isolation from error. But error may
be the vitalizing principle of critical discourse.[17]

Empirical studies of reader-response, such as those of Janice Radway,
are not open to the charge of constructing normative behavior on the
model of something that is too good; frequently they preserve instead
two different types of reading behavior—a behavior either overdetermined by the dullest and most conservative consensus, or behavior so
adrift from consensus, so innocent of the experience of community building, that it is illegibly subjective.[18] Of course, both dull readings and off-

the-wall readings are objects of intense interest in themselves. They cannot explain, however, how texts or readings are historically conditioned. The experimental quality of empirical reader-response research seems to be an attempt to arrive at an objective democratic "norm" that, like the "too good" norm of reader-response criticism, does not practically occur except as an artifact of the experiment.

Historicity, which is controlled out of existence in empirical research, reemerges in the classic studies of reception—"reviews of reviews"—which themselves have become outmoded.[19] The principal flaw with the standard history of reception is the teleology of the method. The traditional reception study is done on a highly canonical author. The starting point of a reception study is therefore the end of the history it covers: the unchallengeable canonicity of the author. How did we get here? the study asks, and proceeds to interest itself in progress toward unquestioning acceptance of the subject author. Dismissals of the author seem laughable; acclaim (especially of the crying-in-the-wilderness sort) seems wonderfully prescient. Teleological history elides the essence of historicity, recasting contingent outcomes as inevitable by producing causes for them, obliterating the dynamics of past argumentative strategies.

The recent trend toward "de-canonization" studies has produced the teleological inverse of this traditional model, seeing how the academy moved to exclude the subject.[20] We cannot speculate about nonreception beyond the point where an author disappears from critical discourse. But in part, I hope in this study to gain insights, very indirectly, into the process of the exclusion of noncanonical writers. Writers who are now reentering the canon, like Elizabeth Stuart Phelps, Sui Sin Far, Elizabeth Stoddard, and Frances Ellen Watkins Harper, are intrinsically the equal of Emily Dickinson or Walt Whitman in the New Critical values of complexity, irony, and verbal technique.[21] If the New Critical canon held no place for these writers, it was because institutional forces interrupted their transmission, not because they were continually read and continually rejected (on aesthetic grounds) by generations of scholars.[22] We cannot directly observe the institutional forces that worked to de-canonize those writers who were completely invisible during most of the twentieth century. We must instead try to understand how the critical principles that constituted the ideology of the canon were generated and defended by the specific historical individuals active in the stabilizing selection that enabled the canonical authors to survive in their niches during the mid-twentieth century. In such a study, test cases like Dickinson, Moore, and Bishop—as women who survived against long odds—are illuminating examples.[23]

I would not argue, however, that Dickinson, Moore, and Bishop constitute a feminist tradition. I am encouraged here by the work of Betsy Erkkila, who has sharply observed, in *The Wicked Sisters* (1992), that the literary history of American women's writing is characterized as much by disruptions and failures to communicate as it is by nurturant enabling. "In recognition of the struggle among, between, within, and *for* women which is the very ground of feminism as both social movement and critical and theoretical practice, 'the wicked sisters' is meant to suggest the oppositional nature of feminist literary discourse, a discourse that has challenged the hegemony of the white masculine subject in literature and elsewhere and undermined traditional assumptions about the study of literature."[24] I suspect that "traditional assumptions" here means as much "assumptions about the nature of traditions" as it means "masculinist assumptions," and the oppositional readings that Erkkila sets up among the nontraditional set of writers she studies—Dickinson, Moore, Bishop, Rich, and Brooks—confirm this suspicion. Erkkila's basic realization that it is not always helpful to place female writers in a line of filiation has great potential as a framing assumption for work on these writers' texts.

Erkkila defines her feminism in this way: "It is about changing the traditional binary male/female at the base of Western metaphysics, transforming traditional social orders of power and dominance, and radically altering our very ways of knowing, seeing, and being in the world."[25] I believe in that project, and I think I can contribute to it in a limited but useful way. Much of what I do in the following chapters is a kind of "showing the flutes," as Margaret Mead might put it, of the male sodality that so long dominated American criticism, and for which the poetics of presence was a powerful means of gendering texts in order to preserve the privileges of the male artistic voice.[26] One of the advantages of being a male critic in strong sympathy with feminism may be the ability to return to the discourse of the fathers and imagine one's way subversively into it.

The second and more serious way in which feminism is a part of my own horizon of expectations lies in Erkkila's sense of feminism as a project that aims to change the male/female binary opposition and to imagine new ways of knowing. These new ways of knowing are very much *en procés* in the mid-1990s; "queer theory," which impinges briefly on my discussion of Bishop, is starting to break down absolutes of sexuality that have so constrained thought about gender, most notably in the work of Martha Nell Smith on Dickinson. The strongest part of her work—which I will critique later—is a reappraisal of the uses of thought about sexuality in reading Dickinson.[27] Erkkila's own sense of a "post-feminism" is another such new way of knowing, one that sees the implications of feminism as leading many discourses out of the oppositions of gender.

The poetics of presence should be abandoned as an assumption of reading. Such an abandonment presents problems even for postfeminism, because the power conferred on authors and readings by presence is a hard thing to give up. But until texts are freed from their current role as elements in the construction of authorial images, it will be hard to break free from gendered readings that limit the potential of texts to be read—and to change minds and actions—across the boundaries of sex. I am talking mainly of readings that are gendered male: the masculinist appreciations of Whitman and the masculinist diminutions of the women poets that I discuss in later chapters, readings that demand assent from men and silence from women about supposed eternal verities of sexual inequity. I simply do not think that feminist countermoves can be successful if they rely just as uncritically on the values of presence.

I don't expect this argument to be accepted without resistance, and I expect that many readers—feminist, nonfeminist, and antifeminist—will reject it in principled ways. But one of my aims remains that of opening texts up for transgender readings that establish points of contact across texts, while foregrounding the living cultural struggles of readers and downplaying rhetorical struggles over the data of authors' lives.

Such transgender readings (which stay mostly at the level of potential here while I reconstruct a history of decidedly intragender readings) cannot be achieved if readers feel they must first escape their own historical situation. An acceptance of the historicity of one's own readings, as the abandonment of any positivist urge to demonstrate the absolute efficacy of one's own critical procedure, has an enormously vitalizing effect on one's own critical judgments. A caricature of the history of literary criticism in twentieth-century America might take one from what the author meant (the old historicism), to what the text means (New Criticism), to what an ideal reader would understand the text to mean (reader-response criticism), to why the text cannot mean (deconstruction), to a demonstration of what the text might have meant to those deluded enough to believe it could mean anything (the New Historicism), to what the author meant but could only express subversively because of her sex ("pre-post" feminism). These divergent critical paradigms share the same basic concern of textual essentialism; they focus on making conclusive statements about the significance (in Hirschean terms) of the text.[28] But that very significance is an evolving, emergent phenomenon, historically produced by interpretive communities as they act on the text.[29] Many of those communities, of course, operate from essentialist assumptions, and texts can only have meaning for them if they are reduced to various definitive parastatements about themselves.

Reception theory, by contrast, demands that the historicity of all readings be kept in the critical foreground. By so doing, it frees criticism from essentialisms—even from the deconstructive essentialism of exposing the lack of definitiveness of texts and their readings. I hardly mean to suggest that feminist critics have never taken this critical historicity into account; writers like Susan K. Harris, Nina Baym, Cathy N. Davidson, and others *have*, and often centrally.[30] I simply want to insist on the continuous necessity to see the historical situation of any reception as an opportunity rather than a constraint. If in imagining the future we are constrained by our past, one imperative is to understand that past so that we can see exactly where our present is located.

Historically, texts have mattered to their readers, and they continue to matter (for diverse reasons) to readers at the present moment. Any immanent, intrinsic meaning of a text, no matter where one locates it, is essentially a fiction. But the meaning a reader develops from a text is not a fiction. That meaning (properly, "significance") reorients the attitude of the reader toward life and language, however trivially or ephemerally. Too often when a reader develops a significance, the consequence is a countervailing desire to abandon that significance for a corrected, authorized version with the imprimatur of a cultural institution—whether classroom or Cliffs Notes. When we instead see readings as contingent rather than conclusive, the critical imperative then becomes not to resolve, or unify, or erase that contingency, but to answer it. The function of critical self-consciousness, in a reception-theory model, is less to ensure objectivity by controlling for all of one's imbedded assumptions than to acknowledge that objectivity is impossible.[31] And studying the history of reception shows the tenuousness and imbeddedness of systems of reading that supposedly guarantee objectivity or detachment.

Texts may be seen as emergent phenomena.[32] Emergent phenomena are real enough, but amount to more than the sum of the things that produce them. Texts contain formal and generic elements that are emergent with respect to the actual existence of the text, especially since they are largely relational features; the form and genre of the text, and indeed its linguistic status, are only perceptible in relation to an evolving historical context. One function of traditional historicist criticism, obviously, is to freeze the historical context of a work at the instant of its production and thereby to deny reception, especially the continued reception at the critic's present moment, any ability to shed light on formal or generic features of the text.

In a survey of reception history, we can identify features of texts, ranging from semantic to cultural, that have been unintelligible to one generation of readers and all-important to another. Significances of texts are lost and produced and regained in the course of reception history. Texts appear, almost of their own accord, to unfold in the process of their reception, to exhibit new significances as new communities ascribe those significances to them. The potential that a given text has for unfolding new features is another way of describing the old concept of a classic as an eternally relevant book, Jauss's concept of recovering the original negativity of a masterwork that has become familiar because of horizonal change, or Umberto Eco's concept of an "open" work.[33] It seems unlikely that any text can unfold without limit, though the point that Walter Miller's *A Canticle for Leibowitz* makes about the interpretive volatility of scriptural texts (like the blueprint of the Blessed Leibowitz) when they are cut off from the cultural matrix of their production should be taken seriously.[34] The Bible is clearly the most widely extended text of Western culture, with a historically real but practically unfathomable multiplicity of available interpretations. Texts, because they are produced within a system of cultural codes and communities that pre-orient their intelligibility, retain, as long as some cultural mechanisms make it possible, some constraint over interpretation. When the text ceases to have that constraining power, it ceases, like the Etruscan language, to have intelligibility, and therefore ceases to have a reception history. (If Etruscan is deciphered and Etruscan texts become part of world literature anthologies, some Rosetta stone of cultural continuity will have been the key, confirming the principle of continued constraint.)

Harold Bloom's concept of the "strength" of a text may be another way of talking about the potential of a text to unfold—that is, to *negatively* constrain—its readers.[35] This is counter-intuitive; one would suppose that "strong" texts impose their "meanings" particularly well, particularly unalterably, on future communities of readers. But a text that fails to unfold will be one that can be dealt with without the necessity to engage in creative misprision. A weak text is limited by its very clarity and unequivocality. A text that is "strong" in the Bloomian sense, however, may pose recurrent problems for poet and critic alike, because its concerns will be continually extensible into the interests and the language of its interpreters.

This dichotomy is close to Umberto Eco's notion of "open" versus "closed" texts, but it's different too. Eco adds the notion that a closed text *because* of its monotonic message can mean anything, while an open text remains bound.[36] An open text—strong, or potentially evolving, in other terms—is bound more heavily by the constraints of the community—but not because of its intrinsic complexity alone. Strong texts are usually perpetuated in traditions of reading that allow for strongly determined patterns of unfolding. Closed, monotonic texts often escape from these communities and their traditions—schools and other prestige institutions—and enter a submerged or a revolutionary interpretive community. The classics don't get loose from constraints on the latitude their interpretive communities allow them; Superman and Eugène Sue do.

Critical readings within such constraints can be seen as representing performances of texts, or at least recordings of those performances. In *An American in Paris*, Gene Kelly tells Nina Foch as he sells her one of his paintings, "Y'know, a writer, a composer, they can always buy a copy of what they create; but with a painter, it's the original that counts." (She replies, "I never thought of that"; in Hollywood, women do not theorize.)[37] Kelly—performing a text by screenwriter Alan Jay Lerner—anticipates a later observation by Gérard Genette, that copying has a full and honorable (or dishonorable) place in the visual arts, but that a copy in the textual arts—literature and music—is intrinsically meaningless.[38] A copy of a text does not "matter" for itself, as transcendent object; only external conditions (marginalia, descriptive bibliography, provenance) give it value. In Genette's terms, or Gene Kelly's, the dichotomy between textual and nontextual arts is valid. When one asks where "art" exists, however, one sees that both Kelly and Genette are operating from a perspective dominated by production rather than reception. The score of a musical work, as text, is endlessly iterable; one production suffices for all its performances. But each performance, as record collectors know, is unique. The same is obviously true for drama, but less obviously true for poetry, and still less for fiction. Performances of poetry have a conditioning effect on reception: witness innumerable classroom discussions of *The Waste Land* knocked stone cold dead by a tape recording of T. S. Eliot. But a poem is no less "performed" for being read silently from the page than it is in oral interpretation. And one reader's silent performance of *Barchester Towers* is somewhat different from another's, though both may be heavily conditioned by Nigel Hawthorne and Donald Pleasance.

It is in the context of performance that critical readings can be the best gauges of past potentialities of texts. The overpowering impulse when one sees a text on a page is to arrive at a determinant reading—or a determinant dissolution of meanings—rather than to acknowledge a continuing potential for performability. Some performances work better than others, and some performances make stronger impressions on their audience than others. But each new reading of a text demands a new performance. One way of reading poetry is to study the tradition of performance as attentively as the student actor will watch films or ask older actors to read a line as the great performer of *their* childhood would have read it.

The classroom is where these performances are continually rehearsed and directed, and the writing of this book was provoked more by participating in performances by the interpretive communities of the classroom than by reading theory "in the study." In classroom discussion, a text very often acts as if it constrains readings of itself. The notion that texts can do *anything* to readers may seem philosophically obtuse, and I have no doubt that in a strictly philosophical analysis, that's just what it is. But in the social struggles that surround reception, people often behave as if the text constrains their opinions, just as jurists behave as if constitutional law and precedent constrain theirs. Precisely because interpretive communities precede the production of texts, texts encode the expectations of interpretive communities. Communities that form to interpret newly produced texts are constrained in part by limits that prior communities placed on the production of those texts.

Nevertheless, texts can be carried very far by later interpretive communities away from the encodings of previous communities. Multiple communities are constantly at work, creating a dialogic haze of disagreement about the values and meanings encoded in a text—a haze evident in late Victorian opinion on Walt Whitman. But the powers of reification possessed by interpretive communities are very resilient, constituting a sort of hermeneutic "Plexiglas principle" that infuses texts produced within those communities' horizons of expectations with resistance to critical bending and breakage. The Plexiglas principle in teaching is not an invisible hand, of course—it is the hand that marks the papers. Authorial intention—as a creation by the instructor, not as something numinously present in a text—is a component of this resilience, as biographical and other paratextual materials (interviews, letters, drafts, journals) are synthesized and reified by scholars into a validating authorial image. ("That's *not* what the author meant.") Contextualizing, whether primary (source or influence) or ancillary (the *Zeitgeist*) is another reifying tendency that stiffens texts and their interpretations; that's why professors give "background lectures."

Philological scholarship can have the same effect. I once had an argument with a student who glossed the word "disinterestedness" in Moore's "Marriage" as "indifference." I explained that the word could not carry that connotation; it must mean "impartiality." Moore could not be capable of such semantic sloppiness as to intend "disinterested" as a synonym of "uninterested." I was right on my own terms, playing and winning a pedagogical power game by invoking presence as if I could conjure Marianne Moore out of the ether to chastise a semantically care-less graduate student. But in the 1990s, "disinterested" means "uninter-ested," and it is unlikely to return to the meaning I presume Moore held for it, and which I certainly did hold (for fear of my fifth-grade English teacher) when I grew up as Moore's late contemporary. The old mean-ing "impartial" is being buried and forgotten. A twenty-fourth-century scholar may argue desperately and unverifiably that in certain early twen-tieth-century texts the word connoted "impartiality"; footnotes based on that scholar's suggestions may be appended to anthologies four hundred years from now. Changing linguistic behavior exerts an external pres-sure on interpretive communities against which the text must ultimate-ly be powerless, preserved only in a sort of cryonic cocoon of scholarly apparatus.

The larger interpretive community impinges on the classroom and on everyday scholarship (lectures, papers, syllabuses) in the form of anthologies, their introductions, literary histories, and those essays and books that become important enough (by the same contingent process-es that construct the "literary" canon) to be widely perceived by stu-dents as the sources of authority. I want to take some time here to es-tablish a provisional, synchronic picture of the *seuils* to the American canon that most decisively function, in the mid-1990s, as its surround-ing arbiters.[39] I hope to establish some of the history of these *seuils* in the more diachronic approaches of the chapters that follow, especial-ly chapter 2; but the immediate task here is to develop a sense of what a graduate student or advanced undergraduate today experiences as the frame of critical wisdom about the American poetic tradition. My pur-pose is to justify my treatment of Whitman's reception at such length and to confirm my sense of his centrality—a centrality that is still be-ing consolidated today.

Roy Harvey Pearce's *The Continuity of American Poetry* (1961) pro-vides one still current paradigm for the study of American poetry be-cause of its insistence on a "basic style" of American literary artists. The enduring strength of Pearce's critical formulation is certainly due to his conception of that style, however, as open-ended, antiformal, and self-conscious.[40] In seeing an essence to American poetry, Pearce chooses to formulate it as including many diverse essences. His book continues to persuade students to revise the literary history of the nineteenth centu-ry away from the reception record and toward a retrospectively imposed canon, validating the achievements of Poe, Emerson, and Whitman as against more formally conventional poets like Bryant, Halleck, and Longfellow—or indeed Sigourney, Larcom, and Thaxter.

In substantial agreement with the outlines of Pearce's paradigm,

Harold Bloom has done influential work in centering the American poetic tradition on an Emersonian Whitman whose major twentieth-century legatees are Stevens and Ashbery.[41] Bloom's emphasis on the freedom of the individual voice to struggle for "strength" within a milieu of tradition, however patriarchally Darwinian it is, can potentially be used to recenter attention on the "individual talent" that, in the wake of Eliot's famous essay, was often overwhelmed by its partner "tradition." But that's obviously not how Bloom uses it; he is the arch-tradition-builder, and students looking for articles to supplement their research papers will find scores of Bloom's Chelsea House introductions in the library. Bloom relates nearly every American writer back somehow to Emerson and Whitman. One can open the introductions virtually at random and read a capsule of the Bloom version of tradition: "The central strain in our literature remains Emersonian, from Whitman to our contemporaries like Saul Bellow and John Ashbery, and even the tradition that reacted against Emerson, from Poe, Hawthorne, and Melville through Gnostics of the abyss like Nathaniel West and Thomas Pynchon, remains always alert to transcendental and extraordinary American possibilities."[42]

Major revisions of the canons of American nonfiction, autobiography, and fiction have not taken nearly as strong a hold in the teaching of poetry. The formulations of Pearce and Bloom possess the field of the American poetic canon even in the 1990s; much recent work attempts minor shufflings of the canonical pack but no major rewriting of the rules of the game. The widely used anthologies still begin with Bradstreet and move through Freneau and Wheatley to Bryant, even when they discard the schoolroom poets; from Whitman forward there is even more homogeneity. Whitman and Dickinson begin Ellmann and O'Clair's *Norton Anthology of Modern Poetry* and end the first volume of the *Norton Anthology of American Literature*; the more revisionist *Heath Anthology* swings either way, shrink-wrapping Whitman and Dickinson so that the instructor can end the first volume with them or begin the second.

Just as the physical geography of teaching American literature—what books one can use—is still heavily determined by the central presence of Whitman, so too is recent scholarship. Terence Diggory's innovative borrowing of Yeats from the Anglo-Irish division as a catalyst for an American "tradition of the self" is intriguing, especially as that tradition of the self mirrors the critical tradition of a poetics of presence; but Diggory's tradition is decidedly one of Whitmanic white males.[43] Mutlu Konuk Blasing argues vigorously against the view of an American poetic tree sprouting from a central precursor such as Whitman; in its place, however, she plants four shrubs, rooted respectively in Poe, Emerson,

Whitman, and Dickinson.[44] Blasing's modular traditions have considerable heuristic value for reading poets not usually brought together in the received canon, but little historical usefulness. Jeffrey Walker fastens *Bardic Ethos and the American Epic Poem* (1989) firmly onto the founding image of Whitman; Thomas Gardner's recent study of Berryman, Kinnell, Roethke, Duncan, Ashbery, and Merrill is entitled *Discovering Ourselves in Whitman* because, as Gardner reasonably explains, "the fact that Whitman's influence has been generalized now as one set of tensions within our cultural heritage is perhaps the strongest evidence we have of his continuing 'presence.'"[45] Most influential of all on the current horizon of expectations is the PBS television series "Voices and Visions," which has wide currency among students and deserves credit for exciting so many of them to read poetry. It begins with Whitman and Dickinson and moves on to Frost, Stevens, Williams, Pound, Moore, Eliot, Hart Crane, Hughes, Bishop, Robert Lowell, and Plath—as good an empirical definition as any of the high canon of the 1980s and 1990s.[46]

"Traditions," David Bromwich reminds us, "are made from books. That does not mean a set list of great books. Few institutions have ever adhered to a single such list for more than a generation."[47] One is tempted to reply that removing James Russell Lowell from an anthology and replacing him with Robert Lowell isn't exactly iconoclasm. But at the same time it would be absurd to deny that the received canon is a product of sharp struggles in the past that resonate and continue till the present day. Even a canon that appears unchanged on the surface, so that Whitman plays the same role for Paul Lauter that he played for Louis Untermeyer generations earlier, is the product of a continuous process of stabilization and defense.

Even Harold Bloom's own sense of Emersonian and anti-Emersonian traditions in American writing, though he resolves both into a transcendentalist impulse, shows the impact of such stabilizing struggles. Bloom realizes that if one's tradition starts with Whitman, it is annoyingly opposed by Poe (as we will see in chap. 2). In the introduction to *The Oxford Book of American Verse* (1950), which remains widely available, F. O. Matthiessen says that "in the broadest terms, most of our later poets could be described as descendants of Whitman or as descendants of Poe."[48] (Blasing's fourfold tradition can be seen as squaring this bipolarity.) In turn, Matthiessen's bipolar tradition is akin to, though not derived from, Philip Rahv's "Paleface and Redskin" (1939), an essay that, as Sanford Pinsker has recently shown, continues to exert at least a secondhand influence on thought about and teaching of American literature.[49]

Rahv's essay is a stark opposition of literary types. "While the red-skin glories in his Americanism, to the paleface it is a source of endless ambiguities. . . . The paleface . . . tends toward a refined estrangement from reality. . . . The redskin . . . accepts his environment, at times to the degree of fusion with it."[50] The type of the redskin is Walt Whitman, of course; the type of the paleface is Henry James. Rahv's sympathies are with the palefaces: "At present the redskins are in command of the lit-erary situation, and seldom has the literary life in America been as in-tellectually impoverished as it is today."[51] (J. G. Holland said much the same thing fifty years earlier, and William Bennett was saying much the same thing fifty years later; it is all a bit like "these ballplayers today don't play for the love of the game like they did when I was young.") But while he excoriates the redskins and their promoters, Rahv's lan-guage betrays him: the redskins possess "Americanism," they retain an organic connection to their American environment; the paleface pro-duces great literature only when he is able "to transcend or to deviate sharply from the norms of his group."[52] True American literature is still located on the Whitman side of the tradition, as much as Rahv dislikes the fact.

The betrayal of the surface of "Paleface and Redskin" by its own sub-text is true as well of its title, which is more than a gratuitous piece of racialism. American literary nationalism shows a deeply engrained guilt over the word "American" itself, which belongs properly (despite its European etymology) only to the Native American. The Americanist half admits that "Americans" are only posing as such, conceding under-neath that the true Americans are those who tap into Native energies. At some point in literary history (the point when Walt Whitman takes his pre-appointed place) Native energies become entirely and legitimate-ly the property of white Americans, but the anxiety does not cease then. Rahv renames the Whitman tradition "redskin," in a sort of dream-lan-guage gesture toward the realities of symbolic expropriation.

Rahv's canon has not endured as well as his dichotomy. His palefac-es are James, Hawthorne, Melville, Eliot, and Dickinson; his redskins are Whitman, Twain, Mencken, Anderson, Dreiser, Lewis, Faulkner, Wolfe, Sandburg, and Hemingway. If one were to poll students today, one would find most of Rahv's redskins had become palefaces—or in today's idiom, "dead white guys." What the split between the ephemer-al canon and the resilient bipolarism indicates is that we are dealing with a permanent process of canon formation. The process works like a con-vection current. The dead white guys of the received canon are on the surface, cooling quickly. The vital new writers are bubbling up from be-low as we enlist them to show our hipness and *épater* our elders. As the dead white guys are sucked below, they become reheated by the energies that drive canon formation and reappear on the surface—as happened notably to Melville and Dickinson after the Second World War.

When teaching American literary history as chronology, one must start somewhere, and the starting place is either a paleface who serves as straw man or a redskin who serves as *sipapu*, a connection to autochthonous energy. That point of origin is usually Whitman, who is endlessly useful as a source of convective energy, attracting young writers and young students to his image as they pass through the maturational cycle from young redskin to venerable paleface. If one teaches *American* literature, it is tempting to provide a point of origin where one says: "Here is where *we* finally broke from England/Europe/the dead weight of the past. Finally we are reading the real *American* literature."

Rahv concludes: "The sole question that seems relevant is whether history will make whole again what it has rent asunder. Will James and Whitman ever be reconciled, will they finally discover and act upon each other?"[53] One could answer in hindsight that they were already being fused in the mind of F. O. Matthiessen, an Eliot scholar who would link Whitman, Hawthorne, and Melville in *American Renaissance* and then turn his attention to Henry James. The post-Matthiessen face of American literary studies so thoroughly reconciled the split between James and Whitman that it may even be said to have enlisted James, the type of the paleface, in the new energies—Puritan and paradoxical—which gave American literature coherence as a discipline in the 1950s and 1960s.[54] As we have seen, Matthiessen compensated his enlistment of James by driving Poe further into paleface territory, where he became the sinister redskin *in potentia*, to emerge with new powers in the readings of Daniel Hoffman.[55]

The key challenge that Matthiessen's all-male canon has undergone is that from feminist criticism. Some feminist critics work from within, like Joanne Feit Diehl, whose *Women Poets and the American Sublime* (1990) starts by going "From Emerson to Whitman," in a familiar pattern, but then breaks off sharply to consider "the possibilities—if authority is associated with the patriarch, then the woman poet cannot so easily experience the identity between self and all-powerful other. . . . If, on the other hand, the woman poet experiences this external power as feminine, as the mother, her "inspiration" does not impart the gift of tradition."[56] Others work from a largely unprecedented framework that challenges the belletristic and intranational assumptions of the discipline of American literature; Annette Kolodny might be the best example of this trend, as she seeks to redefine the possibilities of "American" textual study itself.[57] Yet another route to the critique of the canon is to attack it directly, as in Judith Fetterley's concept of the "resisting reader" who will not accept the power of certain canonical texts over her reading experience.[58]

Nina Baym exemplifies the feminist direct attack in her sharp deconstruction of the assumptions of canon formation itself, in "Melodramas of Beset Manhood" (1981). In the terms I've developed to explain Philip Rahv's dichotomy, Baym shows here how the palefaced men of the tradition reacquire energy from male critics and are reinvigorated to assume their full canonical place as redskins. Becoming canonical, in Baym's analysis, entails "a fiction which . . . can be taken as representative of the author's literary experience, his struggle for integrity and livelihood against flagrantly bad best-sellers written by women. Personally beset in a way that epitomizes the tensions of our culture, the male author produces his melodramatic testimony to our culture's essence—so the theory goes."[59] Lighting out for the Territory to escape the smothering influence of feminine culture, the author/work/hero (nicely knotted by Baym into a complex of presence) goes native there and emerges with power to reenter the canon. American literary scholarship appears continually to be driven by the urge to sort into the me and not-me; Baym replies, "What a reduction this is of the enormous variety of fiction written in this country, by both women and men!"[60]

Baym ultimately faults these critically constructed melodramas for not being essentially American; but her America is an America of bewildering dialogic diversity. I do not mean to suggest from these last few examples that the only challenges to the received Americanist canon have come from feminist critics. One cannot ignore (though they fall out of my immediate scope): the work of African American critics like Henry Louis Gates, Jr., and Hortense Spillers; the impact of the anthology *Aieeeee!* in bringing Asian American writers forward; the writings, both creative and scholarly, of Hispano-Americans like Denise Chavez, Américo Paredes, and Rolando Hinojosa; Native American literary theory as it evolves in the work of Leslie Silko or N. Scott Momaday; queer theory as refracted through anthologies by George Stambolian and Joan Nestle and Naomi Holoch. The potential of feminism, as Erkkila implies, is to unite all these challenges to the received canon (they all include women) and become a challenge to power itself, as power has traditionally (in both senses) been conceived as a masculine, majority attribute. The criticism of Diehl, Kolodny, and Baym does just this.

In the place of the continuity of American poetry, I prefer to envision a discontinuity. Within such a discontinuity (which extends into the work of individual authors, of course), texts gain emphasis at the expense of authors' overall styles, reified (or "fossilized") poetic genres, or constructions of periods, or movements.[61] Texts can even gain emphasis at the expense of chronology, as heretical as this may seem in a historicist framework; since all texts must be read in a single synchronic framework, the reader's "present," their value is ultimately for and within that present, despite the gravitational force exerted by historicist rehearsal of presumed "past" meanings of texts. The canon of American poetry is evolving toward such a discontinuity, if slowly; newer anthologies like the evolving Norton and the Heath contain progressively more poets and fewer poems by each, with more anonymous, traditional and "folk" verse of all periods, challenging the trend begun in 1950 by Matthiessen of including fewer poets but more of each one. Teaching will gradually follow this course away from the major-author approach, but not without a struggle. My aim here is to contribute to the struggle for decentering and disjoining the canon by complicating and disjoining the voices of some canonical poets.

We will have occasion to see some nascent melodramas of beset manhood in the critical prereception and reception of Walt Whitman. Sexual and class prejudices are at the heart of both Whitman's preapproval and the delayed confirmation of that approval. The critics who established the conditions for preapproval of Whitman's poetry were mostly bourgeois men; the critics who completed the canonization of Whitman were also mostly bourgeois men. Early critics were put off by his working-class origins, by his trades of printer and carpenter; his racial status too, because he was part Dutch and not pure Anglo-American, was inhibiting for those critics who desired a "true" American poetry. Later critics nominated Whitman as the fulfiller of a poetry of presence, once concessions to Victorian prejudices were no longer necessary. Criticism in the 1850s was largely played out in the journalistic press—which meant women readers and men's preconceptions of how writing ought to conduct itself in a mixed company of readers. Critics then, and throughout the nineteenth century, were appalled by Whitman's frank treatment of heterosexuality; his homosexuality rarely even registered on their explicit prejudices. Poetry criticism by the 1910s had decisively entered highbrow and academic realms where there were either no women listening or where the listening women were aggressively unfeminine, like Harriet Monroe and Amy Lowell.[62] In these realms the "feminization" that had been seen by progressive males as sapping American literature of vitality was finally marginalized. Both the prehistory and the history proper of Whitman's reception were inseparable from issues of sex and class which frame the essential continuity of critical assumptions from the 1810s to the 1910s.

If twentieth-century critics could admire Whitman's treatment of sex because there were no longer many women listening, they could be free of class anxieties for an analogous reason: within the universities where criticism of poetry had largely retreated, the working-class and immigrant populations were not listening either. Or if they were, lower-class men were being assimilated to the upper classes; ethnic immigrants were being assimilated to an Anglo identity that they frequently defended more strongly than Anglo-Americans did. The poetics of presence has ultimately been of use, and continues to be of use in the American classroom, as a tool for this assimilative process.

The reasons for the enduring power of a poetics of presence are complex. Connecting one's own reading of a text to the biographical personality of its author has a "natural" appeal that proliferates, with its own kind of organicism, even in the face of decades of relentless antiintentionalist theory. Establishing a documentary trail of associations, carrying out the author's testamentary will, finding a single or typical voice for the author—indeed, establishing authorship itself—these are still part of the basic toolkit of literary scholarship.

Reading a text for its embodiment of a living authorial presence is a deeply satisfying activity; one ought at least to acknowledge this. Holden Caulfield wished he could call up Hardy because he dug that Eustacia Vye, and his pleasure in connecting verbally with the author behind *The Return of the Native*, or that author's character, is both innocent and emotionally sincere, however illogical such an urge might be (like my urge to invoke Holden as if *he* existed, or Ray Kinsella's fictional urge to seek the fictional Salinger in *Shoeless Joe* by the real W. P. Kinsella). There is more immediate (if guilty) pleasure to be gained from reading when one has convinced oneself that one is hearing a direct communication from the author of a text than when one reads for the pleasure of observing a text bounce off the walls of its own textuality and deconstruct its own textual pretensions.

But ultimately one must confront the real-life implications and results of a commitment to presence-based reading. Such a commitment seems to spring from the critical need to master a text, to be able to recreate the conditions of its origin, to be able to locate the text as symptom of neurosis or perhaps as evidence of preternatural genius. Presence-based readings attempt to exhaust the process of reading, which is akin to the process of desire, in some moment of ultimate fixation, when all reactions and life processes stop in an enraptured contemplation of the artistic object. (It's positively theological.) One contemplates a masterpiece, and one finally knows the secret of the masterpiece, and one receives a perfect revelation from its creator.

Such an attitude toward the ends of criticism is not merely stultifying in that it fixes a canon and an unalterable scale of values, and hardly just because that canon and that value scale are likely to be politically reactionary. Nor do I object to the politics of presence because of abstract political dogma (as in the vaguely left-wing air of Derrideanism), nor because of its logical absurdity (the Derrida of "Signature Event Context"). I object to the poetics of presence for working in the classroom to deny the freedom, and in a real sense the identity, of the reader.

The poetics of presence has so directed the course of American literary history that most canonical poets have been valued for a personally identifiable voice in their poetry. When one reads a poem that has the distinct vocabulary of Dickinson, the unique syllabic meter of Moore, or the restraint and irony of Bishop, one is often struck by the direct and powerful illusion of personal communication from the voice of the author. How nice it would be to have such a poet for a friend, one thinks, for a confidante. In fact, of course, one does no injustice to the memory of these women to suspect that it would not have been nice at all to know them. Elizabeth Bishop was a very unhappy person, and Emily Dickinson was troubled by everyday life to an extent that made communication with her all but impossible even for her long-time friends. Marianne Moore comes out of the pages of Charles Molesworth's currently definitive biography as someone who put barriers of class and education between herself and the unwashed world in a typical upwardly-mobile way.[63] It is ironic that most of us who are academic readers of their verse years after their deaths would never have registered socially on their consciousnesses while they were alive. All three were upper-middle-class white women with elite educations; Dickinson and Moore had the distinct (and distinctly correct) self-images of literary ladies. If the reader is the descendant of Slovak or Irish immigrants, or of Appalachian poor whites, if he or she graduated from public high school or state university (I am all of the above), I distinctly doubt that Emily Dickinson would have given that reader the time of day—for class reasons quite apart from any agoraphobia or manic-depressiveness. Nor would that reader have delighted in the patronizing reception she or he might have gotten from Marianne and Mrs. Moore.

My point is simply this: that in addition to the general philosophical attractions of a poetics of presence, it also serves the particular political purpose in America of blurring the class barriers of the past to the point of erasure. We can participate in a sort of retrospective democracy of the spirit by returning to texts by Cooper, Hawthorne, Henry James, or Marianne Moore and inserting ourselves as their ideal audience, assuming that when these authors talk about "gentlemen" or "Americans" they mean "people," they mean those socially and politically assimilated descendants of ethnic Americans—Irish, Italian, Mexican, Jewish, Polish, even African—who now teach, and write about, their work. When reading oneself back into the role of narratee for the American classics, one tends to assume that they would translate their sentiments into gender- and class-neutral language if they knew how; assume, in short, that they would understand and accept us. Readings based on presence import a democratic tolerance, but a tolerance merely, into the work of American writers who might have been served by "our" ancestors rather than dining with them.

In chapter 10 of *Walden* one comes across Thoreau's sentence, "But alas! the culture of an Irishman is an enterprise to be undertaken with a sort of moral bog hoe."[64] It is an offhand remark and can be contextualized for students in many different ways, the most pleasantly available of which is simply to propose that Thoreau had a pig-ignorant view of Irish people.

But is it offhand? What if that sentence is more central to *Walden* than "The mass of men lead lives of quiet desperation" or other equally quotable remarks? Thoreau's undeniable commitment to classicism, belles lettres, and freedom of conscience would then all pivot around the central necessity for a racially irredeemable immigrant serving class to underpin his "Economy." Readers are faced with several options: they can imagine their way back into the Anglo-American perspective of Thoreau in a sort of retroactive poetics of presence—even though most of the readers of this passage are likely to have more Irish than English ancestors. (I would argue that this assimilative identification still occurs more likely than we hope it does, especially if there is a present-day immigrant group that the student reader can summon up as a private analogy to Thoreau's Irish.) Or one could ignore the remark, treat it as truly offhand, and construct a private edition of the "real" politically correct *Walden*. Or one could confront the text and extrapolate the deconstruction of it that I have suggested above. But canonical inertia may suggest a safer course—to try to enlist Thoreau himself as a multiculturalist, as someone who satirizes anti-Irish views and anti-immigrant ideology generally.

And in this last (and tremendously attractive) option, there lies the problem of the poetics of presence as a basic assumption for reading, teaching, and constructing syllabuses. Keeping a sense of Thoreau as a hero can become more important than confronting the text—more important because one reinforces one's own political argument with authority borrowed from him while propitiating an older generation of scholars and teachers for whom Thoreau is more unqualifiedly heroic.

One negotiates Thoreau; one keeps him canonical. But one obliterates the facts of nineteenth-century social history in so doing.

Thoreau was not a multiculturalist; multiculturalism was inconceivable for him historically. The poetics of presence constructs a heroic identity for canonical authors, making them endlessly available as sites for whatever values readers hold to be heroic, because the form of heroism is more elastic than the content of the texts it is derived from. By making already canonical writers ever newly heroic, critics construct what I call retroactive fictions of identity. A retroactive fiction of identity works two ways: we see ourselves as peers of the heroic author and the heroic author as a mouthpiece for our ideas. But even that word "we," though rhetorically useful, begs a logical question: who are "we" as Americans? It is more the medical "we" (how are we feeling this morning?) than the editorial we (or than the Lone Ranger's "We're surrounded," to which Tonto replies, "What you mean we?"—though there are times when any scholar confronted by the plethora of "we's" in the theoretical discourse of Americanist studies has empathized with Tonto). It is the medical "we" because a fiction of common identity has an ultimately therapeutic purpose, uniting a classroom in a common goal of progressive movement toward social health.

But discontinuties, which are all too historically real, entail perceptions and acknowledgments of difference. Foregrounding the reader in the ways I do here entails the responsibility for the reader to recognize and use those differences, and to avoid the retroactive blending of historical struggles (which often have never ceased) into a bland narrative of progress over sociological obstacles. A canon supported by a poetics of presence is therefore a continually charged political institution, even when its components seem as apolitical as the lyrics of Emily Dickinson. (And the works of many Anglo-American writers can easily appear apolitical simply because they have been long canonical.) Teaching (where the work of scholars has far more impact than it does in books like this one) can perpetuate the process of assimilation, a process that involves a rehearsed past where the personalities critics construct from textual traces act out social dramas. Readers censure, judge, extol "people" who are amalgams of their textual constructions and ethical values. These habits will die hard, but I would argue that "we" need to let the tradition of presence go and pay more attention to the immediate moral effect of reading on "our" lives. Such an insistence does not mean the abandonment of history, or I would not be writing this history of reception. People only come to know themselves through the perspective of the past—if it is a true perspective and not a mall-booth photograph where late twentieth-century faces look out of cutouts where the heads of Transcendentalists should be. And I would not argue for the abandonment of scholarship, but instead for the use of scholarly senses of textuality in facing the moral dilemmas of teaching.

TWO

Whitman as the American Homer

> The coming centuries will place Walt Whitman
> high on the list of glorious names, the first voice of
> a united, crystallized, original America, a bard who
> sang democracy, our great citizenship, God-love,
> and the comradeship of the throbbing, suffering,
> hoping, majestic human heart.[1]

Walt Whitman's fame preceded him. It existed years before his birth;
years after his death, the need for Whitman to exist is still in clearer
focus than the texts of his poems. In 1915, Van Wyck Brooks suggested
that Whitman could be the "focal centre" of American culture and explained why he felt the need for such a focus. Whitman, says Brooks, is
a poet in "the most radical and primitive sense of the word (the sense
in which it was held by Whitman himself), a man, that is to say, who
first gives to a nation a certain focal centre in the consciousness of its
own character. . . . A *focal centre*—that is the first requisite of a great people."[2] The requisite came before the poet did, both historically and in
the rhetorical structure of *America's Coming-of-Age*. Brooks devotes the
first two chapters of the book to an explanation of the need for a focus
in American culture and the problem of finding a suitable candidate for
the focal role among currently canonical authors. After rejecting all the
others, he offers Whitman in his third chapter, posing the requisite first
and then supplying the material to meet it. Brooks's requisite was felt a
hundred years earlier by John Knapp, who called in 1818 for an American literature that would establish the glory of the American nation as
the classical writers had done for Greece.[3] By 1922, when Stuart Sherman could say of Whitman's predecessors and contemporaries, "They
have sadly dwindled—most of them—they have lost their warmth for
us, they have become irrelevant to our occasions," Whitman had achieved

that status of American Homer, with all previous American poetry reduced to the status of pre-Whitmanic remains.[4]

The role of American Homer, however, was written before *Leaves of Grass* and without Walt Whitman in mind. There were earlier candidates for the role, especially William Cullen Bryant and the elder Richard Henry Dana—neither of whom maintained the central place for which early critics had nominated them.[5] Those early nominations came out of a sense even in the 1810s that the American golden age was present (indeed passing) and must call forth its poet. Edward Tyrrel Channing demanded a "native" poet who would capture "the splendid barbarism of your country, when the mind was in health and free, and the foundations of your character and greatness laid for ever."[6] "Barbarism" here is an odd metaphor, coming from the man who would epitomize American cultivation as Boylston Professor of Rhetoric at Harvard; but the metaphor is a common one in American criticism. The sense that a barbaric America must produce a barbaric founder-poet informs Park Benjamin's 1839 peroration: "It would, perhaps, not be too extravagant to say that the poetical resources of our country are boundless. Nature has here granted every thing to genius which can excite, exalt, enlarge, and ennoble its powers. Nothing is narrow, nothing is confined. All is height, all is expansion. . . . Shall there not be one great poet—that man whose eye can roam over the borders of our land, and see those things of which we have spoken? Needs not the spirit of prophecy answer, 'Yes?'"[7] The unfortunate punctuation that makes Benjamin's final exclamation seem so tentative ("Yes?") hints that critics were more inclined to identify an unmet than an actualized potential. In the 1840s, Margaret Fuller still put all of American literature in the future: "It does not follow because many books are written by persons born in America that there exists an American literature. . . . Before such can exist, an original idea must animate this nation and fresh currents of life must call into life fresh thoughts along its shores."[8] The impact of Ralph Waldo Emerson's evocation of American poetic potentials in "The Poet" (1844) depends precisely on the continued *absence* of the American Homer: "We have yet had no genius in America, with tyrannous eye, which knew the value of our incomparable materials, and saw, in the barbarism and materialism of our times, another carnival of the same gods whose picture he so much admires in Homer."[9] Whitman's excitement when Emerson said of *Leaves of Grass* that "it meets the demand I am always making" must be understood in the context of so many others *before* Emerson making that same demand. It was more than just an idiosyncratic Emersonian demand; it was like the expectation of an entire people for a cultural Messiah. American critics considered long and seriously of Walt Whitman before he was born.

The founder-poet was always conceived of as a present figure. The demands of a new democratic ideology meant that he would have to somehow embody democracy, while the very newness of the nation entailed his living presence as a voice; he could not be situated in the distant past, as the supposed Ossian had been in Scotland. (For such a rediscovered past, American critics had to wait for the twentieth-century arrival of the eighteenth-century poet Edward Taylor.) As a present poet, the American Homer would be original and monologic, with an essential connection in particular to the American ecosystem.

American criticism between 1810 and 1860 is laden with organic metaphors. These metaphors coexist in the criticism with literal invocations of the American landscape, flora, and fauna, as materials in and figures with which to express the birth of an American poetry. Coexistence bred confusion; the interests of American literary independence entailed a critical vocabulary in which organic metaphors are not recognized or qualified as metaphors. In fact, part of the poetics of organic presence is an insistence that metaphor is itself inorganic, even poisonously mediate. Edward Tyrrel Channing argues for Native American poetic materials while simultaneously attacking metaphor: "A nation should keep itself at home, and value the things of its own household. It will have but feeble claims to excellence and distinction, when it stoops to put on foreign ornament and manner, and to adopt from other nations, images, allusions, and a metaphorical language, which are perfectly unmeaning and sickly, out of their own birth-place."[10] Channing, arguing here against classical and British models for American writing, is, on the face of it, attacking imported metaphors without denying the appropriateness of native ones. But the break in parallel construction between "images, allusions" and "a metaphorical language" conveys an overtone of resistance to *all* metaphorical language because of its distancing effect, which is similar in kind to the distancing effected by using a foreign diction that needs translation into native terms. A salient feature of Whitman's language, which made it all the more eligible for centrality, is its relative lack of metaphors.

Organicist poetics adopts the language of the organism so readily that it presents organicism as direct observation, not as a figure of speech. The early nationalist critics think automatically of American literature as a living organism. Margaret Fuller worries about the organism's nutrition: "The winds from all quarters of the globe bring seed enough, and there is nothing wanting but preparation of the soil and freedom in the atmosphere, for ripening of a new and golden harvest."[11] And almost sixty years later, George Edward Woodberry tries to identify weeds in the American literary garden, speaking of "the pseudo-romantic English school, which was the tap-root of Byronism and in [the elder] Dana sent out a wandering shoot overseas."[12]

If the organic was a value, the wild organism was doubly valuable. For early American critics, "culture" and "cultivation" are negative terms. William Cullen Bryant characterizes colonial American poems as "rare and delicate exotics, cultivated only by the curious."[13] When Margaret Fuller wants to convey her fullest disapproval of Longfellow's poetics, she speaks of his work as "a tastefully arranged museum, between whose glass cases are interspersed neatly potted rose trees, geraniums, and hyacinths, grown by himself with aid of indoor heat."[14] For Fuller, Longfellow's verse is made up of "clean and elegantly ornamented streets and trim gardens," while Bryant's is "like leaving the highway to enter some green lovely fragrant wood."[15] The distrust of cultivated society that runs through the writing of the American Renaissance is of a piece with the value placed on wildness in the poetics of the period, a value that led to the expulsion of "society" poets like Fitz-Greene Halleck and Charles Sprague from the canon at an early date.

Walt Whitman would come to be seen as an even more perfect embodiment than Bryant of the poetics of organicism. Richard Harter Fogle explained in 1955 that "Whitman is the most extreme, the most expansively daring of vital organicists. He goes furthest in identifying art with life and nature in organic form. His organicism means literally the word made flesh. . . . The archetypal organic body of Whitman's vision is America."[16] But the hold that organic ideas had on American critical thought can perhaps best be seen in the work of a critic who denied the importance of Whitman—on organic grounds. Barrett Wendell's commentary on Whitman takes the form of an elaborated metaphor of artistic tradition as a tree with a healthy trunk and large branches, whose offshoots represent artistic experiments doomed to wither. "Oddity is no part of solid artistic development; however beautiful or impressive, it is rather an excrescent outgrowth, bound to prove abortive, and at the same time to sap life from a parent stock which without it might grow more loftily and strongly. Walt Whitman's style is of this excrescent, abortive kind."[17] Wendell's concept of Walt Whitman as a great sucker threatening to destroy the live oak of American literature turns Whitman's own organicism back on itself. The scale of values here is in fact suggested less by the tenor than by the vehicle of the organic metaphor. Taking vegetative health as the Aristotelian mean of artistic perfection, then both overcultivation and overgrowth represent excessive vices to be avoided, and gardener Wendell must prune Whitman away. To make his point even more damning, Wendell puts Whitman's supporters on the side of too much culture: "the public to which his prophecy made its way was at once limited, fastidiously overcultivated, and apt to be of foreign birth."[18]

For other critics, less Aristotelian in their insistence on a mean of organic perfection than Wendell, the very fact that Whitman espoused organicism is reason enough to see him as the heart of the American literary organism. For Brooks, the problem with America is that the nation is "a welter of life which has not been worked into an organism";[19] but Whitman offers the promise of becoming the central nervous system of this welter: "The real significance of Walt Whitman is that he, for the first time, gave us the sense of something organic in American life."[20] Organism is here completely removed from the realm of metaphor; Brooks makes an exact scientific identification of a nation as an interdependent colony of coral-like beings. True to racialist sociological paradigms of his day, Brooks identifies America as a community of separate tribal races, with the ancestral founding tribe—for Brooks, the Anglo-Americans, of course, not the American Indians—as the special bearer of some sort of racial mission. Brooks praises Whitman especially for providing "the raw materials of a racial norm."[21] In turn, Brooks's own influence among American critics was due in part to his own conspicuous racial identity as an Anglo-American; Bernard Smith speaks of the authority that America's Coming-of-Age possessed because its author "was a native, brought up in the traditional home of our own dearest literary heritage," "not a 'foreigner,' not a Catholic, not a Jew."[22]

Organicism in American criticism has a long-standing association with racialism. Racialist ideas lie under both the troubling early twentieth-century "tribal" concepts and under the earlier, romantic idealism of Margaret Fuller. Fuller, whose "American Literature" is inseparable from the organic metaphors in which its argument is couched, presents the role of criticism itself in terms that combine nationalism, organicism, biblical parable, and market capitalism, thereby anticipating Social Darwinism: "There will always be a good deal of mock poetry in the market with the genuine; it grows up naturally as tares among the wheat, and while there is a fair proportion preserved, we abstain from severe weeding lest the two come up together; but when the tares have almost usurped the field, it is time to begin and see if the field cannot be freed from them and made ready for a new seed-time."[23] There is a certain amount of figural confusion here between criticism of texts, moral winnowing of character, and selective breeding of a people. Fuller's concerns often seem more racial than literary. Defending American literary nationalism in "American Literature," she maintains: "What suits

Great Britain, with her insular position and consequent need to concentrate and intensify her life, her limited monarchy and spirit of trade, does not suit a mixed race continually enriched with new blood from other stocks the most unlike that of our first descent."[24] The full force of American genius will not be expressed, Fuller says, "till the fusion of races among us is more complete."[25]

Such an endorsement of racial "fusion" was by the turn of the twentieth century alien to the thought of many American critics; but the basic assumption in Fuller's essay, that different ethnic groups have different essential traits that can mix in interbreeding, is an enduring commonplace. Bliss Perry starts from the notion of racial characteristics in his 1906 biography. One of the conditions of Whitman's intellectual development, for Perry, was a "stout ancestry of mingled strain"; the poet's mother "Louisa Van Velsor was of mingled Dutch and Welsh blood, with an English strain for tempering."[26] Perry's gardening metaphors move uninhibitedly from literary forms and traditions to human families to personality types. For Anglo-American critics in the first decades of the 1900s—the 1910s and 1920s—facing a great wave of European immigrants who were beginning to move into American schools and other cultural power centers, Whitman's very ancestry, mostly British with a picturesque and venerable Dutch component, was a powerful reason to approve of Whitman's poetics.

The racialist assumptions of American literary organicism are important to bear in mind when considering the nature of American literary nationalism as a whole, which is imbued with those assumptions. Early literary nationalism is often seen, particularly by academics within the discipline of American literary studies, as an admirable ideology. In its formation, however, it was the ideology of Anglo-Americans bent on freeing Anglo-American racial culture from Anglo-Saxon racial culture. Given the virtually exact identity of the literary dialects of English on either side of the Atlantic, this was a project informed with paradox from the start. Can there be an American culture that expresses itself in the English language while being free of the influence of contemporary British culture?

Clearly American critics have always thought there *could* be, though the question has become far less important now that the United States has outgrown England and, through the media of films and television, come to dominate the culture of the former metropolitan nation. Retrospective readings of American literary history, especially in textbooks and anthologies, continue to this day, however, to stress the growth of a purely American tradition in English. This tradition is often said to begin with Walt Whitman, whose formal models, oddly enough, include

Smart, McPherson, Blake, and the English Bible. But American critics of the early nineteenth century clearly believed that they were participating in decolonizing, to use Ngũgĩ wa Thiong'o's term, the American mind.[27] For critics like Channing, and indeed for most of the writers in the *North American Review* in the 1810s and 1820s who followed the ideas of its founder, William Tudor, the independence of American writing from British was a cause of first importance.[28] Edwin P. Whipple, in 1844, strongly felt a need for an independent American tradition, with an emphasis on manliness that is a rare overt expression of the assumption that true poetry has a masculine gender: "If we have a literature, it should be a national literature; no feeble or sonorous echo of Germany or England, but essentially American in its tone and object. . . . We want a poetry which shall . . . speak out in the high language of men to a nation of men."[29] The anxiety of British influence weighed heavily on Emerson, who chafed at "our long apprenticeship to the learning of other lands,"[30] and on Fuller, who was concerned that "we use her [England's] language and receive in torrents the influence of her thought, yet it is in many respects uncongenial and injurious to our constitution."[31] Constitution here appears to mean the American intellectual health in general, conceived in organic terms as a single body politic, not the Constitution itself (a document written, after all, in English).

The strongest feeling of intellectual dependence is perhaps conveyed by Edward Tyrrel Channing's critique of classical education in "On Models" (1816). An exclusively classical training means that a child's role models will be ancient and heroical, says Channing. "The effect of this is, in many cases, to make what is foreign, artificial, and uncongenial, the foundation of a man's literary habits, ambition, and prejudices. It is hardly possible that a man, thus trained and dependent, should not lose self respect, and come to think every thing vulgar at home."[32] Channing's formulation of intellectual dependence and its mechanisms is remarkably close to Ngũgĩ's analysis of how a colonial power uses "cultural bombs" to conquer a subject people: "Since culture does not just reflect the world in images but actually, through those very images, conditions a child to see that world in a certain way, the colonial child was made to see the world and where he stands in it as seen and defined by or reflected in the culture of the language of imposition."[33] The situations are different and the force of cultural imposition is different (in Channing's case, a classical curriculum imported from the British educational tradition; in Ngũgĩ's case, the English language itself), but the solution in each case is a vigorous literary nationalism that resorts to native linguistic strategies, that reestablishes the immediacy of the contact between the mother tongue and the physical environment.

Ironic, of course, is the cultural situation made invisible by Chan-ning's reading of Anglo-American dependency on a dominant culture. Anglo-Americans themselves, as a colonizing people, were in reality on the other side of Ngũgĩ's cultural dynamic, imposing English on Indian cultures and reducing Indian languages to a state of extreme cultural dependence. The anguish felt by American intellectuals who saw them-selves colonized by British and classical cultures is analogous to that of white Virginians in the 1770s who saw themselves as enslaved by the British. The very dynamic one people so cheerfully enacted with regard to another was the great source of grievance in their relations to a third.

The long-standing and extremely complex relation between Anglo-Americans and Native Americans in nineteenth-century intellectual history is beyond my scope here and has been studied elsewhere.[34] But it is worth noting that practically none of the literary nationalists of the period 1789–1855 advocates even a study of American Indian culture, let alone an empowering of Indian voices. A very rare exception is John Knapp: "Let us hasten to acquaint ourselves with the earlier native. Let us hasten;—for already has the cultivator levelled many a monumental mound, that spoke of more than writings might preserve."[35] Even at that, Knapp's language has an antiquarian tone, a sense that archaeological study of "the earlier" Indians will be more productive than going out and talking to living, breathing ones. But implicitly, even as the issue of native voices in American literature is marginalized out of sight by Anglo-American rhetoric of the early national period, the deep concern with making American literature native, indeed autochthonous (if only retroactively so), reflects a nagging sense of double belatedness and dou-ble anxiety. Epigones of the British tradition on the one hand, usurpers of the American landscape on the other, the literary nationalists desired a condition of purity that could only come from a purgative starting over, a new inscription on an empty landscape.

The double belatedness expressed in early American literary nation-alism was sharpened by various internal struggles in the American in-tellectual community. There was no necessary consensus on the relations of American literature to English, no fore-ordained growth of the Amer-ican spirit toward literary independence. Some critics were undisturbed by the close connections of American literature to the English tradi-tion. Edgar Allan Poe, as so often, held an idiosyncratic position, see-ing an unproblematic continuity between American and British liter-ary English. "The principles of the poetic sentiment lie deep within the immortal nature of man, and have little necessary reference to the world-ly circumstances which surround him. The poet in Arcady is, in Kam-schadtka, the poet still. The self-same Saxon current animates the British and the American heart; nor can any social, or political, or moral, or physical conditions do more than momentarily repress the impulses which glow in our own bosoms as fervently as in those of our progenitors."[36] For Poe, English literature is English literature regardless of geography and regardless of who's writing it. Poe was not alone in this view; parts of his argument had been anticipated, indeed taken further in the direction of an embrace of transatlantic literary continuity, by Robert Walsh. Walsh used his Philadelphia *American Quarterly Review* as a vehicle for attacking New England critics in general and literary nationalism in particular. This is Walsh, reviewing Samuel Kettell's anthology *Specimens of American Poetry*, in 1829: Kettell "suggests that 'the cultivation of literary talent has been retarded by the state of *dependence* as to literature in which we have continued, to the writers of Great Britain.' We reject the advice and the suggestion as worse than problematical. . . . Dependent we are, and must continue to be for some time; and so far from having been *retarded* generally by British literature, we owe to it the present comparative ripeness of our knowledge and taste."[37] *Pourri avant d'être mûre*, a literary nationalist might retort. Walsh was ultimately a loser in the struggle to define the terms of American literature; his importance lies in showing that there indeed *was* a struggle, and that it had regional and social circumstances that persisted well after the strugglers themselves passed from the scene. Even William Cullen Bryant, so often seen as making an early break with English traditions, did not align himself in his criticism with the extreme nationalists, saying of the growth of an American tradition after the Revolution merely that "on our becoming an independent nation, a different spirit began to manifest itself, and the general ambition to distinguish ourselves as a nation was not without its effect on our literature."[38] The matter-of-factness that Bryant exhibits in 1818 would be a feature of his criticism throughout his career; by refusing to weigh in with the extreme literary nationalists, Bryant in part made himself increasingly irrelevant to the processes that would eventually canonize Whitman, instead of him, as the central American poet.

Concern with American literary dependence on England was still strong at the turn of the twentieth century and was an immediate context for the crucial reception of Walt Whitman. George Edward Woodberry, who placed a strong emphasis on the regional environments of American literature, dismisses colonial American writing with the comment that "the secondary character of American literature in its first century, its inferiority in mass and quality to the contemporary productions of England and France, is everywhere acknowledged."[39] Woodberry goes on to reject Dana as a candidate for the great American poet,

because in Dana's work "poetry and fiction were blended, but neither element disclosed American originality except by some modification of his
English exemplars in respect to the setting of the works."[40] Woodberry
grudgingly allowed only that Whitman had written "a few fine lyrics," but
he admitted that Whitman had fulfilled the task of cutting himself free
of English influence: "To become what Whitman was, Americans, who,
more than Englishmen, are the heirs of all Europe, must first denude
themselves of that larger civilization with which they are integral, and
be an Ishmael among nations."[41] *America in Literature* is interesting as
an early example of the reception of Whitman into the canon, seeing
him as having met some of the requirements for the role of American
Homer but not as having met them very well. Woodberry continues the
line of rhetoric, familiar from Fuller and Emerson, of insisting that the
great American poet has not yet shown himself.

But Van Wyck Brooks, who saw Whitman as fully central, wrote even
more eloquently against American literary indebtedness to Britain than
Woodberry did: "Literary English with us is a tradition, just as Anglo-
Saxon law with us is a tradition. They persist not as the normal expressions of a race, the essential fibre of which is permanently Anglo-Saxon, but through prestige and precedent and the will and habit of a
dominating class largely out of touch with a national fabric unconsciously
taking form 'out of school.'"[42] Brooks here challenges the assertions made
seventy years earlier by Poe. But he does so with some ambivalence.
Where Poe unabashedly identifies the American national character with
the English ("The self-same Saxon current animates the British and the
American heart"), Brooks sees the Saxon component in America only
as a "dominating class," a *part* of "us" that has gained centrality through
historical accident. The convolution of expression in Brooks's second
sentence shows how central that class (his class) still was to his thought
in 1915. "A race, the essential fibre of which is purely Anglo-Saxon" is
apparently *not* what America is; America is something else, where literary English has never taken root. But Brooks leaves open the suggestion, with almost a hint of nostalgia, that a Saxon "race" might still exist permanently untouched despite permanent exile; and while his
explicit sympathies are with the life burgeoning "out of school," his audience and his allegiance are inside.

Critics were drawn to Walt Whitman at the turn of the twentieth
century because they read him as doing what poets like Dana did not:
"disclosing American originality," in Woodberry's significant phrase,
which suggests that such an originality is innate, requiring revelation
rather than construction. Originality here is used in a collective sense,
indicating one tradition's break from another. But individual originali-

ty is also one of the most pervasive values of the literary nationalists who wrote before and after Whitman. Woodberry's devaluation of Dana for insufficient originality was the opposite conclusion, reached by the same method, to that of Edwin P. Whipple in his construction of a canon of American poetry in 1844. Whipple placed Charles Sprague first among American poets and Dana second; his high regard for Dana is because "Mr. Dana is, perhaps, our most original poet. . . . He seems never to have written from hearsay, or taken any of his opinions at second-hand."[43] Whipple's criteria are the same, but his judgment different, from A. H. Everett, who in 1831 elevated Bryant at the expense of Dana, whom he saw as a mere imitator of Wordsworth. Everett's praise of Bryant is indistinguishable from Whipple's praise of Dana: "[Bryant's] imagery is the true and lively expression of nature not transmitted through the pages of a thousand preceding writers, till it has become no better than a mere conventional jargon; but taken fresh at first hand from the breathing face of the divine original."[44] For Everett, as for many other contemporary critics, the connection between originality and nature—and hence, between originality and organicism—was strong.

The emphasis on originality in American criticism before Whitman is in one sense continuous with what Thomas McFarland has identified as the "originality paradox" in romantic thought: the insistence on valuing texts, in an age when technology, population growth, and economic development produced more and more of them, increasingly by their idiosyncrasy and unlikeness to other texts.[45] American critics of the romantic and postromantic periods absorbed from Coleridge a scale of values that related originality to individuation of style, and the degree of a poet's individuality directly to the value of the poet's work. In Coleridge, this relation works to the advantage of Shakespeare and Wordsworth: "A person of any taste, who had but studied three or four of Shakespeare's principal plays, would without the name affixed scarcely fail to recognize as Shakespeare's a quotation from any other play, though but of a few lines. A similar peculiarity, though in a less degree, attends Mr. Wordsworth's style, whenever he speaks in his own person; or whenever, though under a feigned name, it is clear that he himself is still speaking, as in the different dramatis personae of the 'RECLUSE.'"[46] Coleridge conceives of a scale of individuation of poetic voice; Shakespeare is highly individuated; he also mentions Milton as being so. Wordsworth is slightly less so, but his language is still highly individual.

The American canon-makers first saw Bryant as highly individuated, later saw Whitman as the most original poet, and later still would add Dickinson, Poe, and others to the canon in relation to their perceived degree of individuation. The idea of degrees of individuation implies that at some level there is a common mass of poetic diction that most rank-and-file poets do not rise above; often, that common mass—Jauss's "unsurveyable production of works that correspond to the traditional expectations or images concerning reality"—is a rhetorical assumption rather than a demonstrable fact.[47]

The American Romantics combined the general terms of the originality paradox with the special needs of literary nationalism, so that originality was inseparable for them from a new American view of things and from the direct, unmediated presence of American nature and the American voice in texts. Margaret Fuller reiterated earlier critics' praise of Bryant on the score of originality, saying that "his poetry is purely the language of his inmost nature,"[48] but for her, originality had even more of a charged connotation; as the guarantee of the poet's presence in the text, originality is for Fuller the highest virtue, equivalent to Truth: "No man can be absolutely true to himself, eschewing cant, compromise, servile imitation, and complaisance, without becoming original, for there is in every creature a fountain of life which, if not choked back by stones and other dead rubbish, will create a fresh atmosphere and bring to life fresh beauty."[49] Angus Fletcher has seen the extreme idiosyncrasy of poets like Whitman and Poe as a sort of attempt to express a truth that flows only very uneasily into common language. He finds in their verse a surface opacity that conceals universal truths that are difficult of utterance: "The idiosyncratic author embeds the logical issue right in the utterance of this text, just beneath the surface, and thus leads the reader to notice always how the text is being uttered, to notice a certain opacity of the text."[50] In a sense, Fletcher reproduces a feature of the critical consensus that developed long after Whitman and Poe. For their contemporaries, these poets were indeed original but hardly as stunningly remarkable as they now seem, when they are practically the only poets from the period represented in anthologies and literary histories. Mid-nineteenth-century American critics made manifold distinctions among the styles of poets who now blend together for us: Longfellow, Bryant, Dana, Percival, Sprague, Sigourney, Willis, Very, Larcom, Whittier, Halleck. All these poets were held to be original in one way or another by the critics who promoted them; often (as in the debate over Dana) a poet would be seen as original by one critic, derivative by another. From the perspective of criticism 150 years later, the crucial dynamic may be scale-dependence.[51] Looked at from a broad vantage point, it is easy to tell apart writers who work in different languages or different genres. In a given language and genre there are historical, dialectal, and various contextual conditions that establish an individual voice. Among writers who come from similar historical, regional and educational circumstances, there are individual verbal mannerisms, and between writers who have mastered similar verbal styles there are even more minute identifying marks of personality, verbal mannerisms that reveal a writer to readers who know that writer's work well. Being so far from writers like Sigourney and Halleck on all these levels, we now find it difficult to distinguish between them.

One example of the distinctions that operated for contemporary readers but not in nearly the same way for us can be seen in a pair of reviews by Edgar Allan Poe. Poe is an extreme case because he read more obsessively for scansion than other critics of his time, but he was not a pedant. He expected that his readers would understand his analyses of versification, and he made them clear and deliberate.

In reviewing Lydia Sigourney's "Friends of Man," from her collection *Zinzendorff,* Poe says, "the versification throughout is of the first order of excellence. We select an example."

> The youth at midnight sought his bed,
>   But ere he closed his eyes,
> Two forms drew near with gentle tread,
>   In meek and saintly guise;
> One struck a lyre of wondrous power,
>   With thrilling music fraught,
> That chained the flying summer hour,
>   And charmed the listener's thought—.[52]

Several years later (but there is no reason to think his critical standards or his ear had changed in the meantime), Poe reviewed Elizabeth Oakes Smith's "The Acorn," with this severe reservation: "the rhythm . . . is imperfect, vacillating awkwardly . . . rendering the whole versification difficult of comprehension." Here is Poe's own choice of quotation from "The Acorn":

> They came with gifts that should life bestow;
>   The dew and the living air—
> The bane that should work its deadly wo,
>   The little men had there;
> In the gray moss cup was the mildew brought,
>   The worm in a rose-leaf rolled,
> And many things with destruction fraught
>   That its doom were quickly told.[53]

The reader's ear and sense of form may differ from mine, but I would argue that after 150 years English readers can perceive an "etic" difference between these stanzas (they do technically differ in a perceptible way), but that for us there is no socially meaningful, or "emic," difference: both are conventional in the extreme, "Victorian" to the hilt. Both poems are written in the common meter that can also be found in different stanza combinations in "The Walrus and the Carpenter," "The Village Blacksmith," and "The Ballad of Reading Gaol." They alternate four- and three-stress lines; they rhyme *abab* (and they would resemble Dickinson's common meter, except that she almost never rhymes *abab*). The difference is exactly the one Poe perceived (to summarize his extensive technical analysis): Oakes Smith's poem employs trisyllabic substitutions (it allows three syllables in a foot, as well as the usual two). Where all of Sigourney's long lines are exactly eight syllables long, Oakes Smith's range between nine and ten; where Sigourney's short lines are uniformly six syllables, Oakes Smith's are six or seven. This was a very big deal in early nineteenth-century prosody; one of Bryant's first critical articles dealt with the trisyllabic substitution in great detail, and he was often criticized strongly for employing it. But no critic is about to devote a review in *American Poetry Review* or *Poetry* to slating someone for trisyllabic substitution any time during the 1990s or 2000s.

In the context of convention where Elizabeth Oakes Smith could seem drastically different from Lydia Sigourney, Walt Whitman took originality in form to a new level. But Whitman's originality did not immediately bring him high canonical rank. His dissimilarity to previous writers is the theme of most initial reviews of the 1855 *Leaves*; as Edward Everett Hale noted in 1856, "he has a horror of conventional language of any kind."[54] Whitman's highly distinctive style quickly became the target for pastiche and charge. The role of these parodic genres in displaying a period sense of individual style is crucial. *Pastiche* (in the sense of playful imitation) and *charge* (in the sense of satiric imitation) are dependent on a firm sense that there is an individuality to be imitated.[55]

American poets of the late eighteenth century, like John Trumbull, were devoted to burlesque—the use of a conventional style for inappropriate subject matter. American poets of the mid- to late nineteenth century were increasingly aware of the possibilities of pastiche and charge. American poets of the late eighteenth century are insulated from pastiche by the conventional style of their burlesques; American poets of the mid-nineteenth century are targets for various imitations of their idiosyncratic styles, ranging from charge (against Longfellow) as in "Hiawatha's Photographing" by Lewis Carroll to the pastiches of Poe by James Whitcomb Riley, which approach the status of forgery. The many and various imitations of Whitman are somewhere along the scale.

But while Whitman was imitable, he was not always intelligible even to his imitators. With the value placed on originality came a corresponding rejection of the overly original—much like the rejection of wildness that accompanied critical organicism. Bryant placed as much value on originality as any early nineteenth-century critic: "There is hardly any praise of which writers in the present age, particularly writers in verse, are more ambitious than that of originality. This ambition is a laudable one, for a captivating originality is everything in art."[56] But one could have too much of a good thing: "Whoever would entirely disclaim imitation, and aspire to the praises of complete originality, should be altogether ignorant of any poetry written by others, and of all those aids which the cultivation of poetry has lent to prose. Deprive an author of these advantages, and what sort of poetry does any one imagine that he would produce? I dare say it would be sufficiently original, but who will affirm that it could be read?"[57] Bryant's eminently logical point about the dependence of texts on conventions for their very readability foreshadows Barrett Wendell's organicist attack on Whitman as an "excrescence" seventy-five years later. For Wendell, pure organicism is incompatible with true originality; organic truth means an adherence to classical norms of expression.

The canonizing critics who answered Wendell's arguments used several strategies. One we have seen used by John Macy—to assert that Whitman was the founder of a mode of poetry and therefore completely readable in retrospect. Macy also adopted a feature of Whitman's poetics that the poet himself had realized was inherently self-contradictory: the notion that an idiosyncratic poet could utter the "word enmasse."[58] For Macy, Whitman could be a founder of a tradition, a lonely prophet, and a perfectly representative common man all at once. One of Macy's moves was to redefine America to make room for Walt Whitman: "The indifference of democracy to its greatest poet seems a paradox, but the indifference does not exist. America is not a democracy; it is a vast bourgeoisie; the democracy which Whitman celebrates has not arrived on the earth."[59] To get around the objection that Whitman's forms are unreadably idiosyncratic, Macy decenters form by detaching it from "true" originality and by insisting that the poet himself was confused about the connection: "Whitman himself made much of the fact that he departed from the tradition of regular metres, and (as genius is frequently mistaken about itself) he thought that his departure was essential to his originality, whereas it was only one expression of his originality, and not the capital expression. His true originality lies in the use he made of the metres he chose and not at all in the fact or the degree of their technical difference from other poetry."[60] Macy's emphasis on the spirit rather than the letter of literary form is appropriate in a work called *The Spirit of American Literature*. Setting up a dichotomy between spirit and form in Whitman's texts allows them to be read as both individual and representative.[61] George Santayana, in the course of a long, ever-retreating rearguard action against the canonization of Whitman, was often one of Macy's opponents; but Santayana may have crystallized Macy's solution in a sentence from "The Genteel Tradition in American Philosophy" (1911): "When the foreigner opens the pages of Walt Whitman, he thinks that he has come at last upon something representative and original."[62] Perhaps the native would not; but Santayana *was* a foreigner and hence implicates himself in a certain acceptance of Whitman as the embodiment of a necessary paradox: the nonconformist representative. In achieving his dissent from the canonization of Whitman, we might further note, Santayana relies on the authority of the assimilated immigrant who has learned to think as a native—and therefore to reject Whitman as something fit only for exotic or exoticist tastes.

In the mid-twentieth century, R. W. B. Lewis reached the ne plus ultra of valuing Whitman for his originality; and Lewis conceived of Whitman's originality in terms that show how the monologic nature of that originality was central to critical appreciation of Whitman.

> There is scarcely a poem of Whitman's before, say, 1867, which does not have the air of being the first poem ever written, the first formulation in language of the nature of persons and of things and of the relations between them; and the urgency of the language suggests that it was formulated in the very nick of time, to give the objects described their first substantial existence.
>
> Nor is there, in *Leaves of Grass*, any complaint about the weight or intrusion of the past; in Whitman's view the past had been so effectively burned away that it had, for every practical purpose, been forgotten altogether.[63]

Lewis celebrates here the very process that had so worried Bryant 125 years before: that American poetry in the attempt to be original would forget, erase, the traces of previous poetries and verbal acts that had informed the classical and British traditions. Such an erasure is a move that guarantees the sealing-off of the poet's voice against dialogic intrusion. Lewis, in celebrating the monologic plunge of the word into virginal territory, retains a key feature of value that both Whitman and American criticism owe largely to Ralph Waldo Emerson. It is a crucial insistence in Emerson—almost an article of faith—that the American poetic landscape is empty, devoid of these previous acts of recognition, whether native, colonial, or foreign. The world of objects is indeed "virginal" for Emerson; it is one of his favorite tropes. "The perpetual admonition of nature to us, is, 'The world is new, untried. Do not believe the past. I give you the universe a virgin to-day.' "[64] Poetry is a sort of begetting on this untried nature, and "the religions of the world are the ejaculations of a few imaginative men."[65] (Whether the poetic theorist is a sort of master procurer goes less developed here.)

The debt of both Whitman and other American poetic theorists to Emerson can be, and often has been, overstated. For us, the apparent inescapability of Emerson is a function of the same institutions that have made Whitman central to American poetry. Emerson has become central to the American essay, and major author anthologies often give the impression that Emerson, Whitman, and Poe were the only Americans thinking about poetry in the mid-nineteenth century. But as Benjamin T. Spencer pointed out in 1957, Emerson's ideas on poetics, in "The American Scholar" and later,

> essentially were a synthesis of what had been developed by scores of authors in the two preceding decades and what was to be reiterated by scores of authors in the two subsequent decades. For as during this period the concept of the nation as a balanced system of contracts yielded to the concept of the nation as an organism, so the neoclassical idea of national literature as the embellishment of orthodox political or ethical principles yielded to the romantic idea of a literature which would be an organic phase of the whole national life and which would derive its very style and tone from the state of the national health.[66]

Still, Emerson's contribution to American poetics has its uniquely important qualities; in particular, he took the general call for a founding American poet and elaborated that call into a detailed exploration of the relationship between a national literature and an individual poetic voice. Emerson's poetics, like that of Channing and Fuller, was haunted by a sense of belatedness. *Nature* (1836) begins with a lament: "The foregoing generations beheld God and nature face to face; we, through their eyes. Why should not we also enjoy an original relation to the universe?"[67] The foregoing generations are left imprecisely defined, obviating the point that they too "saw" the universe through the eyes of tradition. For Emerson, his is the *first* generation to be helplessly embedded in history. The dichotomy between original and latecomer governs all of *Nature*; the essay is largely the self-definition of an epigone.

Faced with a sense of being modern and therefore inferior to an "original" past, one might try to recover that past (classicism) or to defend one's own modernity. Emerson does neither. Instead, he asserts that history does not exist. Historical contingency, "painfully accumulated" out of individual struggles, simply is not real. Language, as an area for work, becomes a clean slate, always and everywhere, once we run our idealistic eraser over it. A proper attitude toward the world "beholds the whole circle of persons and things, of actions and events, of country and religion, not as painfully accumulated, atom after atom, act after act, in an aged creeping Past, but as one vast picture, which God paints on the instant eternity, for the contemplation of the soul."[68]

With the slate clean, a national literature can be constructed from scratch. "The Poet" is Emerson's central essay about the creation of a national literature. Emerson starts from the furthest circle out, the poetry of the Over-soul, and shows how that transcendental poetry filters in to poets who are circumscribed by time and place. "Poetry was all written before time was, and whenever we are so finely organized that we can penetrate into that region where the air is music, we hear these primal warblings, and attempt to write them down, but we lose ever and anon a word, or a verse, and substitute something of our own, and thus miswrite the poem. The men of more delicate ear write down these cadences more faithfully, and these transcripts, though imperfect, become the songs of nations."[69] The paradox in these lines is stunning: the "songs of nations" are precisely those poems least corrupted by "something of our own." To be truly national, a literature must be most universal. The corrupting influence—"something of our own"—is the living language itself, in the form of the dialogized word, that causes the miswriting of a sacred cadence. In American terms, this "lower" centrifugal world of language is the world of all the country's living dialects, bubbling up into belles lettres in the work of Thomas Morton ("New English Canaan"), Ebenezer Cooke ("The Sot-weed Factor"), Brackenridge, Halleck, Royall Tyler, temperance novels, sensational fiction, sentimental poetry. Their contribution to the "monument" of the American language does not register at all with Emerson, or with Brooks, Fogle, Lewis, Matthiessen, and twentieth-century anthologists and critics in general, until very recently.

Indeed, a feature of attempts to define an American literature, from John Knapp in the 1810s to Susan Howe in the 1980s, has been the attempt to seek some centripetal force in American poetic and literary language.[70] Theorists have themselves differed dialogically about where to locate this center, but the idea that a pure national literary language will be monologic is essential to American literary nationalism. The founder poet will erase the past, utter new Adamic words, and thereby found a tradition. He will center American culture around himself and his essential spirit.

A monologic poetic language is always, for Bakhtin, "posited" rather than "given"; in most nations, this monologic, centripetal impulse is the idealistic impulse of normative literary tradition and of the educational institutions that guard and refine it.[71] But in nineteenth-century America such a recourse to tradition was impossible, because the only available tradition was itself the colonizing force to be escaped. Hence it was attractive to posit a new kind of American English that would embody the centripetal impulse of monologic art while being wholly original. Stuart Sherman, writing in 1922 in response to Santayana, believes Whitman to have been committed to this centripetal project: "In the life-long evolution of his work, he was seeking a concord of soul and body, individual and society, state and nation, nation and the family of nations, some grand chord to unite the dominant notes of all."[72] Whitman's own physical oscillation between health and illness, as publicized by his disciples, fused this organicism with the biographical record; as Betsy Erkkila notes, "there had always been a curious correspondence between Whitman's body and the body politic of America. His body seemed at times a kind of national seismograph, registering disturbances in the political sphere."[73] In Sherman's criticism, organicism and monologism fuse with the poet's self; his art becomes indistinguishable from his life as both evolve together; the poet's body becomes gradually fused with other bodies and the body politic. Because of his success in this project, Sherman says, "Whitman still with astonishing completeness lives. He lives because he marvelously well identified that daimonic personality with his book, so that whoever touches it, as he himself declared, touches a man, and a man of singularly intense perceptiveness."[74] "Literally the word made flesh,"[75] as Fogle would say of Whitman and his poetics, was Sherman's assessment of Whitman. This is enthusiasm of a level that verges on a blasphemy that twentieth-century critics did not have to avoid as scrupulously as their predecessors did; but the essential value in Sherman's criticism, the presence of the poet himself in his texts, is a direct legacy from nineteenth-century criticism.

Among John Knapp's values was the presence of the spirit of the poet in the text: "The words of the poet are like the breath of life to him that hears them worthily."[76] As part of their canonization of Bryant, critics like Everett and Fuller had focused on the immediacy with which the poet's thoughts and voice could be experienced in his work. But for one of the most typical of nineteenth-century critics, Edwin P. Whipple, presence became the value overriding all others.

Whipple is now so completely forgotten that it comes as a shock to see his name included as recently as 1955 (with Emerson, Poe, and others) in Fogle's list of great American critics.[77] But for writers of Whitman's generation, Whipple, his exact contemporary, was perhaps the default-value implied reader for American literature, the median point of the *kulturragende Schicht* of the American Renaissance.[78] His essays in the *North American Review* expressed the literary taste of the Boston and Concord elites; he was also a popular Lyceum lecturer and member of literary clubs and salons. Perhaps most powerful of all Whipple's roles was his position—thanks to his friendship with James T. Fields—as chief reader for Ticknor and Fields.[79] In this capacity, Whipple held a power to make literary reputations, the centripetal force of which for nineteenth-century America is hard today to comprehend fully. (Probably Gail Hamilton's satire on Ticknor and Fields, A *Battle of the Books* [1870], best conveys the sense of awe in which that publishing house was held by aspiring writers.[80]) It is difficult to suppose that Walt Whitman himself held Ticknor and Fields in awe—though it is just as difficult to imagine him spurning them if they had somehow decided to embrace his work. But he knew and acknowledged Whipple's importance, printing excerpts from Whipple's 1844 review of Griswold's *Poets and Poetry of America* in reissues of the 1855 edition of *Leaves of Grass*.[81] Whipple shared common ground with Whitman. Neither man had attended college, and that was rare among the white male literary figures of the day. Both held antislavery views and emphasized the holistic nature of bodily and intellectual health; one of Whipple's best-known essays was the 1849 piece "Intellectual Health and Disease."

Whipple's critical ideas were the ones widely diffused through literary America in the 1850s. They can now be read as a set of critical traditions that would provide a fall-back point for future generations long after Whipple himself was forgotten. Central to those critical ideas was the notion of authorial presence in the literary work. In "Intellectual Health and Disease," Whipple attacks the view that the creative mind is a collection of distinct faculties: "We do not say that Milton's imagination wrote Paradise Lost, but that Milton wrote it. There is no mental operation in which the whole mind is not present; nothing produced but by the joint action of all its faculties, under the direction of its central personality. This central principle of mind is spiritual force,—capacity to cause, to create, to assimilate, to be."[82] *Paradise Lost* is therefore not the creation of any of the romantic faculties, nor of language, tradition, convention, collective or personal unconscious, fancy, or imagination primary or secondary. Whipple cuts through the Gordian knot of Coleridgean thought on creativity and attributes literary creativity to the author as a realized, whole human being.

Whipple applied his poetics of presence to the evaluation of his contemporaries. Like many other critics of the period, Whipple admired Bryant; but where Fuller had admired Bryant for his closeness to nature and Everett had admired him for his originality, Whipple concentrated on Bryant's personality: "He is so genuine that he testifies to nothing, in scenery or human life, of which he has not had a direct personal consciousness. He follows the primitive bias of his nature rather than the caprices of fancy. . . . His style is literally himself. It has the form and follows the movement of his nature, and is shaped into the expression of the exact mood, sentiment, and thought out of which the poem springs."[83] One can imagine two kinds of readers of such criticism—poets like Walt Whitman eager to transfer such praise to themselves by fulfilling its critical imperatives, and critics wishing to displace Bryant and finding the terms in which Whipple had treated Bryant well adapted—pre-adapted, in evolutionary terms—for reading Whitman.

The critics who would be most responsible for the canonization of Walt Whitman would be most responsive to the poet's own insistence on presence. Stuart Sherman's sense that Whitman "with astonishing completeness lives" is one of the most dramatic indications of the importance of presence for Whitman's advocates; but in 1906 Bliss Perry had commended Whitman's purpose in *Leaves of Grass* of writing "a book which should embody himself and his country"—thereby uniting the demands of nationalism and presence.[84] Brooks, again, epitomizes the trend: "It was the main work of Whitman to make fast what he called 'the idea and fact of American totality,' an idea and fact summed up with singular completeness in his own character and way of life."[85] For the generation of American critics between 1900 and 1920 that did so much to canonize Walt Whitman, the critical project of reading and explicating texts was not at all distinct from the biographical project of assessing the author's life. It is not so much that these critics made a conscious decision to link criticism and biography as that the values of Whipple and his contemporaries came out of the Victorian age essentially unchanged. The paradigm within which Brooks worked, however different in political aims and institutional settings from that of Whipple, was identical to his in the insistence on linking a poet's work and his "character" (to use one of Whipple's favorite critical terms).

The values of the poetics of presence were the uncritically accepted common ground for generations of American critics. The critics who established expectations for an American Homer did so in the context of a poetry of presence, and critics who promoted Whitman held those values. So too did critics who denied Whitman a place in the canon. At first, Whitman did not register, did not seem conventional enough even to be readable in the terms of an American poetics. He represented the kind of originality that Bryant had questioned—the originality that severs itself so completely from tradition that it becomes indecipherable. Josiah Gilbert Holland, editor of *Scribner's Monthly*, waged a long anti-Whitman campaign in his magazine, dedicated to proving that "his form of expression is illegitimate—that it has no right to be called poetry; that it is too involved and spasmodic and strained to be respectable prose, and that there is no place for it, either in the heaven above, or in the earth below, or in the waters under the earth."[86] Holland experienced a cognitive dissonance upon reading Whitman, a dissonance too great for him to overcome. He expresses his bewilderment by lineating in Whitmanic fashion some passages of what he can recognize as prose—though he considers it overly poetic—by Emerson and Carlyle. He compares them to passages from Whitman; the result, to Holland, is that Whitman's work still fails, even when placed next to what he considers poor prose. To a reader in the 1990s, Holland may seem impossibly hung up on genres, but for his time he reflects the importance of the received formulas for placing and interpreting verse. Holland's criticism always stresses the normal, the familiar, the established; inveighing against "literary eccentricity," he seems in retrospect to be one of the most eccentric of critics. In 1878, Holland pronounced Bryant, Longfellow, and Whittier to be the greatest American poets, and predicted that they would continue to be the American classics when "their countrymen will have ceased discussing Poe and Thoreau and Walt Whitman"—a prediction that will have to be borne out in the twenty-first century or later, at this point.[87] Holland was a very late follower of Robert Walsh in perceiving no need for an American literature separate from that of England; he was one of the last literary antinationalists.[88] But as a touchstone of the most settled literary tastes of the late nineteenth century, Holland is a telling example of the bewilderment that Whitman presented to readers on account of his overoriginality. Many readers felt with Holland that "how an age that possesses a Longfellow and an appreciative ear for his melody can tolerate in the slightest degree the abominable dissonance of which Walt Whitman is the author, is one of the unsolved mysteries."[89]

Holland's bewilderment in the face of his age's catholicity of taste is a sharp example of what Jauss calls "the noncontemporaneity of the contemporaneous . . . the multiplicity of events of one historical moment."[90] Placed in the context of the overall reception and rejection of Whitman during the last twenty years of his life (1872–92), Holland's incomprehension may go further; it may signal that Jauss is not necessarily correct in believing that "this multiplicity of literary phenomena nonetheless, when seen from the point of view of an aesthetics of reception, coalesces again for the audience that perceives them and relates them to one another as works of *its* present, in the unity of a common horizon of literary expectations, memories, and anticipations that establishes their significance."[91] The case of Whitman suggests that there was no "common horizon," or rather that the contemporary audience is itself a heteroglot phenomenon, and that any individual reader will variously align herself or himself with other readers within the totality of that audience to constitute an interpretive community for a given work.

A reader who found himself in Holland's community for the reading of Whitman, but outside it in other ways, was Thomas Wentworth Higginson. In an unsigned review of "Recent Poetry" for *The Nation* in 1881, Higginson aligns himself strongly with Holland's views on the subject of Walt Whitman. Higginson finds Whitman's treatment of sexuality "nauseating" and, ever the chivalrous feminist, is repelled by "the sheer animal longing of sex for sex—the impulse of the savage, who knocks down the first woman he sees, and drags her to his cave" in the poems.[92] This nausea is a buried undertone in Holland's more formalist criticism; in a private 1880 letter to Richard Watson Gilder, Holland referred to Whitman's early work as "smut."[93] Higginson also joins Holland's critique of Whitman's prosody, approving only of "O Captain! My Captain!" (In 1900, Higginson would say that Whitman "has phrase, but not form—and without form there is no immortality"—after a decade of saying the opposite about Emily Dickinson.[94] Critics are frequently at dialogic odds with themselves.)

But the core of Higginson's objection to *Leaves of Grass* is his personal disgust with its author. Here Higginson arrives at the same judgment as Holland but for the opposite reasons, invoking not formalism but nationalism and the poetics of presence.

> We cannot quite forget what Emerson says, that "it makes a great difference to a sentence whether there be a man behind it or no." . . . One can be aroused to some enthusiasm over the pallid shop-boy or the bookish undergraduate who knew no better than to shoulder his musket and march to the front in the war for the Union; but it is difficult to awaken any such emotion for a stalwart poet, who—with the finest physique in America, as his friends asserted, and claiming an unbounded influence over the "roughs" of New York—preferred to pass by the recruiting-office and take service in the hospital with the non-combatants.[95]

To read Higginson's criticism by his own demands of presence is to recognize the sheer bad taste of its author, a distinguished Union veteran who had no need to be defensive about his own service and little call to disparage the work done at military hospitals. But frequently, one of the blind spots of the poetics of presence is its disembodiment of the present critic who embodies all texts but his own Olympian judgments. Higginson seems provoked into this stance not only by his own values but also by those of his opponents, the Whitman cultists, who could not imagine anything less than perfection in their poet—and consequently presented a portrait of him as difficult to reconcile in all its aspects as the multiplicity of experience presented in *Leaves of Grass* itself.

For many of his contemporaries, Walt Whitman did not exist; sometimes, he existed in a form that would be unrecognizable to readers today. Even when mainstream Victorian readers were sympathetic to Whitman, they tended to transform him into a sort of Good Gray Santa Claus. Here is the description in Arthur Gilman's *Poets' Homes* of Whitman at the age of sixty: "He is a great favorite with children, and bachelor as he has been all his life, his nature is as sweet and gentle, his heart is sympathetic and young, as tender and true as if he were the happiest grandsire around whose knees sunny-haired children clung."[96] That is one Victorian Whitman who is hard to imagine today; there were also the Christ-like Whitman, the heroic Whitman (because of his war work), the "esoteric" Whitman, the occultist's Whitman, the Whitman of "O Captain! My Captain!" whose poetic image was inseparable from the burgeoning myth of Abraham Lincoln.[97]

Perhaps most revealing for the persistence of presence as a central value in the reception of American poetry is the curious and now almost unintelligible debate that broke out sporadically—for the latest time in the 1930s—over whether Whitman was a poseur. A main thread that runs through cultist appreciation of Whitman, academic acceptance of him, and High Victorian venom against him is an assumption that the Whitman persona is to be taken at face value—that Whitman is a poet of presence, whether one likes his particular presence or not. Should he be found to be pretending to be that persona and not biographically faithful to it, he is to be excoriated. A minority of critics in the 1930s—Mark Van Doren being the last of the line—treated Whitman as a sort of confidence man of literature; they saw his poetic form, his b'hoy personality, his mysticism and his cult equally as pure pretense.[98]

The unintelligibility of the poseur charge today stems from its powerlessness to erase the texts of *Leaves of Grass*, *Democratic Vistas*, and *Specimen Days*. If Whitman was a poseur in his personal life (in whatever sense one cannot be "oneself") one is still left with the text of Whitman's work, which would remain the same whether he had ever worked in his life, ever met a "rough," ever been to New Orleans, or indeed ever lived in America. We might tend in fact after postmodernism to value a writer whose work was total artifice over one whose work was realistic reportage.

But the poseur charge was a meaningful one in its day, enough to mobilize the forces of academic criticism and indeed to focus even the following generation of Whitman criticism on biographical interpretations, centrally Henry Seidel Canby's *Walt Whitman: An American*.[99] The focus on critical biography as an approach to Whitman's texts continued in definitive work by Gay Wilson Allen and Roger Asselineau.[100] The emphasis on scholarly accurate "critical biography" in the post–World War II period is itself a continuation of a poetics of presence that has its roots farther back than Whipple. The project of critical biography is akin to the process Boris Tomasevskij describes in "Literature and Biography": "Legends about poets were created, and it was extremely important for the literary historian to occupy himself with the restoration of these legends, i.e., with the removal of later layers and the reduction of the legend to its pure 'canonical' form. These biographical legends are the literary conception of the poet's life, and this conception was necessary as a perceptible background for the poet's literary works. The legends are a premise which the author himself took into account during the creative process."[101] It has been well demonstrated that Whitman took biographical legends into account when composing his texts and himself.[102] But what is of even more interest in Tomasevskij's formulation is the process of "restoration" of biographical legend. It is easy to dismiss Gilman's Santa-tizing of Whitman as fantastic Victorian hyperbole. It is harder to see a scholarly opinion that Whitman *personally* corresponds to the democratic, or modernist, or even deconstructive ideals of a later critical paradigm as a project about presence, and therefore of the very same nature as Gilman's.

Criticism that adheres to the poetics of presence must employ the biographical project. If a poet succeeds in achieving immediacy through the poetic deployment of originality, organicism, and a centripetal, monologic voice, then readers must be reassured that they are experiencing intimacy with someone who will edify them, or at least not molest them. Tomasevskij's formalism prevented him from connecting all biography with literary biography; he insists, in his essay, on the difference between a biographical legend created for the purposes of reading primary texts (something intraliterary, organically connected to textual analysis) and the poet's "real" life, which can be recovered through documentary scholarship but remains strictly marginal to interpretation of the poet's work (and therefore external to the discipline of literary study). But it is impossible to reconstruct the trace of a "life" without reconstructing the trace of a text, even in biographies of people who were not bellettrists. In literary biography, even the purgation of legend from a project that remains the "life" of a writer cannot be separated from Tomasevskijan ideal biography, which—sanctioned by authoritative scholarship or not—is a component of all acts of reading.

Partly from a desire to avoid the imperatives of ideal biography, throughout this study, I avoid citing authors' comments on their own work, including their general commentary on poetics. One of the main components of ideal biography is the paratextual material that accretes around the texts of primary interest for the nonscholarly reader. A key method in literary interpretation is for the interpreter to gain access to, assemble, and process such paratexts, which are allowed a decisive confirming value in reading and teaching one's readings to others. When one reads *Madame Bovary* in the Norton Critical Edition, for instance, one reads it through Flaubert's parallel account of its composition, which then becomes the determinant of the degree and nature of the authorial presence in the work. "Madame Bovary, c'est moi"; and for authors as diverse and as un-Flaubertian as Walt Whitman and Elizabeth Bishop, paratexts like *With Walt Whitman in Camden* and the interviews that Bishop granted to Anne Stevenson have become ways for an authorial voice outside the text in question to reclaim authority over that text, to reassert the present self—and in turn, ways for other interpreters to doubly validate their own readings. In such cases, strangely enough, the paratext can become more important than the text. It has simply proved too confusing to separate the author as focus of critical construction from the author as critical constructor; my practice instead has been to treat critical statements by Dickinson, Moore, and Bishop only when these writers reflect on Whitman or on one another (he read none of them, because he did not, apparently, read the first editions of Dickinson's poems in 1890–91).

Tomasevskij's insights lead us directly to consideration of the American poet who has been most plagued, or blessed, with biographical criticism, Emily Dickinson. Two of the critics who were most involved in constructing negative biographies for Walt Whitman—T. W. Higginson and J. G. Holland—were among Dickinson's literary correspondents; in fact, they were among the few people in the literary establishment who knew about Dickinson's poetry while she was alive. Higginson went on to construct much of Dickinson's early ideal biography himself.

Dickinson offers a very significant test case for the nature of the reception of American poets. No one could say of her that she would have to have been invented by the critical establishment; indeed, she is anomalous in so many ways that she functions more as a permanent embarrassment to literary history than as an enabler of traditions poetic or critical. And in the absence of presence—the absence of a coherent construction of a poetic biography either by the poet or by her contemporaries—many competing ideal biographies have been constructed. The values of presence and its components, which work so wondrously for reading Whitman, are strained sometimes past recognition in accommodating Dickinson and her various ideal biographies.

The key force in this strain is, of course, gender. Emily Dickinson was white, upper-middle-class, immaculately Anglo-American, and almost *too* New English; she was as socially acceptable in the studies of twentieth-century academics as she had been in nineteenth-century Amherst. But male critics serving (in J. Hillis Miller's sense) as host to Dickinson were constantly aware of her gender and the difference it posed to the gender they shared with all the rest of the canon.[103] That difference is the central dynamic of the reception of Dickinson's poetry.

THREE

Dickinson: Reading the "Supposed Person"

Emily Dickinson became canonical in terms of, and in spite of, the template provided by the Whitmanic American Homer. She did not explicitly invoke the energies of Whitman's poetics, so her readers could not make a direct connection between the two poets; in fact, they were sore pressed to make her work cohere at all. But when they employed the narratizing power of gendered readings to make her work cohere, Dickinson emerged as a feminine version of Whitman, a suppressed, private, thwarted persona with energies of her own that were no less shocking than Whitman's. In this chapter, I chart the largely male project of overcoming the surface obstacles to narratizing Dickinson, from 1890 to 1945—at which time a growing sense of the importance of Dickinson's work and the imperfection of available texts led to the end of the period in which she became canonical and made way for the revisionist and reconstructive senses of her work that followed the 1955 variorum edition.

What was Dickinson's critical assessment of Whitman? In a letter of 25 April 1862 to T. W. Higginson, Emily Dickinson says: "You speak of Mr Whitman—I never read his Book—but was told that he was disgraceful—."[1] That was the only time Dickinson ever referred to Whitman in her writing, indeed the only thing either of the two most canonical American poets of the nineteenth century ever wrote about the other. As a refutation of the notion that canonical writers have a "book-centered" existence that revolves around other members of the canon, the remark is startling.[2]

Of course, Dickinson's remark may not be all that it seems. There are several different ways of interpreting her statement:

1. It may be an outright lie. She makes many evasions in these letters to Higginson, and this may simply be another one. She may have read Whitman's poetry and was trying to cover up her debt to that poet by claiming ignorance. She feared charges of derivativeness; in her fifth letter to Higginson, she says, "[I] never consciously touch a paint, mixed by another person."[3] On the other hand, there is no evidence that she ever read any of Whitman's work.

2. Therefore, it may be the complete truth. Dickinson was not notably hip; her literary tastes did not run to Flaubert, Dostoevsky, or the Pre-Raphaelites. Instead, she idolized George Eliot.[4] At least to male correspondents during her lifetime, Dickinson maintained a strict self-censorship about sex and her body. It might not have taken more than a few guarded descriptions of the sexuality of Whitman's work by Holland, Samuel Bowles, or another of her friends to put her off reading Whitman altogether. Nor does she mention Whitman in her less-guarded correspondence with Susan Gilbert Dickinson.

3. It may be something more confusing than truth or lie. Dickinson undoubtedly knew the contours of American poetry criticism and may have had a fair idea of Whitman's relation to it, as filtered through early Whitman criticism like Hale's piece for the *North American Review*. Her poetics is in so many ways the exact opposite of Whitman's that one can posit a dialectic response on her part, conscious or unconscious, to the poetics of presence that Whitman fulfilled and that critics had developed in the decades before the 1850s. She was a woman, and most American critics and poets were men; that in itself resulted in her internalizing a poetics of reticence that is opposite to Whitman's exhibitionism.[5] Whitman is garrulous; Dickinson is sparing of words. Whitman uses a poetic form that is freer of metrical constraints than anything ever seen in English; Dickinson adopts a traditional English form, the hymn, and exploits its constraints from within. Whitman's poems imply an audience of generalized common men (sometimes women too); they are paradoxically addressed to individual people who are not concretely realized. Dickinson's poems often have specific addressees, especially Susan; these poems are private and concrete in their rhetorical situation even when their subject matter is death, time, and eternity. And while Whitman's work would come to be seen as the greatest monologic, organic utterance in American literature, the form and development of the Dickinson corpus is radically dialogic and inorganic; her manuscript books and her individual poems defy and resist the demands of the poetics of presence.[6]

In another letter to Higginson, Dickinson makes a famous disclaimer: "When I state myself, as the Representative of the Verse—it does not mean—me—but a supposed person."[7] At least the sentence has sometimes been interpreted as a disclaimer, in the sense of forestalling suspicions that the intensity of the poems might reflect the poet's emotional experience. The assumption inherent in using the term "disclaimer" is the poetics of presence itself: assuming that the poem *is* the poet, any attempt to cut the text off from the signing authority of the author is a subterfuge. George F. Whicher took that line when he argued in 1930 that "her poetry is not the formal mask of a personality, but a living face vibrant with expressiveness."[8] But the poet never made her living face, or her poetics, very explicit. Authorial statements—comments on the genesis of certain works, manifestos of critical principles, attempts to make herself cohere—are precisely what Dickinson avoids in all her literary correspondence. Furthermore, the unstable nature of her biographical image in the whole run of the poems corresponds to Margaret Dickie's conception of a "discontinuous lyric self" within individual poems. "The properties of the lyric—its brevity, its repetition, its figuration—obstruct readings that are determined by a socially limited understanding of the self or its subject."[9] Hence the "I" in Dickinson's poetry, Dickie shows, is not a worked-out character but is "discontinuous, limited, private, hidden."[10] Both within poems and across her lyric output, Dickinson shows a dazzling faithfulness to infidelity, a consistent inconsistency.

Critics who came to the texts of the 1890s editions of Dickinson were confronted with an almost insurmountable problem: how to narratize a dialogic poet. The strongest narratizations were produced by those critics with the most personally invested in Dickinson's success, especially Mabel Loomis Todd, whose efforts benefited from their status as *seuils* to the authorized editions. The strongest resistances to such narratization came in the work of critics so put off by the apparent lack of consistency in the poet's thought that they rejected everything about the early editions.

The extent to which the internal dialogism of Dickinson's poetry led to dialogic rifts in her reception can be seen in one of the sharp controversies of that 1890s reception. The popular Christian press had spoken favorably of Dickinson since 1891; the Unitarian journalist John White Chadwick, in particular, was one of her strongest supporters.[11] But as Dickinson's general popularity began to fade toward mid-decade, so too did the warmth of Christian support for her work. In June of 1892, the *Christian Union*, which had published Higginson's very first essay on Dickinson in 1890, began to find fault with her poetry, and with the persona behind it:

One must close his ears here and there to quite an acrid tone toward the world of which she refused to be a part. It must be remembered that if the artist rid herself of certain criticisms by retiring from the standard of others, still the victory is less than when those irksome incumbrances are borne patiently and are triumphed over. To be sure, a "somebody" is more greatly tempted to pretense; but is not the merit finer if he overcome pretense? Nor can we admire entirely the particular form of "Emersonian self-possession" which this author exhibits toward her Master. We do not believe that the poem entitled "A Prayer" was meant to be irreverent, but it comes dangerously near it; nor can we see any compensating advantage gained. It is the eagle who can look Phoebus in the face, but in certain troubled conditions of the atmosphere much lowlier birds may safely apostrophize him.[12]

Reading "A Prayer" (P-476) in the version presented by Todd in the 1891 *Poems: Second Series* tends to confirm the *Christian Union* reviewer's opinion, perhaps even to strengthen it.[13] The speaker in the poem asks God for heaven and is met with mocking smiles from him and his angels; the poem concludes:

> I left the place with all my might,—
> My prayer away I threw;
> The quiet ages picked it up,
> And Judgment twinkled, too.
>
> That one so honest be extant
> As take the tale for true
> That "Whatsoever you shall ask,
> Itself be given you."
>
> But I, grown shrewder, scan the skies
> With a suspicious air,—
> As children, swindled for the first,
> All swindlers be, infer. (21)

The poem is the most irreverent that Todd was to include in any of the 1890s editions, and one can only speculate at why she let it get past her editorial gate. The childlike persona of its speaker perhaps allowed her to read its treatment of God as a "swindler" as a stage in the spiritual maturation of the speaker, and the poem as a whole as a dramatic monologue. In any case, Todd, sensitive to the power of journals like the *Christian Union*, was not about to argue even for a melioristic reading of the poem, much less defend the poem's anger toward God. Instead, in her preface to the 1894 *Letters of Emily Dickinson*, she simply contradicted the conclusions the *Christian Union* had drawn from "A

Prayer," by reading Dickinson's "irreverence" as a form of reverence: "Reverence for accepted ways and forms, merely as such, seems entirely to have been left out of Emily's constitution. To her, God was not a far-away and dreary Power to be daily addressed,—the great 'Eclipse' of which she wrote,—but He was near and familiar and pervasive. . . . she had in her heart too profound an adoration for the great, ever-living, and present Father to hold a shadow of real irreverence toward Him, so peculiarly near."[14] Todd's is an able defense, turning the poetics of presence back on the negative criticism. The *Christian Union*, finding the poem to be irreverent, accuses the poet of a lack of humility; Todd argues that the poet herself conceived of God in terms of presence and hints that she was an eyewitness to Dickinson's devotions. It would be hard to counter Todd's defense without impugning the poet's personal faith—hardly a genteel critical move.

"In essence, no real irreverence," Todd wrote, "mars her poems or her letters."[15] Readers had to take this assertion on trust, of course, because Todd herself was the source of the poems and letters that had been published. The bitterest of Dickinson's atheisms remained unpublished until 1945, poems like "Those—dying then" (P-1551) and "The Fact that Earth is Heaven—" (P-1408). But Todd did not totally cleanse the 1890s selections from anti-Christian sentiments. "I meant to have but modest needs" marks an extreme, but it is not a unique example; "Safe in their alabaster chambers" (P-216), included in the first series (1890), mocks the "sagacity" of the departed in Christ; "Heaven is what I cannot reach!" (P-239, published 1896) sees the Christian heaven as "interdicted ground." "Not in this world to see his face" (P-418, published 1890) takes up the idea that earthly existence is a "primer" to the kingdom of heaven but concludes: "Might someone else so learned be, / And leave me just my A B C, / Himself could have the skies" (166).

Nor did Todd include the most conventional of Dickinson's Christian sentiments. She rejected "Life—is what we make it—" (P-698), with its picture of Christ as "Tender Pioneer"; she wrote an emphatic "*no*" above the manuscript of "'Unto Me?'" (P-964), with its egregious final stanza:

> "I am spotted."
>   "I am Pardon."
> "I am small."
>
>   "The least
> Is esteemed in Heaven
> The chiefest.
> Occupy my house." (300)[16]

Neither poem was published until 1929. But there were plenty of expressions of faith among the 1890s texts. "I never saw a moor" (P-1052), one of the least equivocal of all Dickinson's expressions of belief in the unseen, was in the 1890 volume. "At least to pray is left" (P-502, published 1891) reads like a sincere call to Christ in extremity, and "Far from love the Heavenly Father" (P-1021) is a lyricization of the spirit of *The Pilgrim's Progress*. The Christian lyrics in Dickinson's early editions range from the troublingly erotic ("The soul should always stand ajar," P-1055) to the downright silly: "Tie the strings to my life, my Lord" (P-279) resembles nothing so much, in retrospect, as "Drop-kick me, Jesus, through the goalposts of life." Several of the poems published in the 1890s are drippingly ironic and make only the most superficial concession to conventional religious attitudes: "I shall know why, when time is over" (P-193); "I went to heaven" (P-374); or "Prayer is the little implement" (P-437). Sometimes the attitude of the Dickinson persona is playful; "Some keep the Sabbath going to church' (P-324) was a favorite even in the Christian press in the 1890s because it rejects ritual in favor of spiritual experience drawn directly from nature.[17] At other times, the speaker assumes an awful indifference:

> I reason, earth is short,
> And anguish absolute,
> And many hurt;
> But what of that?
>
> I reason, we could die:
> The best vitality
> Cannot excel decay;
> But what of that?
>
> I reason that in heaven
> Somehow, it will be even,
> Some new equation given;
> But what of that? (P-301; 166–67)

This poem, which perhaps takes its Boethianism a step beyond the limits of piety, did not register in the 1890s; only Arlo Bates quoted it, and then only to cite it as an example of "the strangeness of some of the mixtures that she offers."[18]

Strangeness indeed. The multiplicity of responses to Christian doctrine, even in those Dickinson texts available in the 1890s, strongly resisted narratization. Within a single poem, like "I have a king who does not speak" (P-103), the Dickinson persona can be either devotee or hardened sinner—attributing the switch to the accident of a dream. Two poems juxtaposed in the 1896 *Third Series* seem deliberately placed by

Todd to enhance their contrast: "Superiority to fate" (P-1081), with its image of the soul laying away a spiritual "pittance at a time" until it has gained salvation, and "Hope is a subtle glutton" (P-1547), with its image of hope as a tantalizing devourer of the faithful. (In 1891, "Hope" had been "the thing with feathers" in P-254.) And immediately below both of these poems is one connected so ineffaceably with masturbation by the readings of Paula Bennett that one is startled to find it smiling at the reader in its Victorian typography.[19]

> Forbidden fruit a flavor has
> That lawful orchards mocks;
> How luscious lies the pea within
> The pod that Duty locks! (P-1377; 42)

The fact that so many voices and personae coexist in the dialogic swirl of Dickinson's texts has never meant absolute defeat for the impulse to narratize her oeuvre. Reading strategies exist that can convert any amount of discrepant data into a coherent portrait of the artist; obviously, the more discrepant the data becomes (as Dickinson's work steadily became between 1890 and 1945), the more resistant interpretive communities become to such totalizing strategies of reading. In 1894, Todd's strategy of asserting Dickinson's essential reverence for the spirit of Christianity—bolstered by her personal acquaintance with the poet and her access to unpublished manuscripts—was certainly tendentious, but it was not unlike later reading strategies in quality. An "objective" reading like Allen Tate's in 1932 would try to see her in "the perfect literary situation" of being "without opinions," thereby equating her artistic diversity with her artistic objectivity (and her own objectivity with the critic's).[20] A reading that stresses Dickinson's rage at a patriarchal God would deconstruct the apparently pious texts and read them as ironic: "I never spoke with God" would become the sinister point of "I never saw a moor," for instance. Readings that reduce *all* these poems to irony, or to playfulness, are available. So is a reading that would show how Dickinson remained immured inside her own patriarchal value system even in the poems that most radically oppose it—since they oppose it only on its own terms and cannot transcend it.

The latitude of narratizations is limited only by an interpretive community's patience with them. It is, for instance, perfectly possible to read all of Emily Dickinson's poems as evidence that she was abducted by those aliens from space who seize earthlings, conduct ghastly experiments on them, heal them magically, and inject them with amnesia serum so that they can only recall the experience via dreams or hypnosis.[21] I refrain from sketching such a reading here (even though it sheds considerable light on "Because I could not stop for Death") because the point has been made. Continuities in the Dickinson oeuvre are in the eye of the theorist. Even highly processed collations of Dickinson poems, like those of the 1890s, resist attempts at finding a "figure in the carpet" and resolve themselves back into the "strange mixtures" that Arlo Bates perceived upon first looking into Todd's Dickinson.

The discontinuity of Dickinson's work posed many problems for the critics who helped make her work canonical early in the twentieth century. Critics who inherited the values of the poetics of presence and a canon with Walt Whitman at its center were faced with the puzzle that Dickinson's work presented even in the simplified, abridged, and thematically arranged editions that Dickinson's poems first appeared in starting in 1890. Out of the mass of conflicting possibilities, these critics chose a Dickinson. At first several images of the poet competed; later the consensus image, that of an oddly reclusive confessional poet, began to solidify. Once its unary central subject emerged, Dickinson's poetry became fit for canonical status.

The form of Dickinson's poetry was the initial obstacle to her canonization. For its early readers, her verse was both conventional in form and inelegant within those conventions. The overwhelming majority of her poems are in hymn forms. The 1890s selections slightly overstate that monotony; the editions published in the 1910s and 1920s tend slightly to obscure it by lineating metrical poems as free verse. I have called her usual form "literary hymn"; her verse is far from unpremeditated chant, barbaric yawp, sea-surge, woodnotes.[22] There is not much originality in Dickinson's formal repertoire. She takes a stock metric form, imbued with associations from Watts, Cowper, and the whole British Protestant tradition, and innovates by moving the form *further* from direct experience, more toward the mediated experience of the silently read page. The one unusual form she uses, free-rhyming, is modeled on Emerson's poetry.[23] Her poetry has all the features of imitation bad ballad verse—failure to rhyme, to scan, to add up syntactically, to round a phrase competently—and 1890s critics were not shy about pointing out these failures. Though both poets constructed "incompetent" verse, Dickinson's formal contrast with Whitman is even greater than it appears: Whitman cut himself loose and wrote as odd-looking a verse as was possible in 1855; Dickinson took the pose of an adolescent unable to master the rudiments of formulaic composition and intensified it. Maurice Thompson summed up, in terms of the poetics of presence, the sense that negative 1890s reviewers had of Dickinson's technique: "Her lack was intrinsic and constitutional. Mere functional derangement of the organ of expression is curable; but here was organic lesion of the most unmistakable type."[24]

Initially, in the 1890s, Dickinson's poetry met with a resistance similar to that which Whitman's met; Arlo Bates noted the similarity in the challenges the two poets' formal oddities posed for readers and concluded that their extreme originality left them similarly unapproachable.[25] An anonymous reviewer for *Scribner's* in 1891 put the case against Dickinson's "formlessness": "It not merely offends by perversely ignoring the conventionally established though rationally evolved and soundly based rules of the game it purports to play, but in announcing thus, boldly, its independence of any aesthetic, any sensuous, interest, it puts a severe strain on the quality of its own substance—handicaps it in most dangerous fashion instead of giving it that aid and furtherance that the best substance is sure to need."[26] This reviewer makes the case for an a priori rejection of Dickinson because of her perceived formlessness. Other influential critics, like Thomas Bailey Aldrich in the *Atlantic Monthly*, signed on to this rejection, citing Dickinson's "poetical chaos" and calling her works *disjecta membra*.[27] Aldrich's terminology is intriguing. If one could play Pierre Menard and write the same words in the 1990s instead of the 1890s, they would indicate high praise rather than high disdain. Critics who reiterated the Whipple values of character and presence, as Aldrich did, could identify disjunction but could not value it. In turn, it was far easier for Dickinson's critical defenders to create a coherence for their poet than it would have been for them to leap forward and overturn the values of coherence and order.

There was no way to praise disjunction in the existing critical vocabulary of the 1890s. A relatively unusual style like Whitman's could be either wholly ignored or seen as something that demanded to be read by its own standards; Dickinson's violations of traditional lyric forms could only be read as conventional failures. So positive critics seem to praise her by making something unrecognizable of her.

Another hindrance to her canonization was the continuing ascendance of organicism. Emily Dickinson's verse was difficult to read as formally organic; its conventional style did not resemble a metaphor or analogue for organic processes. Her mediate approach to the American landscape proved to be a difficulty for critics. Canonizers resolved the difficulty across her biography, where she became the poet of the domestic backyard, subtly disarmed and compressed in her treatment of nature.

The high American organicists—for example, Whitman in poetry, Frederic Church in painting, Louis Sullivan in architecture—have usually been men, with a particularly expansive and ambitious design upon the use of nature in design. The notion that women's ideas about the landscape could have power and artistic validity has not been prominent in American intellectual history; in fact, one senses the move to nature in American writing, from Bryant to Thoreau to Melville, as an escape from the feminized concerns of the city, or human settlement in general—a permanent lighting out for the Territory. In this context, Dickinson's nature poems could receive only a miniaturist's place in the gallery of American nature writing.

Todd and Higginson arranged Dickinson's poems into four thematic groupings in the 1890 edition: Life, Nature, Love, and Time & Eternity. The result was not merely a misleading sense of order but also a bracketing of "Nature" poems as a descriptive genre with little power to comment on the transcendent or sublime. The bracketing consequently abetted the feminizing of Dickinson's concerns about nature, ensuring that they would not escape from the neighborhood of familiar animals, plants, and local landscapes into the great sprawls of landscape that were the poetic preserve of poets like Bryant, Whitman, and Longfellow. As always, Dickinson texts can be found to assist such bracketing. "My nosegays are for captives" (P-95, first published 1891) is the epigraph to the "Nature" section in *Poems*. "Nature, the gentlest mother" (P-790) was given the appropriate sentimental spin by Louise Chandler Moulton's review: "She preferred the companionship of Nature to that of men; and to her finely attuned ear Nature spoke; and she translated for the world utterances unheard by duller neighbors."[28] The final stanza of "The robin is the one" (P-828) was one that Higginson found "most refreshing"[29] when he received it in his regimental camp:

> The robin is the one
> That speechless from her nest
> Submits that home and certainty
> And sanctity are best. (68)

One can perhaps forgive Higginson, in the stress of the front, for being innocently charmed by lines that we might take as sardonic in their irony. But his reading (as he recalled it for the October 1891 *Atlantic Monthly*) suggests that Victorian readers were ready to ignore the possibility of irony in women's poems that draw domestic lessons from nature.

Early Dickinson critics sometimes considered her nature poems the "loveliest"—not always high praise, as it often means the critic did not find them thought-provoking.[30] Sometimes, however, the early critics depreciated Dickinson's "fatal gift of uniting absurd figures with solemn thoughts," as an 1891 lecturer put it.[31] Even Rupert Hughes, a Dickinson admirer, had to concede that "the audacious homeliness of many of her tropes" would hold "much that is torment" for the uninitiated reader.[32]

One of the best examples of absurd figures and audaciously homely tropes from the 1890s selections is the cluster of sunset poems chosen by Todd. It is coincidental, if Dickinson never read Whitman, that she wrote so many poems describing the sunset in distancing metaphors, while his great poem of face-to-face immediacy with the reader is the 1856 "Sun-Down Poem" that would later be called "Crossing Brooklyn Ferry." Recall Whitman's initial description of the sunset in that poem: "Clouds of the west—sun there half an hour high—I see you also face to face" (116). Now, here is a Dickinson sunset:

> She sweeps with many-colored brooms,
> And leaves the shreds behind;
> Oh, housewife in the evening west,
> Come back, and dust the pond!

> You dropped a purple ravelling in,
> You dropped an amber thread;
> And now you've littered all the East
> With duds of emerald!

> And still she plies her spotted brooms,
> And still the aprons fly,
> Till brooms fade softly into stars—
> And then I come away. (P-219; 87)

Eleven of the twelve lines of the poems contain metaphors. The overload of trope in this poem makes it almost impossible to *see* the experience. Other sunset poems suppress the tenor of the metaphor altogether, as in this pair:

> Where ships of purple gently toss
> On seas of daffodil,
> Fantastic sailors mingle,
> And then—the wharf is still. (P-265, published 1891; 88)

> A sloop of amber slips away
>   Upon an ether sea,
> And wrecks in peace a purple tar,
>   The son of ecstasy. (P-1622; 121)

The second poem in this pair complicates the figurative language even further than the first, by introducing the "purple tar," personifying an aspect of the visual image, and then proceeding to dramatize that personification by calling him "the son of ecstasy."[33] The quality of obliqueness in these poems, which verges on riddle, is neither original nor even particularly remarkable in nineteenth-century poetry; in fact, it verges on preciosity. Andrew Lang represented the contempt that many readers British and American felt for such personifications in his remark on another sunset poem, "Presentiment is that long shadow on the lawn" (P-764):

> The notice to the startled grass
> That darkness is about to pass.

This is mere maundering. The grass would not be startled in the least, even if it was informed that darkness was not only "about to pass," but about to take high honours.[34]

Paradoxically, another poem published in 1891 makes mimetic representation of sunsets the ultimate artistic achievement:

> And who could reproduce the sun,
> At period of going down—
> The lingering and the stain, I mean—
> When Orient has been outgrown,
> And Occident becomes unknown,
> His name remain. (P-307; 82)

The feeling of communicative presence in "Sun-Down Poem" by Whitman is brought off by invoking the stability of natural cycles. The speaker sees the sunset; the reader, years later, sees the same sunset. The circle of immediate experience is unbroken. In Dickinson's poem, words overwhelm the experience, whose only persistence is through language. Verbal representations will survive even when "Occident becomes unknown"—a metonym for the death of the poet, of course, but a very strange one to choose, because it suggests that the very experience the poet represents is the one that future generations will know only from that poet's representation.

The sense that representation is fulfilled in the absence of the thing represented, combined with a tendency to represent in as distancing a way as possible, informs "What mystery pervades a well!" (P-1400). The poem expresses fear of water, particularly in wells, notes that the grass does not fear the water (one hears Andrew Lang stirring in protest at this point), *begins* to speculate on the relation between grass and water, and then gives up very quickly, concluding

> But nature is a stranger yet;
> The ones that cite her most
> Have never passed her haunted house,
> Nor simplified her ghost.

> To pity those who know her not
> Is helped by the regret
> That those who know her, know her less
> The nearer her they get. (116)

"What mystery pervades a well!" gave an indication to her earliest readers that the Dickinson texts would not treat nature as comfortable, or sublime, or particularly as American. Except when they did, of course; the
nature poems are as dialogic a mixture as the ones that treat Christianity.

With such an uncertain mixture to choose from, Dickinson critics
used biography to make the poet into a tiny friend of tiny living things.
Since she supposedly never left her home and garden, she could be read
as the poet of the conservatory, the potted exotic of American verse.
Martha Dickinson Bianchi's 1924 description of the poet as botanist is
remarkable for its contextualizing of her aunt's poetics:

> Emily's own conservatory was like fairyland at all seasons, especially in
> comparison with the dreary white winter cold outside. It opened from the
> dining-room, a tiny glass room, with white shelves running around it on
> which were grouped the loveliest ferns, rich purple heliotrope, the yel-
> low jasmine, and one giant Daphne odora with its orange-blossom scent
> astray from the Riviera, and two majestic cape jasmines, exotics akin to
> her alien soul. She tolerated none of the usual variety of mongrel house
> plants. A rare scarlet lily, a resurrection calla, perhaps—and here it was
> always summer with the oxalis dripping from hanging baskets like hum-
> ble incense upon the heads of the household and its frequenters.[35]

The exotic artificiality of the poet's "alien soul" in Bianchi's description
foreshadows William Carlos Williams's treatment of Marianne Moore's
poetry as a "porcelain garden" just one year later. A direct influence is
unlikely; what is happening instead is a gradual construction of a natural setting for the verse of American women poets, a separate sphere that
would not compete with the male territory of the sea, the prairie, the
desert, the forest.

Bianchi's *The Life and Letters of Emily Dickinson* was superseded by the
more scholarly biographies by Genevieve Taggard and George F. Whicher, but its status as the definitive statement of the poet's last living relative made it disproportionately influential on Dickinson criticism during the crucial decades that established the poet in the canon.[36] Percy
Lubbock, reviewing Bianchi's book, rooted Dickinson's poetry in "the
perverse artificiality of her life" and saw her contact with the world as
limited to "the daisies and butterflies outside her window."[37] Theodore
Spencer saw Dickinson's poetics as exotic and ornamental even when
most effective: "like those dry Japanese flowers which blossom out when
put in water, her condensed preservations of experience spread and expand in the reader's mind."[38] The complexity of Dickinson's approach
to nature would be explored in greater depth by Allen Tate and R. P.
Blackmur in the 1930s, but the essential work of drying and preserving
Emily Dickinson had been done.

When one reads 1890s criticism of Dickinson one hundred years later, one gets the odd sense that the negative reviewers saw Dickinson in terms that we might praise her with, while the positive critics shaped the poet in terms we would certainly disagree with, confining her as they shaped her into the limits that they felt were appropriate to a small-town New England woman writer. Her supporters limited and narrowed approaches to her work because of the demands of the critical paradigm of presence. These limitations have the poet's sex as their central motif.

Bliss Carman, in the course of a reading that localizes Dickinson, treats her as the distillation of New England and "a type of her race," maintains that "she must have had the sunniest of dispositions," and speaks of her "tolerant, gay, debonair note of blameless joy."[39] This is the Yankee angel in the house, but she had an out-of-doors counterpart. Arlo Bates treats Dickinson as barbaric in something like the sense that was being used to praise Whitman: "There is a barbaric flavor often discernible, as if this gentle poet had the blood of some gentle and simple Indian ancestress in her veins still in an unadulterated current."[40] In Bates's formulation, however, Dickinson's barbarism has a feminine gender and must therefore be "gentle and simple." Rupert Hughes produced a reading of Dickinson in 1896 that is admittedly identical to his own reading of Walt Whitman: "Emily Dickinson and Whitman, with their unbending comradery with God and humanity, are our best realizations of the distinctively American spirit. . . . Her outlook upon Death (and Walt Whitman's also) is so calm, so nonchalant; her pride so near Yankee brag; her seriousness so close to Yankee humor; so fond of everyday things, in short, so bigly democratic, that I feel in the poetry of both of them something markedly American, something majestic that belongs especially over here in our United States."[41] "Bigly democratic" is employed here as a reaction to Dickinson's mundane imagery and as a defense of her form in the face of poetic rules that Hughes compares to "Oriental despotism."[42] But Hughes also uses the phrase because it was current in the highest appreciations of Whitman and was the keynote of American literary nationalism. For Dickinson to be admitted to the canon of great American poets, she must, somehow, be thought of as democratic, and Hughes tries to do so.

Hughes's reading of Dickinson is frankly banal, all but unthinking; it is one of the dullest examples of the application of Whitmanic values to another poet's work. In one sense Hughes's reading is just a cliché, not an idea; but I would argue that a critical cliché is a sort of second-order ideogram in critical discourse. When "democratic" comes to mean "good" in such a facile way that one can apply it to nearly any text one wants to value, then critical discourse does not become meaningless. It merely takes on meanings that are part of a larger, assumed ideology of social value. In a sense, readings like Hughes's are literary criticism on the brink of quite unconsciously becoming cultural criticism. The unexamined thought is well worth examining.

Gender is rarely important in early Whitman criticism; Whitman is simply a poet, if sometimes a sexually odd one, and his male gender per se is not an issue in his early reception. Gender is a frequent undertone in early Dickinson criticism. Ellen Battelle Dietrick noted, in 1892, the inability of male critics to "review the intellectual products of a woman without constant reference to her sex." For her the double standard in the contrast between Dickinson criticism and the reception of Whitman was clear. She cites Aldrich's "sweeping condemnation of Emily Dickinson's 'incoherence and formlessness' (qualities which are now supposed peculiarly to manifest genius in Walt Whitman)."[43] The gender bias that Dietrick's unseconded critique perceives foreshadows trends in the reception of "Miss Dickinson," "Miss Moore," and "Miss Bishop" that resonate well into the second half of the twentieth century.

In Harry Lyman Koopman's 1896 discussion of Dickinson, the dynamic of gender is combined with the racialism that prevails throughout literary criticism of the period. He adds a scientific flavor to the commonplace view that Dickinson was ahead of her time, seeing her as an example of "adnepotism," a phenomenon where traits that will appear in the future of the race are manifested early in a rare individual. Therefore, she is a preview of the future salience of women writers, since the "position of woman in literature is destined to become increasingly prominent as the race advances."[44] But Koopman conceives of the impact of women on culture not as an assumption of cultural power but as an increasing public representation of the immanence of women:

> Woman is at once more conservative and more lawless than man; more abandoned both to love and to hate; more intense in imagination and sympathy, but narrower; capable of an apparently intellectual enthusiasm that really springs from the affections, and incapable, except in the strongest, of a degree of spiritual self-dependence that is common to the average of men. These are some of the characteristics of woman that are beginning to make their impression upon literature, and some of them help to account for traits in the poetry of Emily Dickinson that would otherwise seem to be purely individual.[45]

Koopman's attitude helps to clarify some of the background of later appreciations of the poet. If Dickinson had been a man, her achievement would have been "purely individual"; since she is a woman, her work cannot be read in gender-neutral terms. Despite his display of scientific objectivity, Koopman feels the thrill of scientific discovery; at last a woman poet steps forward uncensored by Victorian morality, "abandoned to both love and hate," cut off from the decorous support networks that authoresses used to enjoy. For Koopman, it is indeed a thrilling moment in the criticism of American poetry.

Carman's perception that the poet had the "sunniest of dispositions" did not become part of her ideal biography. Instead, the biographical myth constructed in the 1900s began to see Dickinson as a "New England nun," a character out of local-color stories.[46] From Britain in 1924, Percy Lubbock echoed back the ideal biography that American critics had been assembling for a decade: "To this determined little anchoress, so carefully shut up in her provincial cell, nothing was sacred and nothing daunting."[47] Critics involve the anchoress image in sundry corporal acts of mercy: Koopman has the poet "constantly sending delicacies to the sick";[48] Ella Gilbert Ives, in 1907, reports that "during the later years of her life the poet was accustomed to keep a candle burning in her window at night for the belated traveller."[49] Ives does not record what welcome any actual belated travelers got when they knocked on the Homestead door, however.

William Dean Howells, one of Dickinson's first proponents, had argued in 1891 that "she could as well happen in Amherst, Mass., as in Athens, Att."[50] But criticism in the 1910s began to construct an elaborate picture of Dickinson as a quintessential New England character. Elizabeth Shepley Sergeant asked, "[Where] did Emily Dickinson get her daring inspiration? Certainly she did not go abroad for it, but dug it out of her native granite. To me she is one of the rarer flowers the sterner New England ever bore. . . . The peculiar quality of her short concentrated poems is that they bring infinity and eternity within a village hedge; and to her, as to the early Puritan, the great earthly experience was poignantly individual."[51] Sergeant's essay—a 1915 review of *The Single Hound*—is ostensibly an attempt to connect Dickinson with modernist poets; it is entitled "An Early Imagist." But as Dickinson was gaining her still-current reputation as a protomodernist, she was also being circumscribed as a regionalist. Walt Whitman, whose life experiences were mostly limited to Nassau, Kings, and New York counties, became the poet of the entire continental United States; Dickinson was relegated to the subordinate task of reflecting a limited part of the national experience. Just as Whitman spanned and reconciled the paradox of the individual and the mass, he reconciled the universal and the local. Poets further down the organizational chart of the cultural work of American poetry (especially women) were delegated parts of his task, and small-town New England fell to her. Hence she could function within modernism as a provincial voice, one of William Carlos Williams's "pure products of America," granted, but like them, "crazy."

The view of Dickinson as the quintessence of New England persisted in the work of many critics throughout the first half of the twentieth century. The uses of regional identification can be studied in Whicher's *This Was a Poet*, where the regional motif is presented in organic metaphors. "What she actually represents is the last surprising bloom—the November witch-hazel blossom—of New England's flowering time. . . . In the technical details of her poetry she was as native as a blueberry. . . . She translated into poetry the instinct for sound craftsmanship in things of use evidenced by colonial silverware and clock-cases, New England doorways and fireplaces, and Yankee sailing ships."[52] Whicher's appeal to the utilitarian folk art of her region makes Dickinson's style seem representative rather than wildly idiosyncratic. By connecting her verse with solid if somewhat inelegant Yankee things, Whicher continues an analogy begun in 1925, when Edward Sapir called Dickinson a "primitive" artist; he also finds a way to dissent forcefully from the opinion still expressed by poet-critics as diverse as Yvor Winters, R. P. Blackmur, and Marianne Moore: that Dickinson's style was flawed.[53] Instead of relying on a subjective judgment of taste or a demonstration of internal consistency in Dickinson's style (both of which were attempted by Susan Miles and T. Walter Herbert), Whicher invokes regionalism to place Dickinson within a tradition and a grammar of craftsmanship.[54]

Whicher takes his chapter title, "Seeing New Englandly," from the following version of P-285, which appeared in *Further Poems* and is often seen as Dickinson's pronouncement of a regionalist poetics:

> The Robin's my criterion of tune
> Because I grow where robins do—
> But were I Cuckoo born
> I'd swear by him,
> The ode familiar rules the morn.
> The Buttercup's my whim for bloom
> Because we're orchard-sprung—
> But were I Britain-born
> I'd daisies spurn—
> None but the Nut October fits,
> Because through dropping it
> The seasons flit, I'm taught.
> Without the snow's tableau
> Winter were lie to me—

> Because I see New Englandly.
> The Queen discerns like me—
> Provincially. (307)

Whicher reads the poem as an expression of regional loyalty: "She did not seek to emancipate herself from provincial traits. The whole duty of a New England poet was to realize as fully as might be the possibilities of beauty implicit in the New England tradition."[55] Whicher's reading is a creative misprision, reading a positive program into a text that is a bare statement of limitations. The poem presents an alternating list of perceptual paradigms, one of New and one of Old England. The speaker locates herself in the New England paradigm because that's where she's grown up. There is no rejection of the English way of seeing, such as one might expect from a poem influenced by literary nationalism; instead, there is an equation between the local limitations of one way of seeing and those of another. "I see New Englandly" is not an pledge of allegiance but a recognition of a foreclosure of choice.

Regionalism was a way of placing Dickinson's voice so as to diffuse its power and its potential resonances. Conrad Aiken, in 1924, had seen Dickinson as "the most perfect flower of New England Transcendentalism."[56] Contextualizing her as an heir to the Puritans, Aiken observes that, like the Puritans, "The problems of good and evil, of life and death, obsessed her; the nature and destiny of the human soul; and Emerson's theory of compensation."[57] Aiken's reading of Dickinson—as text and persona—is a good early example of the centripetal imperative in Dickinson criticism. Conceptually, Aiken starts from the surface of the poems, which seems to be, formally, "nothing but a colourless dry monotony." "Once adjust oneself to the spinsterly angularity of the mode" and the poems are intellectually multifarious.[58] But the richness of subjects and forms in turn conceals a unified core concern. Dickinson's many poems about nature are, for instance, "not the most secretly revelatory of or dramatically compulsive of her poems. . . . they are often superficial."[59] The center of her poetry is the old Puritan concern with death: "Death, and the problem of life after death, obsessed her. She seems to have thought of it constantly—she died all her life, she probed death daily."[60] Aiken's is a reading that confronts the poems initially as old-maidishly gendered. Below that level there is a brief opening of possibilities, as the poems can expand to address all kinds of social concerns. Below *that* there is a level where the central concern is once again an old-maidish theological worry, an obsession befitting some minor character out of Harriet Beecher Stowe. Reading Dickinson as the essence of her region and its history enables the critic to bracket and control her.

Norman Foerster, in 1921, developed some of the themes that Aiken and Whicher would echo, saying, "There is no better example of the New England tendency to moral revery than this pale Indian-summer flower of Puritanism."[61] Foerster reverses Koopman's theory that Dickinson was ahead of her time; he sees her as an avatar of the Puritan past. "A mystical poetess sequestered in a Berkshire village, . . . she spent her days in brooding over the mystery of pain, the true nature of success, the refuge of the tomb, the witchcraft of the bee's murmur, the election of love, the relation of deed to thought and will. On such subjects she jotted down hundreds of little poems."[62] Foerster saw this textual construct of the "mystical poetess" as corresponding exactly to Dickinson's biography. "She expressed her experience in poems, forgetting the world altogether, intent only on the satisfaction of giving her fluid life lasting form, her verse being her journal."[63] For Foerster, the late Puritanism of Dickinson's poetry must be validated by a heavy insistence on the poetics of presence; imbued with the regional influences that had come down to her from the seventeenth century, Dickinson both wrote and *was* a late Puritan. As such, because she is personally inseparable from her poetry (her "journal"), she represents a seductive challenge to the male reader: "Always she is penetrating and dainty, both intimate and aloof, challenging lively thought on our part while remaining, herself, a charmingly elfish mystery."[64] The challenge to the male critic is the exoticism of this poetic voice, this persona so remote in time and attitude from the reader of the 1920s.

The most salient accomplishment of Bianchi's *Life and Letters* was its oblique confirmation of readers' suspicions that Dickinson suffered from unrequited passion. Bianchi's hint that the poet fell in love during a trip to Washington in the mid-1850s is oblique and excessively mysterious, but spoken with the authority of the only daughter of the poet's only confidante:

> All that was ever told was a confidence to her sister Sue, sacredly guarded under all provocation till death united them—the confiding and the listening—in one abiding silence.
>
> Certainly in that first witchery of an undreamed Southern springtime Emily was overtaken—doomed once and forever by her own heart. It was instantaneous, overwhelming, impossible. There is no doubt that two pre-destined souls were kept apart only by her high sense of duty, and the necessity for preserving love untarnished by the inevitable destruction of another woman's life.
>
> Without stopping to look back, she fled to her own home for refuge.[65]

This mystery, once fomented by Bianchi, has continued alive to the present moment.[66] What matters more than the identity of the lover, of course, is the explanatory value the lover's existence took on in Dickinson criticism. For Genevieve Taggard in 1930, Dickinson was prevented from marrying George Gould by her father and consequently "took life 'over her door-sill' to live with it on curious terms."[67] Taggard goes on to say of this blocked engagement: "Even if it took place as a pure hallucination, so perfectly fitted it seems to Emily's dilemmas, we should still say it was profoundly true."[68] In other words, the explanatory power of a frustrated love affair is so great that if it cannot be documented, we must conclude that it occurred in the poet's fantasies anyway. For so many readers the poems simply do not make sense until read through a love affair. George F. Whicher cautions that "we should not expect to find in fervid love poems an exact statement of actual circumstances"; but he then proceeds to read from the less-fervid love poems a set of clues that enable him to say that "she found in Charles Wadsworth the 'atom [she] preferred to all the lists of clay.'"[69]

When Allen Tate, in 1932, saw guesses about Dickinson's possible lovers as manifestations of the prejudice that "we believe that no virgin can know enough to write poetry," he was not quite accurate; the consensus at the time was actually that no woman *contented* with her virginity could know enough to write poetry.[70] One reason for Dickinson's achievement of canonical status was her availability as the ultimate virginal site for criticism. She achieved her prominence in the canon as a woman who invited male critical fantasies, who spoke—only in her poems, because in life she had to be guarded—most freely of the deepest female longings. One senses a thrill of overhearing what a woman "really thinks," of finally being privy to a monologue that is not edited for "mixed company," in male Dickinson critics from the 1890s to the 1960s. The poetics of presence unavoidably gendered her texts, leading to male curiosity about the immanent female traits revealed in those gendered texts.

If Whitman required circumspection and distancing on the part of some critics who could not, whatever their own sexual preference, assume a homosexual voice in their texts,[71] Dickinson provided the perfect contrast: a woman poet erotically available as speaking persona to the heterosexual male interpreter. Granville Hicks wrote in *The Great Tradition*:

> There was, of course, a whole field of experience, closed to Thoreau, that Emily returned to time after time in her poetry. We may not know who her lover was or why she never married him, but surely no American poet has written so movingly of love and renunciation. Sometimes she spoke with the utmost simplicity; sometimes passion merged with religious aspiration in a cry of fierce and almost agonizing intensity.[72]

Hicks's comment that erotic experience was "closed to Thoreau" is unintelligible unless one thinks one's way back into an ideology that insists, with Byron, that "Man's love is of man's life a thing apart, / 'Tis
woman's whole existence." In Hicks's reading, sexual concerns are gendered feminine; unrequited sexual longing, in particular, is a feminine
experience. The merging of passion and religion in Dickinson's poetry
is irresistibly attractive to the critic here; it becomes a basis for the erotic
appeal of the poetry to the reader. The male God that the poet wor-
ships and struggles against blends with the male lover that biographical
speculation must provide for her, even if he must remain biographically
anonymous (because he does not, biographically, exist). The ecstasy such
a composite figure represents when hypostatized into reality by the poetics of presence is attractive to the male critic who reads himself back
into that very role. If T. W. Higginson didn't understand her, these critics seem to say, at least *I* can. The poet's historical distance from her
readers encourages what Matthiessen would call the "liberties" of first-
name-basis intimacy with the "Emily" of this reading.[73] The same critics would not have dreamed of calling Miss Moore "Marianne"; the late
Miss Dickinson became for a whole generation of male critics the girl
who was dying for them to take her to the prom, the teenaged sister
whose diary they could steal and read.

The extreme of the eroticized reading of Dickinson was reached by
Robert Hillyer, a poet and the distant successor of Edward Tyrrel Channing as Boylston Professor at Harvard. His 1922 essay on Dickinson
builds to a celebration of the poet's diffuse, polymorphous eroticism:

> Living amid the velvet hush of American Victorianism, she blew clarion
> notes of the shocking truth; a daughter of Puritanism, she pushed past
> the rigid image of Fear and took her God confidently by the hand. The
> vast love that was her being was never squandered in such sentimental
> abstractions as Humanity, Nature, and Religion; it was profitably, if wan-
> tonly, poured out for the individuals and objects that she knew, her fam-
> ily, her friends, the hired man, all children, her garden, and the visible
> symbols of life everlasting.[74]

The masculine image of God that the poet takes here by the hand is
excitingly close to the image of the competent, powerful male reader
that the criticism itself creates as persona. The poet, freed by critical
reconstruction from all decorum, can now come on to the hired man.

There is undeniably a mixture of eroticism, family romance, and religious imagery in Dickinson's texts, and as Mary Loeffelholz has shown,
it can be read as a complex and troubling reaction to Dickinson's patriarchal surroundings and the extreme demands they made on women's

sexual and familial identity.[75] But a reading like Hillyer's shows how the same texts are refracted through the liberal, masculine criticism of the modernist period. Male anger against representations of Victorian women as poetesses, spinsters, and maiden aunts is catalyzed by the presence of Dickinson, who seems to reach out to the virile male from her immurement in the culture of ladylike gentility. The continual references in 1920s criticism to Dickinson as a flower, usually a late-opening bud to be coaxed open by sympathetic male power, reinforce the male imagination in its appropriation of women's poetic territory.

The most influential readings of Dickinson from the 1930s downplay gender but are rooted in a poetics of presence that takes the strongly monologic form Edward Sapir had expressed in 1925: "Emily Dickinson's life was all of a piece, her poetry and her letters are but a single expression."[76] Both Allen Tate's promotion of the poet and R. P. Blackmur's careful, thorough rejection of her are based on the critical assumption that poetry should reflect what T. S. Eliot had called "direct sensuous apprehension of thought."[77] Tate finds this unifying force in Dickinson; Blackmur, failing to find it at all because of the poet's heterogeneity, argues that Tate and others have overrated her.

Tate's reading is subtle both in its connection and its disconnection of Dickinson's life and work. He reads the poetry as a direct personal embodiment of Dickinson herself: "There is none of whom it is truer to say that the poet *is* the poetry," he maintains.[78] But having made that claim, he dissociates himself from biographical speculations: "Admiration and affection are pleased to linger over the tokens of a great life; but the solution to the Dickinson enigma is peculiarly superior to fact."[79] Tate therefore refuses to take part in biographical and personal speculation about Dickinson, particularly about any sexual relationships.

Instead, to explain and contextualize Dickinson's poetry, Tate has recourse to a more expansive and intellectualized regionalism than other contemporary critics used. He attempts to see her in "the whole complex of anterior fact, which was the social and religious structure of New England," especially in the problems of theology and its relation to nature.[80] By being completely true to her experience of these questions, Dickinson avoids abstraction; therefore her "work exhibits the perfect literary situation—in which is possible the fusion of sensibility and thought." She never succumbs to "rumination," another Eliotian no-no.[81] Dickinson's withdrawal from society and her avoidance of publication are then intelligible for Tate as evidence of her commitment to a true life of the mind. In this sense, her poetry exhibits her personality intensively without there being lovers behind every love poem; since Dickinson's life was really about intellectual struggle, it is possible without prurient overtones to read her texts as "a magnificent personal confession, blasphemous and, in its self-revelation, its honesty, almost obscene."[82]

When one reaches that sentence, in Tate's final paragraph, it is legitimate to wonder whether the eroticism of other Dickinson critics, having been shown the door, hasn't climbed back in through a window. But whatever the undertones of Tate's rapturous appreciation, his assessment of Dickinson is typical of criticism published on her work before the 1970s. The canonical American poets of the early twentieth century—Eliot, Stevens, Pound, and, except for a few stray comments, Frost—were silent about Dickinson; there is no single essay at any point in her reception that matches the influence of Van Wyck Brooks's chapter on Whitman or Eliot's 1935 preface on Moore. In that vacuum of "major" commentary (which again shows how little the received canon is "book-centered"), Tate's essay is representative of what general New Critical consensus there was, not least because in his terminology and values he was writing as a virtual surrogate for Eliot. Tate constructed a unitary central self for Dickinson's texts, aligned her with Donne and Shakespeare instead of her Victorian contemporaries, and foregrounded her intellectual concerns—dampening biographical rumors, giving Dickinson's work the contours of modernism as filtered through Eliot, and making her poems safe for formalism. Without abandoning the imperatives of presence, Tate read Dickinson as a verbally centered person whose language was essentially poetic but without "moral responsibility."[83] She was magnificently sincere and genuine—in a sort of asocial, disembodied way.

Nature, in Tate's view of Dickinson, is more problematic than in other readings; the poet is not merely an exotic looking at butterflies and robins from her conservatory windows, nor is she explicitly a bud ready for the flowering. Instead, in Dickinson's poetry, "We are shown our roots in Nature by examining our differences with Nature; we are renewed by Nature without being delivered into her hands. When it is possible for a poet to do this with the greatest imaginative comprehension, a possibility that the poet cannot himself create, we have the perfect literary situation."[84] For some reason Tate sees this perfect situation as occurring only in Elizabethan and Stuart England, and in nineteenth-century New England. Whatever the reasons for his canon of historical situations, which neatly adumbrates both Dickinson and Donne, he places the highest critical value on the disjunctive approach to nature that had caused Dickinson's earliest readers such "torment," in Rupert Hughes's phrase.

Tate's criticism has a distinct, austere appeal. In desexualizing the poet while arguing for the excitement of her texts, he at once raises the perceived tone of Dickinson criticism above "mere" gossip and also disarms the potential of such gossip for provoking a feminist appreciation of how Dickinson "wrote the body"—a potential not "reloaded" until the 1980s. When read through Tate, Dickinson became important for the New Criticism because her essence came to be perceived as a lack of intentionality, an unmediated presentation of verbal texture arising from "discipline in an objective system of truth, and . . . lack of consciousness of such a discipline."[85] The poet's failure to publish could now be read without qualms as a magnificent defiance of fashion. The evasive "supposed person" had become a coherent and forceful artistic presence.

Coming after Tate's canonizing essay, R. P. Blackmur's 1937 debunking of "prejudices" about Dickinson was a significant demurral that seems in retrospect as eccentric as Santayana's persistent downgrading of Whitman. But just as with 1890s criticism, the terms in which Blackmur attacked Dickinson now seem to come closer to our sense of the texts than more positive assessments do. Blackmur's central complaint is that Dickinson's "is not a homogeneous vocabulary; its unity is specious for the instance rather than organic for the whole of her work."[86] That comment alone might stand as an epigraph for some of the strongest Dickinson criticism of the 1980s and 1990s; all that need be changed is the critical "value sign," from Blackmur's negative to the positive of a critic like Margaret Dickie. Blackmur was aware that the text Dickinson's editors presented was uncertain, and also that many of the poems, in manuscript, were unfinished. He suggests that a more rigorous selection of texts might enable critics to discover the essence of Dickinson: "with the obvious fragments cut out . . . a clear, self-characterizing" poet might emerge.[87] In the event, it was much less obvious which Dickinson texts were fragments and which were finished poems than Blackmur with his hierarchical assumptions supposed. But the essence of his critique is consistent: great art demands a unified sensibility, and Dickinson does not demonstrate one. "The pattern of association is kaleidoscopic and extraneous for her far more often than it is crystalline and inwardly compelled."[88] Read back through this comment, Dickinson seems like a poetic voice just waiting for Umberto Eco to attack the structuralist notion of the artwork as crystal.[89]

But as Blackmur's argument unfolds, it returns, however formalistic its opening, to arguments based on the poetics of presence, especially the presence of gender. In the guise of linguistic analysis, Blackmur subtly denies Dickinson linguistic empowerment: "In what is quantitatively the great part of her work Emily Dickinson did not put the life of meaning into her words; she leaned on the formulas of words in the hope that the formulas would fully express what she felt privately—sometimes the emotion of escape and sometimes the conviction of assent—in her own self-centered experience."[90] The imperative of originality is particularly strong in this passage; there is no sense that poetry can be made from a dialogic interaction of preuttered formulas, much less any sense that all utterances are ineluctably formulaic. Dickinson's language is, for Blackmur, doubly belated; he senses that Scott was a stronger influence on Dickinson's vocabulary than Shakespeare, making her derivative from a derivation.[91] Its belatedness is attributable to her gender, to her need to live vicariously through the language of males. The only words she had living contact with, says Blackmur, are those "taken from sewing and the kinds of cloth used in women's clothes . . . legal words [because of her father's and brother's profession, and] . . . the names of jewels." The rest of her vocabulary comes from "the stretching of her daily fancy."[92] Hence her words get "out of control through the poet's failure to maintain an objective feeling of responsibility towards language."[93]

Blackmur's critique is internally self-consistent and shares the same values as Tate's, while coming to the opposite conclusion. But even while he constructs perhaps the most objectivist, formalist reading of Dickinson's texts to appear before 1955, Blackmur's conclusions depend on the poet's gender. Having dismissed Dickinson's poetry, Blackmur adds, almost as an afterthought: "She was neither a professional poet nor an amateur; she was a private poet who wrote indefatigably as some women cook or knit. Her gift for words and the cultural predicament of her time drove her to poetry instead of antimacassars. Neither her personal education nor the habit of her society as she knew it ever gave her the least inkling that poetry is a rational and objective art and most so when the theme is self-expression."[94] One could shrug off this comment as representative of the 1930s and the status of women writers then in academic criticism. Or one could perhaps note that it is not a particularly hostile comment; in effect, Blackmur excuses the poet for *not* being born into a "perfect literary situation." But if traced back through Blackmur's argument, his connection of femaleness with limitation is in fact the linchpin of his entire critique. He finds her use of words "out of control" and therefore not "self-characterizing"—not unitary, not monologic—because she fails to put the "life of meaning" into her words. She cannot put the life of meaning there because her gender has only allowed her half a life. Ultimately, we must reject poetry, by these criteria, if we examine the poet's life and find that there was insufficient experience to authorize the texts as embodiments of a lived personal identity. If that lived identity is a woman's, it can be sneered at with impunity. Such was the "objective" criticism of the 1930s.

By 1943 Eunice Glenn was tiring of such criticism:

> The prejudiced, naturally, do not take the trouble really to read her poems; consequently, they are usually willing to dismiss this "Puritan maiden" and her "bulletins from Immortality" with a patronizing shrug of the shoulder and to consign her to those who they think comprise her true audience—female readers who find in her verses a reflection of themselves and their frustrated love. It is much easier to accept romantic criticism than it is to examine the poems firsthand. Emily Dickinson has been put in her place, the wrong place, and kept there.[95]

Glenn specifically exempts Blackmur from her general comment, but it is clear that her attack is on the entire critical fraternity that had sequestered Dickinson in her gender roles. The status of Glenn's essay itself is instructive about the gender assumptions of the academy. A major essay in a respected literary review, at a time when little else was being written on the poet, Glenn's article might be seen as having paved the way for later Dickinson scholarship. Yet it was never reprinted and has virtually never been cited, while the essays of Glenn's male contemporaries have been carefully preserved and acknowledged as formative elements in the critical tradition.

By the late 1930s, Dickinson was in the canon to stay, but in a curious double bind. She was either fixed as the overheard passionate girl (Hillyer), drained into formalist abstraction (Tate), or disparaged because of her sex (Blackmur). These three attitudes have in common a sort of orientalism of gender; they are about how male critics think men should respond to women's writing. They do not even acknowledge a woman's response, like Glenn's, let alone attempt to read the concerns of gender as they are expressed in Dickinson's texts as opposed to Dickinson's ideal biography. At least one Dickinson critic of the 1930s, however, did not emphasize organism or gender and in fact celebrated Dickinson's artificiality—while retaining the value of originality. A review of Dickinson's *Letters* in the January 1933 issue of *Poetry* reads in part:

> As Mr. Trueblood has noted, "What she said seems always said with the choicest originality." Whittier, Bryant, and Thoreau were choice; and to some extent Emerson. Hawthorne was a bear but great. All of these except Whittier seem less choice than their neighbor—"Myself the only kangaroo among the beauty" she called herself, not realizing the pinnacle of favor to which her words of dejection were to be raised.
>
> An element of Chinese taste was part of this choiceness, in its daring associations of the prismatically true; the gamboge and pink and cochineal of the poems; the oleander blossom tied with black ribbon; the dandelion with scarlet; the rowan spray with white. . . .
>
> To some, her Japanesely fantastic reverence for tree, insect, and toad-

stool is not interesting; many who are "helped" by a brave note, do not admire the plucked string; by some the note of rapture is not caught; and by the self-sufficient, Emily Dickinson has been accused of vanity.[96]

This reviewer's voice is enough off the critical center for 1933 that we may suspect the criticism of being more about the critic Marianne Moore than about the book she is reviewing. But even Mooreish phrases like "Chinese taste," "prismatically true," and "Japanesely fantastic" are not far from the vocabulary of Dickinson critics like Percy Lubbock and Theodore Spencer. When considering Moore's reception in the light of Dickinson's—and they are similar in many ways—one should resist the impulse to see Moore as forming a "tradition" of women's poets, immured in patriarchal (and patronizing) readings; however much the reception of Moore's poetry was skewed by gender assumptions, she herself, as critic and commentator, could no more escape those assumptions, as part of the critical preconditions *she* inherited, than any writer could. But if we can see writers as "strong," it is worth noting that Moore's essay on Dickinson is an example of her strength—more eccentric, more self-focused, more about her own texts than about the subject poet's—than almost any other contemporary Dickinson criticism. The formation of an intense personal "prejudice" to counter the prejudices absorbed from the surrounding texture of discourse enabled Marianne Moore to become a poet in the modernist period. The strength of that prejudice could not enable her to escape similarly confining readings once she did become a poet, however. The conservatory that contained Dickinson was sufficient to hold the poetry of Marianne Moore for several decades.

FOUR

Marianne Moore:
The Porcelain Garden

The comparative silence of the American high modernists on the subject of Emily Dickinson stands in notable contrast to their early and en-
thusiastic championing of Marianne Moore. Ezra Pound, Wallace Stevens, William Carlos Williams, and T. S. Eliot did not discuss Dickinson
(except for a few offhand comments by Williams), but they wrote influential essays on Moore, treating her, right from the beginning of her
career, as an equal or even superior artist. One can sometimes sense in
the criticism of the 1950s and 1960s a growing resentment of Moore
among younger male critics who incorporated a distaste for her into their
Oedipal rejection of their male precursors.[1]

In fact, the later critical turn against Moore may have its origins in
the early and easy acceptance she won from her male contemporaries.
That acceptance can be hard to comprehend. Marianne Moore's relation to modernism, when read in retrospect, is a historical fact but a
textual dissonance; she now reads as antimodernist much of the time.
When tastemakers like Pound, Harriet Monroe, Alfred Kreymborg, and
Richard Aldington took up her poetry, she became a modernist by association. Eighty years after her poems first appeared in pioneering maga-
zines like *Poetry* and *Others*, she seems as different from the early Eliot
or the early Pound as she did and still does seem different from Robert
Bridges or Thomas Hardy. One can perhaps see the actions of Moore's
modernist promoters as a kind of preemption. Harold Bloom's theory of
influence, in which poets misprise their precursors to clear poetic territory for themselves, works in the synchronic dimension as well; faced
with an unusually strong contemporary, poets can use their own critical
voices to reduce, contain, or mislead her. From Ezra Pound signing Hil-

da Doolittle's poems "H.D., *Imagiste*," to Henry Miller borrowing Anaïs
Nin's typewriter, Amy Lowell enduring torrents of abuse from male contemporaries, and Laura Riding being demonized by official versions of
her relationship with Robert Graves, the history of women writing within modernism has often been one of management, control, and misdi-
rection by male writers.

Moore's professional relationship with her male contemporaries was
by no means hostile, of course. She was on excellent terms with Stevens,
Pound, and Eliot. Nor was she a passive sufferer at the hands of her male
readers; in particular, when she edited *The Dial* in the late 1920s, she
held power that made her an active participant in molding the tastes of
readers and the careers of others. We have already seen her bending the
reception of Emily Dickinson, if only slightly, in the direction of her
own magnetic critical voice. As Celeste Goodridge has shown in *Hints
and Disguises*, Moore herself was a force to be reckoned with in the reception history of her modernist contemporaries.[2]

The force was reciprocal. Two essays on Moore stand out as disproportionately influential on later readers: William Carlos Williams's 1925
"Marianne Moore" and T. S. Eliot's 1935 introduction to her *Selected
Poems*. The concerns, terminology, and assessments of these two pieces
echo down through the following decades of Moore criticism; strongly
placed independent critics defer remarkably to the readings of Williams
and Eliot. Louise Bogan's 1944 review of Moore's *Nevertheless* repeats
Eliot's 1935 assessment of Moore almost exactly; Wallace Fowlie would
echo Eliot in 1952, Delmore Schwartz in 1960, Hugh Kenner in 1963.[3]
Eliot's contention that Moore's work formed "part of the small body of
durable poetry written in our time" has been ubiquitous, quoted in scholarship and reviews and still alive today as jacket copy on the Penguin
edition of Moore's *Complete Poems*.[4] As the *New Yorker* began to culti-
vate the image of Moore as unofficial laureate of the city and guarantor
of the magazine's poetic taste in the 1950s, it echoed both Eliot and
Williams; Winthrop Sargeant's extensive 1957 profile of her for that
magazine characterizes her work largely in terms Williams had introduced
over twenty years earlier: "kaleidoscopic . . . collage . . . mosaic."[5] Williams's description of "Marriage" as "an anthology of transit" is still an
obligatory accompaniment to the poem in anthologies.[6]

The two essays served different functions in Moore's reception. Eliot's, more unreservedly positive, played the role of irreversible value judgment; when T. S. Eliot said that a book was "durable," it was unlikely
to turn up in neighborhood yard sales. But Williams provided more of
the specific analytical characterizations of Moore's poetry that were to
become current in later criticism. His opinion was hardly negative; his

essay at times becomes ecstatic to the point of obscurity. But in attempting to convey as strongly as possible the special qualities of Moore's achievement, Williams exposes the limits within which he would confine that achievement—limits that later critics would impose even more stringently. Even Eliot's unreserved praise would be strongly misread by Moore critics into faint praise indeed, with his qualifying terms increasingly becoming, in the criticism, qualifying in the damning rather than the clarifying sense.

T. S. Eliot wrote the introduction to Moore's *Selected Poems* twelve years after he had reviewed *Poems* and *Marriage* in *The Dial* (December 1923). In that earlier review, shortly after the publication of *The Waste Land* in 1922, he came as close to a sense of her art as fundamentally dialogic as any critic writing before the 1980s—surely because he was reading her work as the author of that most notoriously dialogic poem in the modernist canon. In 1923, Eliot cites Moore's "peculiar and brilliant and rather satiric use of . . . the curious jargon produced in America by universal university education" and praises her "refinement of that pleasantry . . . of speech which characterizes the American language, that pleasantry, uneasy, solemn, or self-conscious, which inspires both the jargon of the laboratory and the slang of the comic strip."[7] When Eliot goes on to say that "Miss Moore works this uneasy language of stereotypes—as of a whole people playing uncomfortably at clenches and clevelandisms—with impeccable skill into her pattern," he can be seen as appreciating her art for its play with the strata of a living language.[8] Eliot's own prejudices about that living language and its social milieu are now rather insufferable. "Universal university education" as a description of the United States in 1923 can only mean "but you know, my dear, they let *anyone* take a degree over there." But his application of an understanding of heteroglossia in his poetics and criticism at this time results in a sharp sense of what he then shared with Moore: a flair for the juxtaposition of bits of language drawn from many social contexts and many competing dialects and jargons.

The 1935 "Introduction" is more austere. After a preamble on the dangers of judging one's contemporaries (of interest for its anticipation of some of the themes of reception theory), Eliot addresses the "function" of poets: "Living, the poet is carrying on that struggle for the maintenance of a living language, for the maintenance of its strength, its subtlety, for the preservation of quality of feeling, which must be kept up in every generation; dead, he provides standards for those who take up the struggle after him. Miss Moore is, I believe, one of those few who have done the language some service in my lifetime."[9] Apart from the disconcerting image of Marianne Moore as Othello in the final sentence (has she just smothered some Desdemona of English grammar?), this passage marks a subtle maintenance in its own right of an Eliotian poetics. Read back through his 1935 insistence on the centripetal function of language maintenance, Eliot's 1923 appreciation of the pattern of dialects in dialogue in Moore's work seems to see her work as a sort of curmudgeonly showing-up of linguistic barbarisms. In 1935, he is rereading and reorienting his earlier concerns.

In the wake of Eliot's 1935 assessment, readings of Moore would remain devoted for years to polite, though sometimes chafing, respect for her as a guardian of the language. As late as 1963, Hugh Kenner (taking issue with Elizabeth Bishop's misleadingly limiting title for her Moore essay) says that Moore is "much more than 'the greatest living observer.' . . . she has accomplished things of general import to the maintenance of the language."[10] By the mid-1930s, Eliot's criticism had brought Moore into the conservative wing of modernism, where she was to remain.

Tendentious misquoting from Eliot's introduction, which I will now engage in, can assemble an impression of diminution that was surely not his intention. In his introduction, Eliot refers to Moore's use of "minute detail rather than . . . emotional unity," to "her amused and affectionate attention to animals," to her poems as being "something that the majority will call frigid," and, of course, to the place of her work as "part of the small body of durable poetry written in our time." These comments are positive; even the remark about the "frigidity" of the poetry is immediately erased by Eliot's statement that "to feel things in one's own way, however intensely, is likely to look like frigidity to those who can only feel in accepted ways."[11] My misquotations are completely unfair to Eliot's intention; but the fact remains that to call a forty-seven-year-old single woman "frigid," with whatever intention of immediately undermining that statement, has already done the damage one hoped to forestall. Critics' readings of other critics are as tendentious as poets' readings of other poets; the reader is always seeking grounds for misprision. By impressing Moore into the palace guard of "the language," citing her minutiae, her love of animals, and her seeming frigidity, Eliot's introduction leaves the possibility of minimizing misprision very much available. For the succeeding generation of critics, Moore's poetry would change slowly from "part of the small body of durable verse" into part of the body of durable small verse.

The keynote of Williams's 1925 characterization of Moore, and of the diminution of Moore subsequently, is his image of the porcelain garden. As used within Williams's essay, this is a positive image. It is meant to underscore Moore's uniqueness and originality; he stresses that she comes at her subjects "so effectively at a new angle as to throw out of fashion the classical conventional poetry to which one is used and puts her own and that about her in its place."[12] In terms of the poetics of presence, this is extremely high praise; Moore is seen not just as a monologic clearer of territory but as an enabler for other modernists. The originality of the porcelain garden is in tension, however, against its inorganic nature; in the long context of American poetry criticism, Williams describes Moore's work in terms similar to Margaret Fuller's sense of Longfellow as a "tastefully arranged museum."[13] Here is Williams's central image:

> The thought is compact, accurate and and accurately planted. In fact, the garden, since it is a garden more than a statue, is found to be curiously of porcelain. It is the mythical, indestructible garden of pleasure, perhaps greatly pressed for space today, but there and intact, nevertheless.
>
> I don't know where, except in modern poetry, this quality of the brittle, highly set-off porcelain garden exists and nowhere in modern work better than Miss Moore. It is this chief beauty of today, this hard crest to nature, that makes the best present work with its "unnatural" appearance seem so thoroughly gratuitous, so difficult to explain, and so doubly a treasure of seclusion. It is the white of a clarity beyond the facts.[14]

If one reads this passage for Williams's presumed intention, stressing the value markers ("pleasure," "better," "chief beauty," "best present work"), it is an attempt to reorient the demand of organicist poetics that great poetry be "natural." Williams's modernist aesthetic values artificiality against the natural qualities valued by both Romantics and Victorians.

But the passage is also fraught with an overload of revalued adjectives. It sets so many romantic, organicist values against themselves that it undercuts its own intentions, weighing Moore's work down with negatives that must all be shifted to positives at the same time for the positive sense to come across. For Williams, Moore's poetry works by overturning tradition. But since the tradition is one of life, engagement, and experience, and naturally flows from the soil and from everyday speech, her success is therefore termed *compact, curious, mythical, greatly pressed, brittle, highly set-off, hard, unnatural, gratuitous, difficult, secluded,* and *beyond the facts.* This extraordinarily concentrated collection of terms has rarely, before or since, served as positive characterizations in any criticism of poetry. It is precisely this set of terms that comes to represent, in Moore's reception, those values peculiar to her, values that cut her poetry off from dialogic contact with other art and with real life, and that should therefore only be adhered to by other poets at their own risk.

The ambivalence of the *text* of Williams's essay (I am not maintaining that he felt personally ambivalent in 1925 toward Moore or her

---

work) results from its uneasy straddling of both the values of the poetics of presence and the attempt to find something to replace those values. Presence is a complex of values that are difficult to disengage from one another. For instance, the modernist emphasis on originality is a direct inheritance from the nineteenth century and its admiration for William Cullen Bryant. In the essay as a whole, Williams tries to embrace originality while downplaying literary nationalism; in the "porcelain garden" passage, he holds onto originality at the expense of organicist values. Elsewhere in the essay he does not find it easy to get away from organicism. After arguing that poetry must stand in a special place "beyond 'nature,'" he finds that to characterize Moore's verse rhythm, an organic metaphor is necessary: "Without effort Miss Moore encounters the affairs which concern her as one would naturally in reading or upon a walk outdoors. She is not a Swinburne stumbling to music, but one always finds her moving forward ably, in thought, unimpeded by a rhythm. Her own rhythm is particularly revealing. It does not interfere with her progress; it is the movement of the animal, it does not put itself first and ask the other to follow."[15] The walk outdoors as a metaphor for reading Moore is precisely Margaret Fuller's for reading Bryant: "like leaving the highway to enter some green lovely fragrant wood."[16]

And while Williams detaches himself only halfway from organicism, he remains completely attached to the value of monologism; it is in fact the motivating force that explains how the porcelain garden is created. For Williams, Marianne Moore becomes the American Adam, or rather, the American Adam's fussy spinster sister:

> Miss Moore gets great pleasure from wiping soiled words or cutting them clean out, removing the aureoles that have been pasted about them or taking them bodily from greasy contexts. For the compositions which Miss Moore intends, each word should first stand crystal clear with no attachments; not even an aroma. As a cross light upon this, Miss Moore's personal dislike for flowers that have both a satisfying appearance and an odor of perfume is worth noticing. With Miss Moore a word is a word most when it is separated out by science, treated with acid to remove the smudges, washed, dried and placed right side up on a clean surface. Now one may say that this is a word. Now it may be used, and how?[17]

The gendering of Moore's poetics, combined with the gratuitous stray detail of her personal taste in flowers, is strongly evident in this passage. As R. P. Blackmur might have put it (but didn't), Moore was a woman who went in for both poetry *and* antimacassars.

Williams's characterization of Moore's method is almost a direct parallel with Bakhtin's tendentious characterization of the generic impulse of poetry, as he contrasts it to the dialogic art of the novel:

Each word must express the poet's *meaning* directly and without mediation; there must be no distance between the poet and his word. The meaning must emerge from language as a single intentional whole: none of its stratification, its speech diversity, to say nothing of its language diversity, may be reflected in any fundamental way in his poetic work.

To achieve this, the poet strips the word of others' intentions, he uses only such words and forms (and only in such a way) that they lose their link with concrete intentional levels of language and their connection with specific contexts.[18]

Whether such monologic cleansing (stripping, separating, wiping, cutting-out, acid-washing) can actually take place is questionable even in Bakhtin's analysis; as the theorist points out, "dialogic orientation . . . is, of course, a property of *any* discourse."[19] But texts can project the illusion of monologic cleansing of discourse; much of the effect of the "defamiliarization" posited by Viktor Shklovskii as a central principle of literary art is to present the word as something wholly new and strange in contrast to its received associations.[20] And clearly, the importance of monologic "cleansing" of the word is not so much that it can't or shouldn't take place as that readers feel that it can and should. We have seen the critical faith in the poet's ability to make all things new over and over again, from Park Benjamin and Ralph Waldo Emerson to Ezra Pound and to Granville Hicks's exclamation that Emily Dickinson "wrote of birds and flowers as if no one had ever written of them before."[21]

Williams takes the readings of monologic poetics a step further, by making the cleansing impulse the central motivation not only for Moore's work but for modernism in general: "From this clarity, this acid cleaning, this unblinking willingness, her poems result, a true modern crystallization, the fine essence of today which I have spoken of as the porcelain garden."[22] "Marianne Moore" can be read as a confession of Williams's incapacity to write as perfectly and as clearly as Moore does. In a backhanded way, then, the emphasis he places on the immaculate perfection of her poetry frees the poet-critic from serious competition with her. She exists within her *hortus conclusus* while the male poet, drawing inspiration from her presence there, goes out to confront the rough-and-tumble of life. Within the grotto of thoroughly wiped words that Moore has cemented together, she flits around like an angel, hummingbird, nervous woman with a feather-duster—or, indeed, like Emily Dickinson. Williams says of Moore's "Marriage": "There is a distaste for lingering, as in Emily Dickinson. As in Emily Dickinson there is too a fastidious precision of thought. . . . There is a swiftness impaling beauty . . . a rapidity too swift for touch, a seraphic quality, one might have said yesterday. There is, however, no breast that warms the bars of heaven: it is at most a swiftness that passes without repugnance from thing to thing."[23]

Williams, who objected strongly to Eliot's *The Waste Land*, would presumably have seen that poem as passing swiftly *with* repugnance from thing to thing. The value he places on Moore's "Marriage" is more bound up with the absence of repugnance than with the swiftness alone. But the absence of repugnance is also an absence of moral judgment or, indeed, of moral engagement. In Williams's terms a lack of moral engagement, insofar as it entails a lack of didacticism, is a positive feature of Moore's poetry. But in identifying this feature he distances her from real-life concerns. In such distancing, Williams's essay achieves, however unintentionally, its status as a preemptive reading of Moore. Read through Williams, her poetry is monologic but inorganic—an unstable combination of values that never coalesced into a viable poetics in twentieth-century criticism. Her supporters (notably Kenneth Burke) would try to reorient her poems to the values of presence by developing organicist readings; her detractors would close her more firmly within the porcelain garden, stressing her lack of organic contact with her subjects while reading her perceived monologic coherence as the prosaic, didactic rhetoric of a Victorian maiden aunt.

The text of "Marriage" has been very hard to detach from Williams's reading of it as "a pleasure that can be held firm only by moving rapidly from one thing to the next."[24] The poetics of presence, as employed by Williams, seems to act as a sort of lens that cannot keep contradictory—that is, dialogic—texts in focus. As the text is perceived more and more as a dialogue, it loses any meaning but the impression of motion. Sixty years later, Harold Bloom's reaction to the poem is still one of amazement at its disjunction and its heterogeneous range of reference.[25] But if one slows down to consider the poem as engaged with its subject—real-life marriages and their problems—one loses, with Williams, the "pleasure" of the reading experience. Social relevance and even didacticism are suspected; "Marriage" begins to read uncomfortably like a bourgeois novel. Poems about marriage ought to be lyric and descriptive; one thinks of Denise Levertov or of Theodore Roethke.[26] Moore's "Marriage" is satiric, detached from its subject not so much by its author's inexperience as by its reliances on quotation and on trope.

The dialogic potential of the poem continues to unfold, however much Williams inhibited it. "Marriage" foregrounds quotation; it assembles what Charles Tomlinson calls "the fragments of omnivorous reading and looking" into an asymmetrical, nonlinear arrangement.[27] The imperative of presence insists on welding the pieces into something useful; fragments only have a purpose if they can be shored against one's ruins. Tomlinson goes on to say that "the broken things, assembled into the dance of the whole," constitute "a new unity, won from the apparently intractable."[28] Formalist critics, despite their valorization of irony and tension, lacked an aesthetic for the appreciation of sprawling, dialogic texts that are *not* locked into crystalline tensions but operate centrifugally.

Kenneth Burke tries to identify the "specific poetic strategy" of Moore's work. Identifying that strategy as "objectivism," he says: "We might have managed more easily by simply demarcating several themes, like naming the different ingredients that go to make up a dish. Or as with the planks that are brought together, to make up a campaign platform, regardless of their fit with one another. But the relation among the themes of a genuine poetry is not of this sort. It is *substantial*—which is to say that all the branches spread from a single trunk."[29] The essence of Burke's sense of poetry (at least here) is directly analogous—using the same metaphoric vehicle—to Barrett Wendell's sense of a national literary tradition as a tree with various branches and "excrescences." Burke's metaphors are not merely organic; they are also a vivid example of a monologic reading. Unless the object of study can be demonstrated to have an organic coherence and a central vitalizing system, it is not "genuine." The literary work that is not animated by centripetal forces is not alive; it is artificial, fraudulent. When this literary "dish" is eaten, its different ingredients must subordinate their essences to one overall effect. The literary tossed salad is not a "genuine" experience.

Burke's generic distinctions raise a serious problem when he identifies the author of "Marriage" as a "genuine," monologic artist. Are we dealing here with genres of texts or genres of readings? Generic distinctions are relatively localized in readings rather than in primary texts; readings have great power to control generic identifications. Even as centrifugal a text as *The Waste Land* can be subjected to a strong thematic narratization, as it was by the intensive effort of the interpretive communities of the 1950s. The reading of Eliot's poem as a coherent narrative of a Grail quest is one of the best examples of interpretive generic imperatives riding over the resistance of the text.[30]

"Marriage," however, proved even more resistant to narratization than *The Waste Land*—no mean feat. Decades of commentary have been unable to impose a substantial strategy on the poem; Tomlinson's assertion that Moore welds together "a new unity" is not supported even in his essay with any characterization of what that unity might be. Critical response to the poem has therefore tended to fall back on staring agog at it as it goes by. But as deconstructive and Bakhtinian reading strategies have energized the reading of novels, freeing critics from the search for unifying themes in fiction, these strategies have also enabled readings of dialogic poetry. "Marriage" now appears—as its potential has unfolded into the 1980s and 1990s—as a poem that is disjointed *and* is about the lived experience of marriage: a conjunction that formalist and intentionalist readings could not make because of their embeddedness in the aesthetics of presence.

In fact, "Marriage" seems by the 1990s not just to be dialogic in method but to *enact* dialogics; its closing note, "'Liberty and union / now and forever,'" tempts one to discover that the poem is unified in its insistence on heterogeneous yokings. To compose a reading of the poem that would focus on its aesthetic logic would be more than ironically self-consuming, however. It would also continue to miss the importance of the poem and continue to read it as *about* aestheticism rather than as about a common experience. David Bergman's work on Moore's intentions surrounding the poem has shown that it grew for her not out of the impulse of the porcelain garden observer but out of Moore's own anxiety over what marriage meant for her women friends and conceivably might mean for her.[31] But since Moore chose to remain almost aggressively unmarried, critics tended to dismiss the poem's concerns. Operating on the assumption that Allen Tate wryly observed, that "we believe that no virgin can know enough to write poetry," critics dismissed the virgin poet's discussion of marriage with double vigor.[32] Blackmur writes in 1935: "The poem 'Marriage,' an excellent poem, is never concerned with either love or lust, but with something else, perhaps no less valuable, but certainly, in a profound sense, less complete. . . . There is no sex anywhere in her poetry. No poet has been so chaste; but it is not the chastity that rises from an awareness—healthy or morbid—of the flesh, it is a special chastity aside from the flesh—a purity by birth and from the void."[33] Blackmur—consistent with his approach to Dickinson—treats Moore as a poet without experience and one, therefore, whose words can have no impact upon experience.

With a tendency to overkill that perhaps conceals some anxiety over the power of *this* virgin poet, Blackmur invites the reader to compare Moore's animal poems to those of D. H. Lawrence. "In Lawrence you feel you have touched the plasm; in Miss Moore you feel you have escaped and come upon the idea."[34] It is a reasonable, if violently extreme, comparison; to make it fully effective, of course, one has to elide certain passages from "Marriage":

> "I should like to be alone";
> To which the visitor replies,

"I should like to be alone;
why not be alone together?"
Below the incandescent stars
below the incandescent fruit,
the strange experience of beauty;
its existence is too much;
it tears one to pieces
and each fresh wave of consciousness
is poison. (73)

In context, that is a *woman's* beauty, but

he has beauty also;
it's distressing—the O thou
to whom from whom,
without whom nothing—Adam;
"something feline,
something colubrine"—how true! (73–74)

That's not exactly "Tortoise Shout," of course; but there is a sense in which Lawrence's sex poetry is analytical and Moore's chaste poetry is erotic—a sense perhaps stronger today than in the 1930s, when the novelty of Lawrence's explicit language loomed larger on readers' horizons of expectations than it does today. The horizons of expectations that greeted a virgin poet writing of marriage in the 1930s were in turn unavoidably colored, for male readers, by a sense of the inadequacy, the "poseur" quality, of any approach that she might have to sexuality.

Elements of Marianne Moore's ideal biography were naturally inseparable from the reception of her poetry. While readers could construct a biography for Emily Dickinson to suit their own readings, or when convenient deny that Dickinson *had* a biography, Moore's position as a public figure made such expedients impossible. Dickinson could be reconstructed as a passionate, thwarted lover; Moore could not. Not only was the critical move unavailable because of the explicit facts of the poet's life, but the suggestion that Moore's poetry might be erotic or in any way "fleshly" was highly ungallant and impolite. (Even in the case of Dickinson, early speculations on her sexual life were suppressed until they were given sanction by the hints of Martha Dickinson Bianchi, her last living relative.) The decorum that obliged critics to characterize Moore as pure "by birth and from the void," however, did not prevent them from wishing that she were someone different. I have suggested that the personal warmth with which writers like Robert Hillyer addressed "Emily" was a key element in her reception; by contrast no writer except Williams—and he only in a brief memoir when both were in their sixties—ever called Moore "Marianne" in print during her lifetime, or even expressed much personal affection for her. (Even Elizabeth Bishop's restrained "Efforts of Affection" remained unpublished during *Bishop's* lifetime, let alone Moore's.)

Lacking the resource of affection, critics found fault with Moore's poetry as unnaturally detached—attacking the porcelain garden from without, unsustained by Williams's wondering appreciation for it. Blackmur, following on his impression that Moore's poetry is "less complete" than that of a writer like Lawrence, writes: "In Miss Moore life is remote (life as good *and* evil) and everything is done to keep it remote; it is reality removed, but it is nonetheless reality, because we *know* that it is removed. . . . Her sensibility—the deeper it is the more persuaded it cannot give itself away—predicted her poetic method; and the defect of her method, in its turn, only represents the idiosyncrasy of her sensibility; that it, like its subject matter, constitutes the perfection of standing aside."[35] Blackmur goes on to connect Moore with Dickinson as a writer interested both in "sophistication of surfaces" and in "the genuine." The effect is to canonize the poetry while denying its power to engage the reader; it is left-handed praise of the highest order.

And it is gendered praise, akin to Blackmur's later deprecation of Dickinson for the same detachment from life and concern with surfaces. The imperatives of the poetics of presence are not intrinsically hostile to moralizing; much of the canonization of Walt Whitman was predicated on his radical moral transvaluations, while much American resistance to Poe was based on his perceived aesthetic detachment (in the Moore essay, Blackmur cites Poe as an artist interested in surfaces but *not* in "the genuine"). Critical inattention to Moore's ethical and moral concerns has always been accompanied by an undertone of not wanting to be lectured to by an officious spinster. When Louis Simpson wrote in 1963 that "one would be willing to be judged by Mr. Roethke—who doesn't; instead, one is judged by Miss Moore," his ostensible subject was the state of literary criticism; but the word "judged" indicates a strong and abiding resistance to submitting to *any* judgments made by a woman.[36] The ideal woman's voice for male critics was the nonjudgmental tone of passionate surrender—the voice that was being carefully reconstructed for Emily Dickinson. In such a context, Moore's voice grated terribly.

Critics often dodged the obligation to talk about the moral issues in Moore's poetry by deflecting attention to its perceived difficulty. If a poem is too difficult to explicate, it may one day turn out not to have a moral at all. Readers did find her poems inordinately hard to explicate. In one of the very earliest extended reviews of Moore's poetry, Harriet

Monroe quotes Marion Strobel's metaphor for the intellectual effort Moore's poems demand: "If we find ourselves one of an audience in a side-show we prefer to see the well-muscled lady in tights stand on her head smilingly, with a certain nonchalance, rather than grit her teeth, perspire, and make us conscious of her neck muscles. Still, we would rather not see her at all."[37] Morton Dauwen Zabel's 1936 review of *Selected Poems* is geared toward reassuring the reader that Moore's poetry is, contrary to popular belief, not all that difficult.[38] But the popular belief was persistent. Virtually all the commentary in *Time, Newsweek,* and *Sports Illustrated* in the 1950s and 1960s would start from the assumption that Moore's poetry was practically unintelligible and move on from there to discuss her hats, her animals, or the Dodgers.[39]

But it was not just "popular" writers who emphasized Moore's difficulty, of course. In a 1918 *Little Review* piece, Ezra Pound (presumably excluding himself) said of Moore and Mina Loy, "One wonders what the devil anyone will make of this sort of thing who has not in his wit all the clues."[40] Williams warned that Moore's achievement as the finest modern poet could be "only with difficulty discerned."[41] As late as 1966, when academic criticism of Moore began to appear in scholarly journals, we find in *PMLA* Rebecca Price Parkin's reading of "Apparition of Splendor" entitled "Certain Difficulties in Reading Marianne Moore."[42]

An offhand comment of Eliot's in the 1935 introduction may have clinched the point for many readers: "It would be difficult to say what is the 'subject-matter' of The Jerboa. For a mind of such agility, and for a sensibility so reticent, the minor subject, such as a pleasant little sand-coloured skipping animal, may be the best release for the major emotions."[43] Eliot's perception of the difficulty of summarizing the poem has the function here of supporting his own well-motivated misreading of it. Eliot's misprision of "The Jerboa" bends it in the direction of descriptive impressionism. He reads the poem—or at least *refers* to the poem— in what by 1935 had become an Eliotian way. The poem to be genuine for him must contain an objective correlative for emotions. He has no objection at all to that correlative being a tiny animal; what he seems to object to strongly and entirely implicitly is the possibility that "The Jerboa" can be an ethical argument as well as an emotional release. Eliot was developing his own moralistic poetry in the mid-1930s, a deeply conservative poetry that would culminate in the choruses from "The Rock" and *Murder in the Cathedral*. Moore's moral tone—more secular, more socially egalitarian, and ultimately opposed to the ritualistic expressions of hierarchical morality that Eliot would construct—competed with his voice, leading to his elision of her own moral concerns in the poem.

Charles Tomlinson's reading of "The Jerboa" identifies its moral suc-
cinctly, though somewhat reluctantly. Unless one has Eliot's motivation,
it is a difficult moral to miss: "An ideal of ethical preference inserts itself among the facts. . . . and in this insertion the imaginative power kin-
dles to cast light on both the fact and the ideal. In 'The Jerboa,' its hab-
itat, the desert, is preferred to the opulence of the pharaohs because of
the ascetic ideal of the animal's freedom, a freedom which Miss Moore
characterizes as 'abundance' against the 'too much' of ancient Egypt."[44]
Even Tomlinson, in identifying the main argument of "The Jerboa," feels
impelled to start with the factual, observational details of the poem and
then to see the ethical concerns as somehow "inserted" into the factual
pattern. Other critics of the 1950s and 1960s were not even that ready
to see Moore's poetry as ethically centered. Philip Ferguson Legler's extended explication of "The Jerboa" in 1953 meticulously surveys the
poem's details and acknowledges its "humane spirit," but is wary of defending the poem as a moral statement.[45]

The basic statement of the poem, as constructed by Tomlinson, is dialogically and relationally expressed by the contrast between Pharaonic
Egypt and the desert lifestyle of the jerboa. The form of Moore's expression is perhaps as threatening to critics like Eliot as its egalitarian message, because it is essentially a poem about morality as mediated by artistic expression. "The Jerboa" critiques not just Pharaonic excesses but
Pharaonic aesthetics. The material culture that expresses Pharaonic values is based on a wonderfully accurate organicism—a commitment to
organic form at all levels:

> Lords and ladies put goose-grease
> paint in round bone boxes with pivoting
> lid incised with the duck-wing
>
> or reverted duck-
> head; kept in a buck
> or rhinoceros horn,
> the ground horn; and locust oil in stone locusts. (7)

The ultimate result of such a triumph of organicist values is

> a fantasy
> and a verisimilitude that were
> right to those with, everywhere,
>
> power over the poor. (8)

If one did not have the overpowering biographical example of Moore's
personal conservatism in mind, one might be tempted to read these line
as a deconstruction of how the values of an organicist poetics serve a

hierarchy of male interests both sexual ("the ground horn" as a cure for impotence) and economic.

By contrast, the poem's hero, the jerboa, is conceived of in artistic metaphors that express the organic creature inorganically and remind us that its value is mediated through our linguistic and artistic concept of it:

> Its leaps should be set
> to the flageolet;
>   pillar body erect
>   on a three-cornered smooth-working Chippendale
>   claw—propped on hind legs, and tail as third toe,
>   between leaps to its burrow. (11)

The text of "The Jerboa" sets up confusions between the organic and the inorganic, primarily confusions of value: organicist art turns out to be oppressive because it reifies a sense of human control over nature; inorganic art turns out to be the only human way of learning from the self-sufficient, alien jerboa, which can serve as a model for human conduct only when mediated through a language that is disconcertingly unaligned with organicist preconceptions. Such a poem found few readers who would submit to Moore's moral "judgment," though many who were willing to be impressed by its technical virtuosity, or, like Howard Nemerov, to be amused by its "recondite meditations."[46]

That Moore should be a dialogic poet of moral principle is hardly a contradiction in terms; many writers whose method is dialogic leave little doubt about their position in engagement with moral issues: Dickens, Zola, Dostoevsky, George Eliot. Dialogic poems like "Marriage" and "The Jerboa" serve as fields for moral exploration, presenting men's and women's voices, or the aesthetics of the Pharaohs and of the desert rat, in vigorous contrast. "Marriage" is almost impossible to resolve into statement; "The Jerboa," much easier. But the method of both poems is a moral exercise too near "rumination" for Eliot and his contemporaries to value it *as* moral exercise; they had to value it for something else.

As late as the 1960s, the work of Bernard Engel, which stresses Moore's moral and religious emphases, received withering reviews from Oliver Evans in *American Literary Scholarship*, for whom such an intentionalist approach to old-fashioned morality in poetry was beyond the critical pale.[47] Criticism of Moore, all along, had to be logocentric—and had to prevent the poet's words from saying anything. This double bind of Moore criticism is vividly exemplified in the work of Randall Jarrell. As he expresses it in 1953, "She is *the* poet of the particular—or, when she fails, of the peculiar; and is also, in our time, *the* poet of general moral statement."[48] Jarrell's long engagement with Moore's poetry is more messy, and consequently even more instructive about the development of her reception, than Blackmur's. Jarrell first wrote on Moore in 1942, reviewing *What Are Years* for the *Kenyon Review*. His first extensive essay on her, a review of the 1951 *Collected Poems*, appeared in *Partisan Review* in 1952 and was slightly revised as "Her Shield" in his book *Poetry and the Age*, with the addition of some of the 1942 material. A highly condensed version of "Her Shield" later appeared in *Prairie Schooner* in 1963, as part of a retrospective essay titled "Fifty Years of American Poetry." This succession of reviews and essays, covering twenty years, shares a lot of the same actual wording; but the effect of the various expansions and condensations was to leave the final impression, in 1963, of a severely qualified judgment of Moore's work.

Jarrell's most substantial piece on Moore, "Her Shield," is characterized by internal fault-lines; its inconsistencies reveal the critic trying to accommodate both the received tradition of Moore criticism and his own instinctive resistance to it—or, perhaps, to accommodate both his appreciation for the poetry (which must express itself in terms of the positive values of presence) and his reservations about its methods. In "Her Shield," Jarrell defends Moore in a passage that indicates the growing critical consensus about her as the poet of the porcelain garden: "It is most barbarously unjust to treat her (as some admiring critics do) as what she is only when she parodies herself: a sort of museum poet, an eccentric shut-in dealing in the collection, renovation, and exhibition of precise exotic properties. For she is a lot more American a writer (if to be an American is to be the heir, or heiress, of all the ages) than Thomas Wolfe or Erskine Caldwell."[49] There is a failure of logic in this defense— or at best, a large ellipsis—that makes it all the more valuable. To the charge that Moore is a "museum poet" (Burke had called her "antiquarian"), Jarrell responds that she is "American." Blackmur, for one, would simply have agreed, noting that Hawthorne was similar in his antiquarian and exotic interests. Others might note, however, the basic impertinence of the defense. To make any sense at all, Jarrell's remark demands an equation of "American" with "extroverted," and a consequent picture of Moore as somehow representative of the rugged Whitmanic tradition in her concerns. But I doubt that the passage *does* make sense. It merely answers one value label (museum = bad) with another (American = good); to the charge "bad" Jarrell responds "good" without considering whether the labeled values line up as viable opposites or not.

Although he flies at the barbarous injustice of seeing Moore as a shut-in, Jarrell elsewhere in his essay expresses uneasiness at her perceived detachment from physical and emotional experiences. "Some of her poems have the manners or manner of ladies who learned a little before birth not to mention money, who neither point nor touch, and who scrupulously abstain from the mixed, live vulgarity of life. . . . We are uncomfortable—or else too comfortable—in a world in which feeling, affection, charity, are so entirely divorced from sexuality and power, the bonds of the flesh."[50] By 1963, this reservation was almost all that remained of Jarrell's assessment of Moore alongside her greatest contemporaries, except for some understated praise of her powers of observation. His words did not change in the intervening decade, but the emphasis that he and the whole climate of Moore criticism lent to them did.[51]

After her 1952 Pulitzer Prize for *Collected Poems*, Moore's critical reputation went in two different directions at once. For the popular press, she was simply the "Best Living Poet" (*Newsweek*), one of the "Unknockables" (*Esquire*).[52] For the highbrow journals and quarterlies, Moore was fair game for ever-increasing diminution and disparagement. To many creative writers, Moore remained both inspiration and influence; but in the academy, the Moore industry was exceedingly slow to develop, lagging not only far behind the industries on writers like Eliot, Pound, and Stevens but also significantly behind the industries devoted to Edwin Arlington Robinson, Hart Crane, and Robinson Jeffers.

The enshrining of Marianne Moore as an icon of popular culture has been well described by Charles Molesworth and need only be briefly touched on here; just a few passing impressions will clarify the image Moore had for her younger contemporaries: George Plimpton's awe of her as he accompanied her to a World Series game (combined with his portrait of Robert Lowell as a hapless and insignificant figure); the delight the media took in Moore when she was placed in any incongruous situation—learning to dance or to drive, writing about alligators or Edsels, with Joe Louis or with Jim Thorpe.[53] By the late 1960s, Marianne Moore had become hip for generations not yet born the first time she was hip, in the 1910s.

For prestige reviewers of the 1950s and 1960s, however, Moore became less and less hip with the passing of time. Even positive reviews of her new work (she published new volumes of poetry in 1956, 1959, and 1966, and her much-revised *Complete Poems* in 1967) fell back on insubstantial generalities in order to praise her. Lloyd Frankenberg, in 1949, had set the tone of this kind of appreciative criticism: "Technically and thematically, in detail and in the round, the art of this poetry is a self-portrait. This is the most beautiful and complete correspondence of all. Interior illumination has been made to shine out, a symbol of integrity, a symptom of wholeness."[54] Such commentary meets the exigencies of the poetics of presence in connecting the text to the author but does little more. Wallace Fowlie would echo Frankenberg in 1952: "Miss Moore's poetry testifies at every step to this very principle, whereby song becomes more total, more unified, as the spiritual concentration deepens.... Poetry, when it is her accomplishment, a miraculous fusion of life and speech, can represent simultaneously in a single name both a spiritual world and a human being."[55] Fowlie goes on to connect this logocentric poetry with Eliot's notion of durability: "What is most personal to Marianne Moore as a poet coincides miraculously with the purest and most durable forms of the English language."[56] As the newsweeklies were becoming more and more enchanted with Moore's use of Bell Telephone advertising and Yul Brynner in her poetry, Fowlie's kind of criticism seemed further and further from the mark. For one thing, although Fowlie and others made energetic attempts to connect personality and poetry in Moore's work, they were departing from the characterizations that had gotten Moore a hearing in the reception of modernism in the first place. It was precisely Williams's concept of the porcelain garden that had established the image of Moore as a daringly original poet; to go back now and suggest that she was somehow a modern Walt Whitman and her work a syllabic "Song of Myself" was an unproductive critical move.

Negative criticism of the 1950s put Moore within the garden and developed precise, vivid metaphors to keep her there. But even much earlier, the garden was being replaced in commentary on Moore by smaller and more cramped enclosed spaces. Stanley J. Kunitz, reviewing *What Are Years* in 1941, concludes that "the mind of Miss Moore is astonishingly clean. Cluttered, to be sure, like your grandmother's attic; but with everything dusted and in its place, labeled, catalogued, usable."[57] The attic had become an even more compulsive setting by 1957, when John Updike, poking fun at footnotes to poems, writes: "To her credit, Miss Moore employs her notes with a certain sense of housekeeping; the effect of the poetry is that of a sparkling-clean, well-swept attic, and, naturally, if the attic is to stay tidy, there must exist a storeroom, under the eaves, where she can jumble the bulkier objects."[58] In Updike's metaphor, the attic is even more orderly than in Kunitz's; but it has ceased to contain anything "usable." In 1963, Robert Bly's centripetalist essay "A Wrong Turning in American Poetry" critiques Moore for being a breakfront whatnot rather than a focal hearth for the American poetic home: "Marianne Moore's poetry also represents a treasure-house—a feminine one. The objects in the poem are fragments, annexed, and the poem is a parlor full of knickknacks carefully arranged."[59]

As Molesworth has noted, some critics turned against Moore for her evident conservatism. M. L. Rosenthal sighed bemusedly at her praise of President Eisenhower in *Like a Bulwark;* other critics considered her topicality to be diffusing her poetic talents.[60] Both her translation of La Fontaine and her selected prose (*Predilections*) received mixed reviews and were generally seen as trivial publications—though in the wake of the Pulitzer, these volumes were more widely reviewed than any she had published since 1935. The *Fables* had few defenders; Louise Bogan and Hugh Kenner were among its half-hearted supporters.[61] Howard Nemerov set the tone for reevaluation of Moore's whole poetic career by rereading her earlier work in light of the perceived failure of this translation. Starting from the formalist version of the porcelain garden reading, Nemerov says: "Miss Moore has never been a fabulist at all, . . . her animals never acted out her moralities; . . . their function was ever to provide a minutely detailed, finely perceived symbolic knot to be a center for the pattern of her recondite meditations."[62] The poetry that Williams had perceived as "a treasure of seclusion" is seen by Nemerov thirty years later as merely "recondite." We are on the same page of the thesaurus but in a much different register of value.

Critics saved their most disparaging comments for Moore's prose, especially her criticism. When Louis Simpson remarks that he is unwilling to be judged by "Miss Moore," his contempt for her as a critic is so overpowering that one doesn't even notice that he hasn't identified what he objects to; her very name is apparently enough to command the reader's assent: how terrible to have to be judged by Miss Moore.[63] Irving Howe's review of *Predilections* combines diminution, gender hostility, generational antagonism, and a turning of Moore's characteristic association with animals against her: "Miss Moore's little essays are mainly about the poets of her own generation—Eliot, Stevens, cummings, Williams—for whom she feels a loyalty so complete as to preclude any sharp critical judgment. . . . Miss Moore glides around her subject with the determined gracefulness of a large well-trained bird. . . . If anyone else did this sort of thing, one would be appalled. But . . . beware of the blandness of formidable lady poets, never more formidable than when most fragile."[64] In referring to literary criticism as "the greenest land she's almost seen," Howe quotes Moore against herself, and sounds the refrain that had existed in negative and even in positive criticism since the beginning of Moore's reception. In constructing an ideal biography of the poet, her contemporaries delighted in portraying her as someone with no experience at all; Kreymborg went so far as to fabricate an anecdote that has Moore becoming a master of baseball strategy entirely through reading a book on the subject.[65] When Moore as a personality was a novelty in the Greenwich Village of the 1920s, this kind of heightening of her eccentricity (which she did nothing to discourage) was appealing to prestige critics; by the 1950s it had become a source of disgust to highbrow reviewers. Some prestige critics remained attentive to Moore's writing; Kenneth Burke wrote a positive and notably thorough review of *Predilections* for *Poetry*.[66] But others showed the strain of trying to pay attention to the verse of a celebrity. In 1963 Hugh Kenner argued testily for a revival of interest in complex poems like "The Buffalo" and "The Pangolin," saying that "such poems were receiving too casual an attention even before *The New Yorker*, by developing Miss Moore as a 'personality,' left everyone with so misleading a clue."[67] The implication is that artistic personalities created for mass consumption are invariably false, even when the artist herself is complicit in the creation of such a personality. By the 1960s, then, Moore had become not only hip but a source of embarrassment for her own defenders, who now saw her as untrue to her former self and to the demands of verbal precision that her critical immurement in the porcelain garden had entailed.

To judge from the press, by the time of her death Marianne Moore was the best-known poet in America. Certainly she was the best-known poet in the history of New York City, with the possible exception of Bryant. Of living poets in the 1960s, only Robert Frost and Carl Sandburg matched her for media recognition in the United States. The status of her reception just twenty years after her death, however, reveals a total transformation. The public image—tricorne hat and stuffed alligator—is fading slowly; the 1990 postage stamp looked so unlike any familiar portrait of Moore that it did little to revive that image. Millions of New Yorkers walk or ride past Bryant Park every day (even though they may know little about Bryant); the Walt Whitman bridge and even the Joyce Kilmer service area are features of life in New Jersey. But there is no public monument to Marianne Moore. Ebbets Field is gone. Moore's Village apartment is now in the out-of-the-way Rosenbach Museum in Philadelphia. When the guys from Delta House go on a road trip in *Animal House*, they head to Emily Dickinson College, and everybody gets the joke. But Moore is never referred to in popular culture anymore. Nor do her texts form an indelible part of anyone's education; "I too, dislike it" from "Poetry" is the line students remember best, but it hardly rivals "Something there is that doesn't love a wall" or "April is the cruelest month."

The same popular celebrity that made literary critics so uneasy in the last decade of her life made Moore an important figure in American culture—far more important and widely known, however misunderstood, than Walt Whitman was in his lifetime or has been since. But since her death, the fading image of Moore has been balanced by an explosion of academic interest in her poetry. In a sense, the equilibrium of normal literary studies has been restored. Moore is now as generally little known as Williams or Stevens but nearly as much studied in universities. Certainly we in those universities now feel that we have a much better understanding of Moore than readers of the 1960s who saw her work only in a piece of doggerel about the Dodgers and the titles of a few animal poems. But it is heavily ironic that in the history of American rhetoric about the need for a poet who would communicate with the masses, one poet who was a legitimate popular sensation would be so confined by her first critics, so derided by later ones, so completely academicized after her death.

Whatever the chords that Marianne Moore struck in the general imagination, she had no desire to emulate Walt Whitman's poetics of presence. She had no desire to be associated with Whitman at all. The only mention of Whitman anywhere in her writing is a note of the fact that in 1852 he attended a performance of Rossini's *La Cenerentola*.[68] Elizabeth Bishop relates one further anecdote: "On one occasion, when we were walking in Brooklyn on our way to a favored tea shop, I noticed we were on a street associated with the *Brooklyn Eagle*, and I said fatuously, 'Marianne, isn't it odd to think of you and Walt Whitman walking this same street over and over?' She exclaimed in her mock-ferocious tone, 'Elizabeth, don't speak to me about that man!' So I never did again."[69] The textual history of that anecdote is itself a complicated mix of presence and distance. Bishop completed several drafts of the memoir "Efforts of Affection" that contains the Whitman anecdote and much else about her relationship with Moore, but never published any of them during her lifetime. She may have intended to at some time, of course; but the fact remains that she lived into her late sixties and didn't. The essay is not very personal in tone, but it is more personal than anything else written about Moore, who is always "Marianne" in it, as almost never before in print.

The context of the Whitman anecdote in Bishop's essay is a group of other anecdotes, in each of which Bishop tries to get Moore's true personal opinion about a literary figure—usually gay—and Moore keeps fending off Bishop's questions with some superficial remark about the person's appearance or manners. There are closets within closets in that passage from "Efforts of Affection"—was Bishop trying to get Moore to confide in her about her own sexuality, or was she looking for an opening to confide in Moore? Probably neither; probably there is a more complex direction of the text of the memoir itself to its potential (and potentially posthumous) audience. We cannot know what either poet heard through the surface of their superficially amusing dialogue—if that dialogue took place. But we can hear Bishop's concern, as directed through her relationship with Moore, about the people behind texts. Where Moore maintained such a scrupulously public identity that her life was an open book, leaving critics little except the idiosyncratic surfaces upon which to base a presence-oriented reading of her texts, Bishop by contrast led such a hidden life that she defused even the critical quest for presence. Her poetry became all surface, and in the context of Moore criticism and Bishop's perceived status as Moore's protégée, her work met with diminution and resistance beyond that which Moore's met. By contrast to Moore, the academic reinvigoration of Bishop's work has been largely the reinfusion of her texts with a lived and living presence.

The relationship between Marianne Moore and Elizabeth Bishop was far from perfectly nurturant and even, as the arguments in Betsy Erkkila's *The Wicked Sisters* have gone far to establish. For Erkkila, the Moore-Bishop relationship is "an instance of literary difference that reveals at once the complex interplay of gender, writing, and social struggle among twentieth-century writers and the very real difficulties women poets have experienced in seeking to possess each other as mothers, mentors, ancestors, and muses."[70] Far from replacing Oedipal struggle with an untroubled filiation, Erkkila suggests, "the mother/daughter configuration initially strengthened the bond between them, it was also the site of their most intense struggle, and it eventually drove them apart."[71]

The impact of the wedge that feminist criticism is itself driving between the authorial images of Moore and Bishop is problematic for the continued critical survival of Moore's texts. Such a critical struggle is the underside of the iceberg of this rehearsed personal struggle between the authors; there is still a limited amount of space in syllabuses and anthologies for women poets, and they are driven into figurative competition for this space (the real competition is between living scholars and their careers). Moore is currently positioned to lose any struggle between her ideal biographical image and that of Bishop. She is the conservative, the fastidious, the personally Puritanical one of the pair; she is the moralist too, and whatever energy feminist critics have drawn from her morality is likely to dissipate in the face of its nature as, finally, a conventional morality. If critics reduce Moore's themes to personal responsibility and good manners, her reputation will suffer even more in the short run. I think that Moore's texts will ultimately survive their author's image; the authorial image of Ezra Pound, for instance, is repulsive and his morality is to Moore's as Ribbentrop's is to Frank Capra's, but that has not slowed the Pound industry in the slightest. One could only wish for more attention to Moore as a counterweight to the image of Pound; Lois Bar-Yaacov's essay "Marianne Moore, Ezra Pound:

In Distrust of Whose Merits?" is a promising step in this direction.[72] If Moore's texts survive as the representation of a principled conservatism in the expanding canon, and if their dialogic energy is given full play, our sense of twentieth-century poetry will be all the richer for it.

Moore and Bishop provide the best material available at the moment for feminist recuperation because they form part of the "high" *Voices & Visions* canon and are therefore available for scholarly industry in a way other poets are not. It is important to realize that Moore and Bishop *did* become canonical, that their work, while read in a way that virtually denies it political or aesthetic power, was still read and promoted by their mostly male critical contemporaries. Their early canonical status, however second-class it now seems, was the basis for what we might call an infrastructure of institutional concern with their poetry that in turn has fed the rapid and revisionist growth of Moore and Bishop criticism since the mid-1980s. They are not the only women poets to have benefited from an early semicanonical status; Hilda Doolittle and Gwendolyn Brooks, for various and different reasons, were similarly allowed partway into the canon and have begun to generate similar scholarly industries. It is as if the poetics of presence has provided a template for the consideration of American poets. The template, cut from *Leaves of Grass*, fits Williams almost perfectly. It fits Stevens or Eliot less well, but in broad outlines it allows for a broad sense of the importance of their work. It fits Moore, Bishop, H.D., and Brooks quite badly, but it highlights in each case an element of their work that is valuable within the poetics of presence and allows for the treatment of the poet as an adjunct to the tradition. In the case of other women writers, the poet's work is completely obscured by the template and thereby excluded from the main lines of critical consideration. Muriel Rukeyser is too politically strident; Laura Riding, too philosophical; Edna Millay, too popular; Mina Loy, too esoteric; Amy Lowell and Louise Bogan, too dangerous as critical presences; Elinor Wylie, too refined; Dorothy Parker, too crude. And these writers have therefore not yet accumulated the canonical infrastructure that would support a revival of interest in their work. Even with the explosion of critical attention to Moore, Bishop, and a few others, we still have only a very partial, very skewed picture of American women's poetry from the first half of the twentieth century.

FIVE

Constraint and Recuperation
in the Early Reception of
Elizabeth Bishop

The early reception of Elizabeth Bishop is still going on at this moment. Studying that ongoing reception, one can observe the mechan-
ics of constraint that allowed her a limited canonicity during her lifetime, and then how critics, freed from constraint both by her death
and by changes in the politics of literary study, are recuperating a poetic presence for her. The case of Bishop is all the more intriguing because the process of recuperating the poet since her death in 1979,
while linked with feminism, postmodernism, and poststructuralism, has
also been linked strongly with the poetics of presence and the construction of an ideal biography.

The recuperation of Bishop has run in notable contrast to the recuperation of Moore. Barring any sensational discoveries waiting to be made
in yet-unexamined papers in her archives, Moore's life resists a construction of the kind of heroic ideal biography so dear to American literary
nationalism past and present. It is exceedingly difficult to portray Moore
as the representative of a "consensus criticism of the consensus" (in Nina
Baym's phrase).[1] The Whitmanic American Homer is a character whose
power is based to a large extent on his continuous potential for enlistment in the progressive causes of the next generation, whatever they may
be. As Moore's biography is constructed it resists attempts to read her as
potentially subversive and leads to the alignment of her ideal poetic persona with the "message" of the texts themselves: that of a conservative
Christian moralist, unredeemed by the early rebellions that so charm critics
of Eliot or Auden.

But Bishop is potentially subversive in all sorts of ways: as lesbian, expatriate, agnostic, postmodernist, surrealist. The very things that make her interesting have brought on the need to process her image into the mold of Whitmanic hero, because Bishop's potential for enlistment in progressive ideologies is offset by the tendency of her texts to turn strategies of reading based on Whitman and the poetics of presence into persistent problems. What is her national identity—American, Canadian, or Brazilian? If she is American, is her region New England, New York, or South Florida? Do her texts have a lyric perspective, a sequential continuity, a consistent aesthetic or politics? And perhaps most important, what is the significance of her personal sexual identity as a closeted lesbian?

The closet, in fact, may be the most unsettling challenge that Bishop poses for the poetics of presence. Norma Procopiow was the first critic to identify Bishop as a lesbian in an academic article, "Survival Kit"— two years after the poet's death.[2] During her lifetime, Bishop's friends and literary correspondents clearly knew of her sexuality. This suggests that the closet is large and has many recesses, and that Bishop was not absolutely secretive about her lesbianism; rather, she depended on the larger social institutions of reticence to preserve her privacy—and indeed may have seen the matter far more as one of privacy about all intimate matters than as an issue specifically of lesbian privacy. For Bishop, the closet provided a decorous silence not just about sexuality, for instance, but also about alcoholism and depression. She avoided confessional poetry for many reasons.

I am lapsing into intentionalism only to convey the assurance that I am not attacking the memory of Elizabeth Bishop. To say that the closet is a key image in reading her texts is not to accuse her of hypocrisy. Bishop participated in the closet as a meaningful social institution with its own living rules and assumptions, one that still makes it possible in the 1990s for some women to live as sexual partners without presumption by the community that they are violating its sexual norms. In turn, the dynamics of the institution of the closet are essential in the reception history of Bishop's texts. Before 1979, the necessity for Bishop to guard her personal life colors the texts themselves—which are full of masks, personae, indeterminacies, and a rigorous covering of biographical tracks under pseudonyms and fictionalizations. Her own family and personal problems demand much of this covering up; closets in the texts go far beyond concerns over sexuality to involve the masking of family history, places, names, and dates. And far beyond the immediate consequences for Bishop's texts (which then affect all readings of them), the closet had a decisively narrowing effect on pre-1979 readings of Bishop. Basically, the poet's guardedness and the critics' decorum conspired to make ideal biography unattainable—in fact inconceivable; had Bishop been "out" in the 1940s or 1950s, she would have been pushed out of the extreme margins of the canon into the limbo populated by Amy Lowell and Gertrude Stein. Since Bishop herself was notably unwilling to authorize, in paratextual ways, a presence in her own texts (the reverse of Walt Whitman), critics found ways to value her work while marginalizing her into a small corner of the Whitmanic project.

Before 1979, then, Bishop's place in the canon was insecure; she was one of many women poets whose work fit some of the requirements of presence-based readings but failed—decisively, because of the combination of her gender and her reticence—to certify her as a major poet. Bishop was often paired in contemporary reviews with other women poets— Lisel Mueller, Eleanor Ross Taylor, Jean Garrigue, Isabella Gardner—who had and still have this precarious place on the edge of the canon. After 1979, the recuperation of Bishop has unfolded dramatically because of the sudden availability of the poet's life to serve as a compelling, validating presence behind her texts. After her death, Bishop has achieved the kind of fame she could not have had, and would not have welcomed, while she was alive.

In considering the reception of Elizabeth Bishop, this chapter will therefore break into pre-1979 and post-1979 halves—and then consider the implications of the post-1979 reception of Bishop in terms of the challenges her texts can present to the poetics of presence itself. Bishop's work is in a sense a key opportunity for late twentieth-century criticism to break with the Americanist project of presence; if such a break is warranted or desired, it must come from the context of understanding how her reception arrived at the breaking point.

Reading Bishop before 1979: "All Eye"

Faced with a set of texts that appear to immerse themselves in one found object after another, with no centripetal principle, Bishop's early critics had three options within the governing critical paradigm of presence: (1) to assert that Bishop's personal presence *was* to be found there and to construct a totalizing narrative for her verse; (2) to surrender claims for her status as major artist and consider her a minor poet with major strengths in description and observation; or (3) to dismiss her poetry as uneven and desultory. The second option became for many years the consensus critical opinion on Bishop; but it is sometimes difficult to tell that second option from the third. The first widely current piece of academic criticism on Bishop, Steven Stepanchev's chapter in *American Poetry since 1945*, makes an all but disablingly qualified case for Bishop as an important postwar poet. Characterizing her poetry as completely cut off from contemporary historical events and politics, Stepanchev sees Bishop as a "peripatetic poet and geographer" whose "love of geography takes her, as tourist and everyman, to many places on many roads."[3] In Bishop's work, Stepanchev says, "now and then, as in the case of the poem 'Florida,' the poet's exuberance provides a scattering of images whose relevance to the total structure is open to question."[4] One might find the lack of a total structure to "Florida," the state that turns out to be "the poorest / post-card of itself" (33), to be poetically productive. But Stepanchev could only identify the poem in that way, not value it as such.

Even a purposive observer fulfills only a very small part of the project of presence, because observers are by its definition passive and do not move on to the more vital projects of naming and inspiring. In Stepanchev's formulation, Bishop is not even a purposive observer; she is less a camera's eye than a photographic plate. Stepanchev draws on well-established themes in Bishop criticism. Reviews of *North & South* (1946) abound in praise for Bishop's description. Louise Bogan saw Bishop as taking "a Thoreaulike interest in whatever catches her attention," suggesting a desultory quality in that attentiveness.[5] Though insisting that Bishop's poems had moral and personal depths (which he declined to specify), Robert Lowell acknowledged that they were superficially "observations—surpassingly accurate, witty and well-arranged, but nothing more."[6] Randall Jarrell is less reserved: "Her work is unusually personal and honest in its wit, perception, and sensitivity—and in its restrictions too; all her poems have written underneath, *I have seen it.*"[7] Jarrell suggests that the central unifying feature of Bishop's work may be its "restriction," in what he tries to make a positive sense, to personal experience. It is a minimal fulfillment of the demands of presence. If the only centripetal force is the poet's observing eye, the counterforces of dream, delusion, and solipsistic imagination can erode the position of the unmeditating/unmediating observer. Jarrell's "*I have seen it*" tries to conflate the author of "The Man-Moth" and "The Monument" with the author of "Large Bad Picture" and "The Map," all of which appeared in *North & South.*

Description became the default value for readings of Bishop's poems. The interpretive community established by published criticism on the poet so thoroughly agreed that her poetry was both descriptive, or, in a metapoetic sense, *about* description, that it was not only safe but almost obligatory to talk about her descriptions. Positive assessments of Bishop could be supported by such a restraining critical move because accurate description, if sincere and immediate (as in Jarrell's reading), does not conflict with the demands of the poetics of presence. But seeing Bishop as an impersonal observer confined her to one of the smallest and least-valued areas of the Whitmanic tradition. Just as the least well-regarded parts of *Leaves of Grass* had come to be the peripatetic descriptive catalogs—suffered by critics only because of a perceived organic relation to the more emotional, meditative, and narrative things in Whitman—Bishop came to be seen as a poet who was doing just one part, and that the least important part, of the work of American poetry. In 1963 Jarrell would revise downward his earlier opinion of Bishop (just as he had done with Moore), commenting: "The poet and the poems have their limitations; all exist on a small scale, and some of the later poems especially, are too detailedly and objectively descriptive."[8] Three years later, Irvin Ehrenpreis (reviewing *Questions of Travel*) would see Bishop more completely, if more positively, as the poet of objective observation: "In most of these poems she appears as a solitary, meticulous observer, not lonely or even isolated, but so veraciously absorbed in what she hears or sees that she never looks around for companions."[9] In later decades, such emphasis on the small and the simple could slide easily into William Jay Smith's dissatisfaction with Bishop as a "miniaturist."[10] H. T. Kirby-Smith, Jr., wrote approvingly of Bishop's recent poetry in 1972, but only because that work was governed by a "contemplative calm" that lifted it above her early "exercises in description": "All the way through the volume [*Complete Poems*] the purpose appears to be one of rendering what she sees (occasionally, what she imagines) as accurately as possible."[11]

North & South was given largely favorable reviews; occasional qualifications of the praise that Bishop received in the 1940s tend in the direction of the diminution that critics were beginning to practice on Moore. Lloyd Frankenberg characterizes Bishop in terms similar to those that he uses to place Moore as highly canonical, saying that her "method is direct, reticent and gracious" and that her poems embody "perception, precision, compression."[12] But Frankenberg qualifies his praise by noting the diversity of approach in Bishop's work as a whole: "There is no general rhetorical effect to be isolated to summarize Elizabeth Bishop's poems. Each poem discovers and is true to its own method."[13] Again, what Frankenberg means as a qualifying comment has an oddly positive ring after more than forty years. The most negative review of *North & South*, Oscar Williams's in the *New Republic*, also presents her, implicitly, as akin to the fussy Marianne Moore of the tidy attic metaphor. Williams sees the volume as too carefully following its models: "The free verse is delicate and not too free, the preciosity is not unpleasant, the sestina is modern, competent and digestible, the influences from a half-dozen sources are handled with gloves, any thumbprints have been wiped from the shining legs of the poetic furniture at least twice in every other poem."[14] Williams's detection of incipient fastidiousness in the Bishop oeuvre shows that distaste for Moore was beginning to spill over into criticism of Bishop. But Williams's dismissal of Bishop is not on purely *ad feminam* grounds, of course, because the image of "Miss Bishop" it conjures up is unrecognizable from her biography. In fact, Williams had no public biography to go on and began to invent his Miss Bishop in the better-known image of Miss Moore.

At the same time, Moore's own review of *North & South*—the last piece she would publish about Bishop's poetry—is decidedly understated: "With poetry as with homiletics, tentativeness can be more positive than positiveness; and in "North & South," a much instructed persuasiveness is emphasized by uninsistence. At last we have a prize book that has no creditable mannerisms. At last we have someone who knows, who is not didactic."[15] Moore's positive review of Bishop's first book is cast almost completely in negative terms: "tentativeness," "uninsistence," "no creditable mannerisms," but the initial impression is that there is nothing creditable *at all* about the volume. The strongest positive statement is that Bishop is "not didactic," leaving any positive qualities unidentified.

Description remained the keynote of 1950s characterizations of Bishop; in an early academic piece, James G. Southworth says that "the poetry of Elizabeth Bishop, except for some ten poems, is as objective as poetry can well be."[16] The exceptions to the rule of objectivity, for Southworth, are poems like "Casabianca" and "Rain towards Morning," which he reads as intense bursts of private emotion. The effect of Southworth's categorizing is to construct two poles for Bishop's verse: the impersonal and the overly personal, the mirror and the solipsist. There is no sense that any of the poems may serve as arguments or dialogues, whether moral or aestheticist. Southworth's argument would be negligible except that it serves so well as a model for the silencing of female writers in general: they can either write exactly what they see, scholars will argue, or they can write exactly what they feel; in either case, more complicated expressions escape them.

Southworth's essay, however, takes the value of Bishop's work for granted, as most scholarly writing does. Prestige critics in the quarterlies were less agreed. Donald Hall concedes that "her most obvious felicity apart from rhythm is description" but counters that "she has the true imagination which turns obsessions into universals."[17] (If in the 1950s critics valued universals over obsessions, it might be fair to say that their concern with universals rose to the level of an obsession, somewhat blurring the distinction.) Howard Nemerov, concluding that Bishop was interested in descriptive detail for its own sake, tries a variant of the "maintenance of the language" argument in an attempt to ascribe some value to that descriptiveness: "The happiest consequences of this kind of work will be the refreshment it affords the language (which becomes impoverished by the moralizing of descriptive words)."[18] Here we see Bishop as stylish hostess to the English vocabulary, offering it refreshments—another indication, as in Williams's review, of the lack of any convincing biographical image to set her work against.

As so often, the most discerning discussion of a poet comes from more negative assessments. Edwin Honig, reviewing *Poems* for the *Partisan Review* in 1956, finds the same surface qualities that appeared to Hall and Nemerov but fails to discover refreshing universals beneath. "The poems arrest one by their brilliant surfaces and transparency. But underneath is a curious rigidity, a disturbing lack of movement and affective life, betraying a sprained and uneasy patience."[19] We are verging back on "frigidity" here, but Honig elaborates his argument in other kinds of terms as well. From the last line of "The Map" ("More delicate than the historians' are the mapmakers' colors"), Honig deduces "the poet's aim: a scrupulous representation of the world reduced in scale and line to something like a cartographer's depiction of geographical areas. It is a plan for suppressing rather than compressing contours, dimension, tonality, emotion. A slow hard gaze moves behind the deliberately drawn-out ironies."[20]

Honig knows that he is begging the question whether a poetry based on suppression might not be just as valid as a poetry based on the more traditional lyric virtue of compression. His comment that Bishop's verse plans systematically to suppress the usual poetic qualities is highly suggestive. It offers a way to read behind and around the surfaces of the poems, to arrive at a sense of them as correlatives—though maybe not objective—for emotions that are at least the reader's if not reliably the poet's. Honig does not go as far as making that transvaluation; he sees the typical Bishop poem as "a baneful asking of meaningful questions of a meaningless or essentially unmeaningful object. . . . She fails with the image when trying to make it over into a symbol because the nature of the precise image is to defy symbolization. For similar reasons, her forced synaesthesia reduces reality not to poetry but to a dressing up of coy attitudes. . . . Instead of relieving, the devices call attention to, the flatness of her prosaic lines."[21] From the perspective of the 1990s, Honig seems largely accurate in his characterizations; the question, of course, is whether Bishop's texts are to be read as exploiting, or as immured in, the limitations of their lyric method. As Honig himself says,

"I recognize that what I have called her risks and failure may all be un-derstood precisely as her successes by another kind of reader."[22]

Indeed, it can be instructive to read a text from the 1955 *Poems* in Honig's terms, but with the value sign reversed. "At the Fishhouses" seems promising for the experiment, because it is prosaic, ironic, syn-aesthetic, and, starting in imagery, ends in symbolism. It is also charac-terized by what Honig particularly likes about Bishop's work, "good cam-era-eye realism":

> Up on the little slope behind the houses,
> set in the sparse bright sprinkle of grass,
> is an ancient wooden capstan,
> cracked, with two long bleached handles
> and some melancholy stains, like dried blood,
> where the ironwork has rusted. (64)

But even that camerawork is prosaic; and the poem promptly wanders into glaringly flat passages:

> The old man accepts a Lucky Strike.
> He was a friend of my grandfather.
> We talk of the decline in the population
> and of codfish and herring
> while he waits for a herring boat to come in. (64–65)

Coming from a poet who is supremely attentive to detail, this poem is one of an inability to pay attention, to concentrate. (Robert Bly would choose these very lines as the epitome of the flatness of modern Ameri-can poetry, neatly ignoring the rest of the poem.)[23] Instead of compres-sion/concentration, we sense suppression. The bloodstain-like markings on the capstan are suppressed in banal conversation, but the speaker's attention is then caught by the fisherman's knife—and keeps being drawn back to the water. The lyric necessity, which keeps butting up against the suppressions of the prosaic voice of the speaker, is to invoke the sea, to come to terms especially with its power to drown and its incipient fascination for the one who might drown in it. The lyric voice comes up momentarily, to be suppressed partially by a humorous aside:

> Cold dark deep and absolutely clear,
> element bearable to no mortal,
> to fish and to seals . . . One seal particularly
> I have seen here evening after evening.
>
> He was curious about me. He was interested in music;
> like me a believer in total immersion,
> so I used to sing him Baptist hymns. (65)

The sea continues to exert a fascination upon the speaker that ultimately purges her voice of anything but the lyric:

> It is like what we imagine knowledge to be:
> dark, salt, clear, moving, utterly free,
> drawn from the cold hard mouth
> of the world, derived from the rocky breasts
> forever, flowing and drawn, and since
> our knowledge is historical, flowing and flown. (66)

The price of the lyrical "knowledge" that is drawn from this final sym-bolization is silence; the poem ends—and maybe the speaker too, if the poem is read as a dramatic monologue; the poem's dramatic situation ends in sleep, or trance, or suicide. But the poem's dialogic qualities make it hard to read as either prose sketch, lyric, or drama. Any of the genres that participate in it throw the others into disquieting perspective. If "At the Fishhouses" *is* its final lyric summation (as, for instance, Stevens's "Sunday Morning" in its final version *is* the passage beginning "Deer walk upon our mountains"), then the prosaic, ironic passages that proceed it are just so much waste of time (as the dialogue in "Sunday Morning" between speaker and questioning woman is *not*, being instead a produc-tive dialectic). If the poem is essentially its "accumulated details," as Nemerov thought, then the final lyric summation is a false note, a "gno-mic anticlimax."[24] And if the poem is drama, it is not very well realized drama; it is static and impertinent. "At the Fishhouses" is, then, some-thing different, something created out of a dialogic confusion of genres; and Honig's sense that Bishop's "risks and failure" in such a poem could be revalued by other reading strategies seems to be borne out.

The resistance that the early genre-confusing poems met was not near-ly as strong as that which more generically traditional texts, presented as a dialogic collation in *Questions of Travel*, would meet in the 1960s. Unlike Bishop's first two collections, *Questions of Travel*—or at least its opening section, "Brazil"—invites a sequential reading, which might go as follows. The speaker in the opening poem, "Arrival at Santos," is a stranger to Brazil, its language and its landscape. That sense of strange-ness provokes comparison to earlier examples of cultural contact ("Bra-zil, January 1, 1502"), and general questions about the appropriateness of the voyage to another country, in the title poem. But the volume moves through curiosity into a growing understanding of the place and its people—"Squatter's Children," "Electrical Storm," "The Armadillo"—into a sense of familiarity where the poet can write uninhibitedly of Bra-zilian legends and myths in familiar English poetic forms, as in "The Riverman" and "The Burglar of Babylon." The mediation made necessary by the poet's native language being English, not Portuguese, is inescapable; but by the end of the "Brazil" sequence, she has at least become capable of that mediation, as a competent translator who knows she will never be a native. Brazil is now her home, poetically as well as physically.

Such a reading of "Brazil" is now commonplace, though it presents problems for recent Bishop criticism that I will treat in their turn. But the initial reviewers of *Questions of Travel*, still reading Bishop as a peripatetic wanderer, read "travel" in the Sunday-supplement sense, as "tourism." Brazil was yet another stop on the Bishop itinerary, following the dizzy variety of places already visited: Nova Scotia, New York, Paris, Florida, the Middle East. Given this proliferation of settings, Bishop could not possibly be categorized as a regionalist; but she began to suffer the other half of the no-win situation for women writers: an attribution of insincerity and lack of deep experience. The woman writer who stays at home (Dickinson) can be slighted for lack of adventurousness; the woman writer who travels (Bishop) can be dismissed as someone who just wants to cover her suitcase with stickers.

William Jay Smith and Louis L. Martz offer readings that combine impatience and antifeminist bias into a significant mix of pejorative terminology. Smith is disappointed by what he perceives as a *recent* turn toward the feminine in Bishop's work: "Miss Bishop is a miniaturist for whom 'The world is uniquely / minute and vast and clear;' and in which there is 'no detail too small.' . . . Miss Bishop comes dangerously close at times to seeming as ridiculous as an earlier New England poet, Lydia Sigourney, the Sweet Singer of Hartford, was in trying to be grand. What we have always admired in Elizabeth Bishop is what she admires in Herbert, 'the absolute naturalness of tone.' When her work becomes muted and coy, quaint and quilted, that tone is lost."[25] "Ridiculous" is not now an adjective that leaps to mind to characterize either Bishop *or* Sigourney. In the context of 1966 and the audience for this review in *Harper's*, Sigourney's name probably was less denotative than simply associative; Percy Dovetonsils would have conveyed the association better, but he did not have the advantage of being real. Perhaps more revealing is the word "quilted" as a pejorative, because it would seem to have no other purpose than as a gender marker; quilting, associated with women, would carry a negative value opposite the masculine "masterful," even though quilting suggests artistic strengths of design and composition. The needlework metaphor is echoed independently in Martz's review. Discussing the passage beginning "not to have had to stop for gas" in "Questions of Travel," Martz says: "This vignette, as an answer, is not quite convincing. Its appliquéd design plays an appropriate part within an effective poem of questioning, and yet the passage suggests a weakness that runs throughout most of these Brazilian pieces: the presence of a stagy, factitious quality as of some 'quaint' souvenirs carefully arranged upon a masterpiece."[26] Martz goes on to criticize the "Brazil" poems for "jarring contrivance" and "excessively studied naïveté."[27] As with Smith's, the basic impetus for this commentary is gendered; Bishop's verse is weak because it is "appliquéd." (Why appliqué should be a weak artistic technique is illogical except in the gendered connotations it conveys.)

The positive reviews of *Questions of Travel* focus in formalist ways on the continuing development of Bishop's typical poetic strategies. Howard Moss sees a sharpening of the descriptive honesty that had made Bishop famous: "Disinterestedness has become passionate. . . . Reading these poems, we have the sensation of seeing what things are *really* like . . . nothing that has not been isolated to be examined, nothing that has not been delineated sharply has been permitted to be written down."[28] One might expect this approach to the "Brazil" poems to raise certain problems, especially about what business the North American poet has isolating elements of South American culture for examination, like a botanist in the rainforest. But only one American critic of the 1960s read *Questions of Travel* primarily to critique its political engagement. Peter Michelson is troubled by the book because it fails to engage contemporary American politics, as he senses her poetry has continually failed to do going back to the Second World War. Because *Questions of Travel* avoids the issue of Vietnam, Michelson feels uneasy about "that atemporal quality in her work that one thinks of as feminine."[29] But he neither rejects her work nor attempts to relate it indirectly to the more "serious" masculine issue of the war. Instead, Michelson holds on to a value for Bishop's work by placing it in a feminine counterpoint to wartime concerns, saying, "the place for her kind of poetry is to insure the lyrical affirmation of what war denies—the human sensibility."[30] But for Michelson, Bishop's is a limited, partial sensibility, passive-aggressive in its inattention to vital matters that are left for men to worry about.

At times, *Questions of Travel* was read more as an adjunct to the canonization of a male poet than as an independent work by Bishop. The most highly praised poem in the volume, which contains several of the current common anthology pieces ("The Armadillo," "First Death in Nova Scotia," "Sandpiper"), was its last poem, "Visits to St. Elizabeths." The poem, which offers successively more complicated views of Ezra Pound to the tune of "The House That Jack Built," is discussed reverently even by Martz, who calls it "a magical ballad of incremental repetition."[31] Frank J. Warnke agrees, saying that "the device of incremental repetition . . . has seldom been used more masterfully."[32] In 1970, Daniel Hughes saw "Visits to St. Elizabeths" "not only as one of Miss Bishop's best poems but as one essential to her *metier* and her tragic scene."[33] The poem does present Pound as a tragic figure—not as misunderstood or as undeserving of his torment, but as tragic nevertheless. Its tone is double-edged:

> This is a Jew in a newspaper hat
> that dances weeping down the ward
> over the creaking sea of board
> beyond the sailor
> winding his watch
> that tells the time
> of the cruel man
> that lies in the house of Bedlam. (134)

By turns, the poem calls Pound "tragic," "talkative," "honored," "old," "brave," "cranky," "cruel," "busy," "tedious," "the poet," and "wretched." The text thereby constructs a deepening, ultimately empathetic, portrait of Pound. Aside from the questionable taste of that effort itself, the poem presents a further problem by introducing the "Jew in a newspaper hat" who wanders the ward mocking Pound and his beliefs. But the Jew is himself a ridiculous figure, a madhouse inmate—perhaps driven to madness (in one stanza he is the "widowed Jew") by fascism and the Holocaust, but nevertheless a crazy stock character who, when set alongside the "poet" or the "wretched" Pound, presents a much more troubling aspect than when he is allowed to tease the "cruel" or the "tedious" Pound.

It will not do to belabor "Visits to St. Elizabeths"; but neither would it do to elide it. The poem is a permanently embarrassing feature of Bishop's work, and a good deal of the initial acceptance of *Questions of Travel* was connected to the inclusion of this poem. The late 1960s saw not so much a rehabilitation of Pound (who had always had powerful admirers in the U.S.) but a renormalization of his work: its return to anthologies, general literary histories, and undergraduate curricula. Bishop added her voice to that renormalization with the publication of her poem on Pound, so that in a small but perceptible way the beginnings of her canonicity were linked temporarily to the recovery of his.

In 1973, *Salmagundi* published Jan B. Gordon's "Days and Distances: The Cartographic Imagination of Elizabeth Bishop." While the overall tone of Gordon's critique is negative, specific analyses of Bishop's poetics are presented as neutral observation—and in just twenty years have acquired the sound of positive aesthetic judgments that it took Thomas

Bailey Aldrich's similar critique of Dickinson nearly one hundred years to acquire. Gordon suggests some of the sources of Bishop's unique poetic strength:

> The poetry often lacks a distinctive teleology. We see no possibility of a therapeutic progression in a world so relativized that "North's as near as West" precisely because hers is at best a two-dimensional craft. There is a certain surface tension always present in Elizabeth Bishop's art that is at least partially the result of the loss of *privilege* in every sense in which we might typically use that word: the narrator's sense of an advantage to perspective; an access to secrets unknown to other protagonists in her poems; or even the subtlety of an untrustworthy vision which might confer aesthetic advantage by granting the reader the right to acknowledge a false subjectivity.[34]

Of course, the most typical sense of the word "privilege," which has little to do with aesthetics, is precisely the one that adheres to Bishop's work: the *cultural* privilege, based on economics, of North over South, city over country, college over factory. If abnegations of the aesthetic of privilege could entail the depriviliging of those cultural biases as well, we might welcome them.

Gordon goes further, in an even more thorough deflation of Bishop's poetics that has the odd potential, twenty years later, to breathe remarkable life into it: "We have the trappings of direction and guidance without the emergence, real or promised, of presence. . . . Her images are never organically related nor are they presented in any of Imagism's characteristically durational clusters."[35] In the terms that American formalists inherited from the critics who elevated Walt Whitman to canonicity, there could be no more thorough dismissal of a poet's work; in the 1990s, Gordon's perception of a decentered poetic in the work of Bishop has revolutionary potential to overturn the poetics of presence.

Nonetheless, it was certainly not Gordon's intention to catalyze antipresence readings of Bishop or other poets. Indeed the influence of "Days and Distances" was to provoke totalizing defenses of Bishop, like Ruth Quebe's "Water, Windows, and Birds," which finds the center of Bishop's poetics in an organic relation of image and theme.[36] Quebe wrote, of course, after the publication of *Geography III* in 1976 had crowned Bishop's career and made her canonical position much less assailable. There has been no substantial demurral from the value consensus that Bishop is worth studying without qualification or defense since the poet's death in 1979.

The reception of *Geography III* was well prepared; most of the poems had already been published in the *New Yorker* or elsewhere, and David Kalstone previewed the book's contents in a 1975 essay in *Ploughshares*.[37]

Geography III was all but unanimously given respectful reviews. Even Calvin Bedient's sense that the "ostentatiously prosaic" quality of many of the poems made them "tepid" and "genteel" is counterbalanced by his praise of "The Moose" as "one of the most nearly perfect and unambitiously profound long poems in modern American poetry."[38] The physical presence of Bishop at Harvard may have had much to do with the more positive reception of the volume; she was now a central elder figure *socially* in the world of American poetry, no longer a hard-to-place expatriate. The powerful entry of Harold Bloom and two critics associated with him—David Bromwich and John Hollander—became the pivotal fixture of her canonical place.

The cumulative effect of their reviews (which were not necessarily coordinated) was to set Bishop's work above mere reviewing and to turn her into literature. Bloom grants the poet sweeping powers: "Bishop's art is as unmistakable in its authority as the poetry of Wallace Stevens and Marianne Moore demonstrated itself to be, at an earlier time."[39] Bloom takes the opportunity to import a retrospective sense of unquestionable authority into Moore's very questioned career. He does the same for Bishop, saying of the last lines of "The End of March": "We *need* that trope of the lion-sun, and it is Bishop's authority that she both re-induces the need or limitation in us, and then restitutes the need by her genius for invention, for rhetorical substitution."[40]

Hollander takes the poet's verbal authority further, into the realm of absolute organic presence: "Bishop's work seems as self-begotten as any in our time. What seems cold in her language is warmed by the breath of its own life."[41] It is late in the day, but Hollander is reiterating the never-failing mantra of presence, Stuart Sherman's insistence that Whitman *lives*, the unanswerable *Christos aneste* of the critical liturgy. The three critics are not, however, mystically convinced of their own objectivity; Bromwich, the most dispassionate of the three, admits that he is asserting largely a personal taste, saying that "The End of March" "seems to me the greatest poem in English since the death of Stevens."[42] Or rather, Bromwich synthesizes his personal preference with the demands of a supposedly self-evident canon, in which Stevens is the major edifice directly to the rear.

The canon Bromwich subscribes to is largely the one transmitted through Bloom. Bloom's own emphasis on the self-evident authority of Bishop's poetry and its natural relation to that of Stevens and Moore suggests a link between his reception of Bishop and the theoretical needs of the American canon he was constructing in the 1970s. Bloom's highly book-centered construct, devoted to finding "the hidden paths that run between poem and poem," needs continual recharging; there must be a contemporary or near-contemporary poet who testifies to its continuance. If the temporal chain of poets engaged in anxiety over their precursors is broken, the whole structure is endangered. So for Bloom, the 1970s became the age of Elizabeth Bishop, making her in turn available as a precursor for coming ages.

Bloom's choice is in fact almost entirely arbitrary. So long as the poet has some plausible relation to the established canon of strong poets (and Bishop's relationship to Moore is a convenient link), any poet will do. Since the fitting of the poet into the relations demanded by Bloom's sense of tradition is so completely artifactual, it need bear little relation to literary history as historically defined by reception. Bloom's own strength as a critic is that he reads and argues so well, and he becomes a powerful constitutive force in his own right *of* that reception history—but it can hardly be argued that his constructs have the status of objective literary history. If history is news that stays news, Bloom's criticism is a review that stays a review—and often it is an exceedingly welcome review, since so few other scholars have been secure enough to express so many negative critical judgments. But ultimately, "we" do not "need" any tropes, any more than we want our MTV; the force of rhetoric persuades us to read (or watch, or buy), and we become interested in what we get—which is half-chosen for us before we demand it.

Read alongside Hollander's and Bromwich's seconding opinions, Bloom's elevation of Bishop to necessary canonical status in 1977 marks the end of the first epoch in Bishop criticism. From the three critical options available to Bishop's readers—assertion of presence, surrender of presence in favor of description, and dismissal—these critics tried the first option. Though the content of their canonizing opinion seems in retrospect no more substantial than Wallace Fowlie's vague appreciation of Marianne Moore's poetry as "a miraculous fusion of life and speech," their value judgments would become increasingly validated by the interpretive communities that formed after the poet's death in 1979 (and which in part, of course, they created). The key interpretive community that formed after 1979 was the community of feminist readers of Bishop, one often at odds in its assumptions and aesthetics with that of Bloom and his agonistic model. But when one turns to post-1979 criticism, one is struck by the fundamental correspondence of the poetics of presence between John Hollander's late transmission of the Whitmanic template and feminist construction of an ideal biography for Bishop.

The Art of Finding: Bishop since 1979

To return briefly to a key distinction made by Tomasevskij: "It is, of course, obvious that . . . authors do have *actual* biographies, and that their literary work enters into these biographies as a fact of their lives."[43] Tomasevskij goes on to maintain that "such actual biographies of private individuals may be interesting for cultural history, but not for the history of literature," a statement that few critics would follow but that calls attention once more to Tomasevskij's sharp distinction between the ideal and actual biographies of writers. The ideal biography is a constructed fiction, just as any narrative must be; the actual biography is the life as lived. To the extent to which Tomasevskij implies that an actual biography can be constructed in any different sense from an ideal biography, or that historical biography is qualitatively different from literary or critical biography, he is clearly self-contradictory.

The implication of Tomasevskij's contentious generic distinctions for studying the recuperation of Elizabeth Bishop is simply that the biographical project of documenting and retelling the actual life is inextricable from the critical use of ideal biography as a mainstay of the poetics of presence. "Actual" and "ideal" biographies share much of the same narrative, of course; and for a writer with little "official" ideal biography to strip away, the creation of both is a concurrent and simultaneous process. But I should be clear at the start: I am not calling for the cessation of literary biography, which is a literary genre in its own right; still less would I advocate censorship or silence in the case of any biographical traces of any author. In fact, I would argue the opposite: the more that is known about an author's "actual biography," and the more quickly it can be constructed and established during or just after the author's life, the less tempting it is to write one's own version of ideal biography. If Emily Dickinson's family had been less bound by conventions that made the revelation of actual biography taboo (or less divided by hatreds that made such revelation emotionally impossible), the whole debilitating construction of the Dickinson myths might have been avoided. In the case of Bishop, Brett C. Millier's 1993 biography *Elizabeth Bishop: Life and the Memory of It* is an exemplary touchstone for the assay of the narratizations that appeared in the previous decade.

As biography tends toward the ideal, it tends to determine readings of texts and sequences of texts. When Norma Procopiow asserts Bishop's lesbian identity in "Survival Kit" (1981), she does so in the service of one of the most strongly narratizing readings of Bishop's literary career ever to appear.[44] Procopiow sees lesbianism as a centrally disruptive component of Bishop's ideal biography and reads her poems as "pointers in her changing psychic condition; they trace a slowly but steadily changing thematic journey that begins with the compulsion to survive (*North and South*), and ends with the equally strong compulsion to surrender (*Geography III*)."[45] In *Geography III*, then, Bishop "finally resolved her sexual and social conflict."[46]

Procopiow's narratization is strong and appealing, pointing to features of the internal Bishop canon that enable such developmental approaches. As perceived collectively or as a sequence of books, Bishop's poetry offers discrete volumes, well-separated in time, with thematic titles and arrangements that seem to demand the very kind of narrative that Dickinson's featureless texts (for instance) resist. We can read *The Complete Poems 1927–1979* and say: here is where the poet was in 1946, here in 1955, here in 1965 and 1976. But the regular publication dates of the volumes obscure the extremely chaotic production of the poems, as Millier makes clear and the bibliography of their initial serial publications confirms. The best example is "The Moose," the poem so important to the 1976 volume; Bishop was writing it before the 1955 volume was published.

With the volumes arranged sequentially, however, formalist techniques for perceiving closure and resolution in individual texts find application on the scale of the *Complete Poems*. It is almost irresistable when performing a poet's career in critical reading to expect initial tensions to be resolved in a final harmonic—in Bishop's case, to play the resonances of "Land lies in water; it is shadowed green" (3) against those, alternately, of "(A yesterday I find almost impossible to lift)" (181, the last line of *Geography III*) or "flying wherever / it feels like, gay!" (192, the last lines of "Sonnet," her last published poem). The intertextualities engendered by such formalist arrangement of a career and life have a kind of moral inevitability; they function almost therapeutically to teach us as readers that a triumphant resolution is the end of every experience.

If there has been a main voice to resist the narratization of Bishop's career in 1980s criticism, it is probably that of Robert Dale Parker. Parker's study *The Unbeliever* is on one level a study of the development of Bishop's voice from "wish" through "where" to "retrospect," descriptive terms that roughly parallel the volumes that Bishop published. But the overtly developmental approach of Parker's book is far from being a narratizing or normalizing one; instead, as his title suggests, the coherence of the career is seen in its poetic skepticism. "Bishop refuses belief and makes her poetry of her refusal."[47] Parker's concept of the unbeliever is implicitly a paradigm for work on Bishop that is analogous to the paradigm Margaret Dickie's discontinuous self offers for Dickinson.

Parker's work also offers a keen sense of how Bishop's poetry was rooted in gendered experience. But such an embrace of the skeptical can become in turn a centripetal force. Much criticism of Bishop in the 1980s repeats one critical move in various manifestations. The archetypal recent reading of Bishop goes this way: her poems apparently lack centripetal force; at any rate, critics haven't been able to detect any. There-fore, the center of her poetry is actually at the margin: in revisions and nonrhetorical questions (Patricia Storace), in mundane daily activities (Victoria Harrison), in the archaic, devalued art of augury (Renée R. Curry), in the side-roads of tradition that provide "an enabling humili-ty" (Jeredith Merrin), in "perversity" (Jacqueline Vaught Brogan), in the very project of subverting phallogocentrism (Lois Cucullu).[48] The mar-gin as alternative center is an attractive valorizing technique in femi-nist criticism, since it allows the political value signs of a text to be re-versed (a marginal text from a male-centered point of view turns out to be politicized in a positive, central, feminist direction) but maintains the central values of the poetics of presence intact, so that the female poet can become a figure of mastery equal to Whitman or Williams. If mastery is a phallogocentric concept, then antiphallogocentric mastery is doubly strong.

Concepts of mastery drawn from the poetics of presence lie behind most feminist recuperation of women writers; indeed it is hard to escape such concepts. Feminist critics argue for the major status of the writers they study, and the major status of a writer is best expressible in the value terms inherited from prefeminist criticism. Bishop wrote great poems, and she is therefore by definition a "great artist"; when one defines her as a great artist, one is drawn to envision her as someone molding lan-guage to her own stylistic and expressive purposes (as monologic), as someone who made bold formal experiments (as original)—and with the values of monologism and originality in place, organicism follows as part of the package of presence. In the vanguard of feminist organicism are readings that see the female poet writing the body, as in Marilyn May Lombardi's fascinating intuition of an asthmatic poetics in Bishop's texts ("The Closet of Breath," 1992).[49] Most feminist recuperations have ad-hered more closely to the terms set out in the early and often antifemi-nist reception of Bishop: vision, observation, and description. Even Lois Cucullu's reading of "In the Waiting Room," which sees that poem as evidence of Bishop's uncompromising radical feminism, is entitled "Trompe l'Oeil," setting itself to confuse the visual tropes of earlier crit-ics. Less radical readings of Bishop's subversion accept description as the main method of her poems and suggest that she worked to subvert an overtly descriptive language, as Jane Shore does in "Elizabeth Bishop: The Art of Changing Your Mind."[50]

Constructs of the margin as center dominate the most recent major critical study of Bishop, Bonnie Costello's Elizabeth Bishop: Questions of Mastery (1991), which begins "by exploring Bishop's optical strategies."[51] Costello's approach is instructive not only for the way in which it hews very closely to established paradigms for reading Bishop, but also for how it negotiates the problem of moving beyond presence. Costello is faced with the image of Bishop formed in her pre-1979 reception—a minor poet with major strengths in description. To maintain an image that is recognizably Bishop's, she must make description central (and it is fair to say that there *is* objectively a lot of describing in Bishop's poetry; if there weren't, the texts would resist this move). But since description is a marginal value in the poetics of presence, Bishop's strategies must be reworked as decentering and subversive. Costello therefore reads Bishop as effecting a transvaluation by means of "directed resistance to idealism and its quest for mastery over nature's plurality and flux."[52] Even in 1991, uncontrolled "plurality and flux" are almost impossible to value in the work of an American poet; Costello must conceive of Bishop's "resistance" as "directed." And so the element of control in the unary subject of presence is reintroduced, to manage the task of subverting itself. When Costello moves to the theme of memory in Bishop, she again banishes "mastery" only to reinscribe it in the very surrender to memory she discusses: "Memory is not, for her, a form of mastery over time; indeed, it often arises as an involuntary force. Bishop possessed a nearly eidetic memory, or at least invents a rhetoric of exact recall. Iconic events in her personal history shape her acts of beholding. Thus memory remains for her a major force of identity."[53] In the process of trying to deal with memory as a factor in Bishop's discontinuous lyric persona, Costello falls back on the idea of memory as "a major force of identity"—the very identity that such irruptions of memory would appear to threaten and dissolve.

Let me emphasize that Costello's formulations are not nonsensical in the slightest. The internal flaws in her argument are actually more like the fault-lines of the whole project of presence imploding on itself, as Costello (like many other critics) tries to preserve a sense of aesthetic value for her subject poet in ways that contradict vitally necessary observations about that poet's essential *lack* of coherence.

If Bishop does cohere in recent criticism, it is most of all in readings that actively engage her sexuality, readings that have only begun to move out of a critical closet since 1989.[54] Feminist critics were slow to follow Procopiow's lead and appropriate Bishop's lesbian status, possibly since (as Cucullu points out) her public persona as the friend and supporter of male and even masculinist poets like Robert Lowell so contradicted the politics implied by her lesbianism. Criticism that deals with Bishop's sexuality is still nascent; there are whole areas of scholarship where it goes discreetly unmentioned.[55] The most substantial critical recuperation of this part of Bishop's life so far has been done by Lorrie Goldensohn in *Elizabeth Bishop: The Biography of a Poetry*; Millier, of course, adds many details of the "actual biography."

Goldensohn's book is a major achievement in Bishop studies because it marks the first time that extensive recovery of unpublished Bishop texts form the basis for a critical treatment. It includes a wry and self-conscious narrative of the Aspern Papers–like discovery of some of this material in Brazil, juxtaposed against critical rereadings of Bishop in the light of it. *Elizabeth Bishop: The Biography of a Poetry* anticipates responses to itself—it is a model of feminist scholarship informed by poststructuralism. My critique of the book, given those imposing features, is directed mainly at a narrow issue of its framing that implicates scholarly projects in general far more than Goldensohn's accomplishment in her particular project.

Scholarly projects of recuperation are, almost of necessity, attempts to provide an intelligible narrative shape to scattered traces of a literary life. That literary life has usually been given narrative shape already, in the author's published constructions of an ideal authorial biography—which is a construction inseparable from the process of becoming an author "before the public." Scholarly recuperation strips away this old published life and gives students a more faithful kind of ideal biography. So we now read Emerson's journals and notebooks interchangeably with his published work, despite the fact that we get thereby an "Emerson" and an "Emerson's thought" that had no existence for his contemporaries and, in a quite real sense, had none for Emerson himself. Most saliently in the early 1990s, scholarship is providing a Philip Larkin who is a grotesque exaggeration of the Larkin who was famous in his own lifetime. The "new Larkin" will, however, replace the old one; it will never be possible again to read the ending of "High Windows"—"Nothing, and nowhere, and is endless"—without a consciousness of the caustic final line of the manuscript draft: "and fucking piss."[56]

Again, one cannot escape the urge and indeed the necessity for scholarly recuperation. One can notice a few things about it, though. The Emerson who bursts out of the journals and notebooks in remarkable diffuseness is someone who, if he had been published to his contemporaries, might have been received in the same tolerant but dismissive way as Bronson Alcott. The Larkin who could have published his own self-mockery and his own asinine knee-jerk criticisms of his contemporaries would have been received as someone akin to the Beats, not as a restrained elegiac lyricist. Therefore, neither the real Emerson nor the real Larkin were part of their literary culture. Nor was the real Bishop. Scholarly recuperation therefore gives us an author in the most printable contemporary state of identity; some Victorian authors (think of Edward

Lear) have gone through several stages of scholarly unmasking. And further, scholarly recuperation, which is more biographical than textual, inevitably makes an author's work cohere around an unexpressed center (which is a reading neatly both postmodern and Romantic). Ever since John Forster's revelations about Charles Dickens's days in the blacking warehouse, reading Dickens has become more and more a matter of perceiving the class anxieties that his works imply but dare not (not even *David Copperfield*) fully articulate. If he had articulated those "real" anxieties, he would have been less like Dickens and more like Multatuli—and he would have been far less the "Dickens" who dominated Victorian literature with his own for-publication image.

If Bishop had a "for-publication" image during her lifetime, it would have been the image of a writer who, like Larkin, found it difficult to publish much but a few poems and even fewer prose pieces. The corpus of her unpublished writing is probably larger than what she did publish, leading to problems and opportunities in the critical reception of such an "imaginary iceberg" of an author. Goldensohn insists on the opportunities opened by her discovery of the unpublished love poem "It is marvellous to wake up together": "If we trace the meshwork, the overlapping circuits in figure and theme across many poems, then the significance of the newly discovered piece begins to assemble as legible pattern, and its startling subject, love's pleasure, opens new ways in which to read all of Bishop's poems about human connection."[57] As we move on to frame Bishop's published treatment of human connection with such newly discovered texts, and with the private biographical narrative as told by Millier, an unprecedented picture of Elizabeth Bishop becomes available: she becomes someone whose reticence is explained by the potential for scandal in her actually unsensational private life. She was always "instinctively building a one-sided picture, omitting the homosexual erotic feelings that would expose her to the hazards of conventional misjudgment," as Goldensohn puts it.[58]

Such recuperation is welcome; its dangers lie in its scope for importing intentionalist variations of presence back into texts that tried to avoid it. One of the great merits of Goldensohn's book is that it resists such dangers; but they lie immediately ahead for Bishop criticism. When both public and private texts are combined into an eclectic biographical image of the author, the salient feature of that image becomes the unexpressed center of lesbian identity—which can proceed to overdetermine readings of the texts by enlisting this eclectic Bishop as a lesbian poet in the mold of Adrienne Rich or Audre Lorde. We now possess a vocabulary for normalizing lesbian relationships, and indeed most of the readers of Bishop criticism find such relationships absolutely normal and healthy. And Bishop was the late contemporary of current Bishop critics; those of whom who knew her found *her* lifestyle normal. Their impulse is to "straighten" an essentially closeted poetry in recuperating it. But for Bishop's early contemporaries, in her 1920s and 1930s youth, lesbian relationships were unstraightenable; the poet's recourse was the closet, which resonates (as Goldensohn shows) throughout her work.

The closet might be seen as an institution of personal nonendorsement of statements, akin to rhetoric's long association in Western thought with lying.[59] There are several preferred strategies for reading closet poetry: transference (which is how the *Immortal Poems* tradition reads Housman, because so many of his poems can be glossed as heterosexual lyrics); denial (as in so many readings of gay poetry that reduce eroticism to friendship); or recuperation (as is beginning to occur with Bishop). A fourth alternative might be to proceed from the beginning made by Renée R. Curry and read Bishop's poems as existing (like Housman's) in their own irrecoverable, but identifiable, historical moment. Curry reads "Crusoe in England" as a poem that works "to delicately unmask a muted lesbian identity"—a strategy unique to a historical moment defined by a closet with several layers rather than by distinctly unmuted comings out.[60] Readings like Curry's allow us to *use* what is now a perceptible historical difference (though only one of twenty years or so) between our moment and that of "Crusoe in England," instead of erasing that historical moment. It is also worth noting that Bishop's writings, though proceeding from the closet, resolutely avoid the homophobia of the closet; personally and textually, Bishop was neither a hypocrite nor a contributor to the literary institutions of power that have sometimes policed closeted literary lives.[61] Her sensibilities run toward the decorous guardedness that is in itself the result of a political reluctance to come out mixed with a knowing sense of gay identities within.

"Given the conventional preoccupations," says Goldensohn, "of either heterosexual or male readers it may be all too easy to discount the power of loving relations between women, also in monolingual and typically North American fashion to slight the full impact on Bishop of her life in Brazil."[62] Goldensohn's own work is the best corrective against such discounting. In centering the life of Bishop's poetry (recall Goldensohn's subtitle) on the years in Brazil, when so much of it was written, she proposes a direction for further study that is exciting, and fraught with other dangers that place the very motives for American academic study of Bishop in question.

Bishop's texts are promising material for a reconstruction of American literary studies because they proceed so transnationally. These texts provide a basis, flawed but usable, for the concept of a trans-American literature, a literature that can be read from America without having to *be* America. Bishop's own mutable national identity, as I have suggested, provides an interrogation of the notion of American authorship.[63] She is as much a Canadian (and ultimately a Tory Canadian, that antithesis of American patriotism) as she is an American, as much an inexplicable expatriate (she should have stayed in Paris and paid court to Gertrude Stein to be explicable) as an upper-middle-class New Englander who, like Dickinson, was born and died in Massachusetts.

Bishop's texts, in fact, may have far more in common with those of expatriate writers in general—with Czeslaw Milosz, Clarice Lispector, or Cristina Peri Rossi—than with those of the intranational figures with whom critics have most associated her: Moore, Lowell, Roethke. The desire of American critics to claim Bishop as an American writer in the face of her transnational identification proceeds, I think, from needs located deep in the projects of American literary nationalism, which are as alive and well as ever (and may always break in as a sort of counterpoint when reading texts that can be associated with the United States).[64] American literary nationalism, as Nina Baym and others have noted, is an ideology that moves very readily to co-opt criticism of America by celebrating a "consensus criticism of the consensus." Americanists present critiques of American culture as a way of managing them, and also as a way of showing the essential democratic values of self-criticism: if we so openly show what's wrong about ourselves, we are always one step ahead of the critics. Bishop is therefore valuable to Americanists as a potential heroic example of our ability to forge tolerant connections with other cultures.

One senses the very beginnings of this celebration of Bishop in recent criticism—in feminist criticism especially, which is aligned with Americanism when trying to show the solidarity of American women with women of the Third World. Goldensohn's reading of Bishop's "The Riverman" as "an annexation of the common dream ground between herself and primitive peoples" is one example.[65] Another is Betsy Erkkila's sense of *Questions of Travel* as incorporating "a more pronounced emphasis on social and political themes . . . in which Bishop's personal identity as alien and outsider is linked with the differences, distances, and struggles between rich and poor, white and black, ruler and ruled in the political landscape of Brazil."[66] Similarly, Lynn Keller admires all the Brazil poems, saying that in them Bishop "points to the kind of language that best maintains and expresses human continuity."[67]

In a sense, Goldensohn's, Erkkila's, and Keller's conclusions about the Brazil poems are predetermined by the demands of studying an American poet from an Americanist perspective. Erkkila and Keller make general claims; Goldensohn focuses on "The Riverman" alone and is very much more tentative about the volume as a whole. Though suspicious of an Americanist reading of the whole sequence, Goldensohn still rescues the poet by reading one poem as a successful fusion of North and South. And the ultimate political dynamic of these poems reflects back in an ironic way on the title of Bishop's first volume. In "The Map," one line of the poem (in a way that was surely intentionally arbitrary) assures the reader that "North's as near as West" (3). The resonance of that line almost fifty years later, after the entire cold war has run its course, may make even the most committed Americanist uneasy. In cold war identifications of the United States as "West," there was often an assumption that being of the West included a deep sympathy with the third-world nations of the South, a confidence that, whatever the predatory intentions of the East against the South, the people of the South shared a fundamental faith in democracy, free enterprise, chewing gum, and other tenets of Americanism. The North-South struggle was temporarily suppressed, at least in many American liberal rhetorics, in the interests of confronting the clearer and more present danger from the East. But the United States was always potentially North as well—the neocolonizer as well as the human rights activist.

The motives for American projections of American values onto postcolonial sites are basically identical with the rhetoric of American literary nationalism that saw Anglo-America itself as a postcolonial site as far back as the 1820s (see chap. 2). Within American cultural nationalism, there is a compelling and permanent need to identify American values as those of a once-colonized, rebellious, developing nation. Whatever their actual relation economically and culturally to the rest of the world, many Americans have taken comfort in a perpetual rehearsal of their tradition as one of the colonies. In the world of American literary nationalism, North's as near as South. But it is far more difficult in the 1990s to see the United States as sharing a resistance to oppression with the nations of the Third World. America has become less and less defensibly the oppressor in a North/South dynamic. After the fall of the Berlin Wall in 1989 (coincidental, but fortuitously so, with new feminist interest in Elizabeth Bishop), we now seem to *need* a heroic poet who can reestablish our solidarity with the South—far more than we need any trope of the lion-sun.

But does Bishop's status as a lesbian expatriate guarantee the solidarity of her texts with the struggles of colonized people of color? Actual biography would remind us that Bishop was an upper-middle-class woman who moved from the American bourgeoisie to an aristocratic position in Brazil; her letters can display a patronizing attitude toward Brazilians.[68] But actual biography is beside the point, because many writers overcome their personal prejudices to produce texts with the potential for tearing down barriers of class and race. Do Bishop's Brazil pieces have this textual potential? Deborah Weiner argues not, in a 1989 essay contrasting Bishop's cross-cultural writing with that of Margaret Atwood: "While Bishop often sees difference in terms of binary oppositions, hierarchically ranked as superior or inferior, with clear separation between self and other and between active and passive, Atwood sees both similarity and difference within and between herself and the other."[69] Therefore, Bishop's texts enact a distorting, lethal dynamic of North over South.

One could answer that Bishop's texts recognize and problematize difference. "The Burglar of Babylon" situates its narrator as a distant and untrustworthy observer whose lot is cast with the privileged Brazilians of the high-rises (116). "Questions of Travel" makes any approach to South America into a moral problem: "Is it right to be watching strangers in a play / in this strangest of theatres?" (93). The things that Bishop chooses to observe in the "strangest of theatres" are things that the North American tourist finds quaint, amusing, or annoying:

> the sad, two-noted, wooden tone
> of disparate wooden clogs
> carelessly clacking over
> a grease-stained filling-station floor.
> (In another country the clogs would all be tested.
> Each pair there would have identical pitch.) (94)

Even if one's sympathies are drawn to the "primitive," unstandardized elements of South American life, the poem continues to formulate the value-laden oppositions that Weiner recognizes. But the experience of a stranger may be unavoidably implicated in the factitiousness of travel writing and the prejudices that support such factitious mediation. The "real" Brazil, as any experienced tourist knows, is not to be found in picture postcards of the Copacabana; but the authentication of one's "real" travel experiences involves the studied collection of "realer" experiences like the clogs and the bird cage. The problem is the inextricability of the observer from the frame. One cannot see the "real" Amazon; the view is blocked by preconceptions and packagings of all kinds. One's relation of well-known "sights" is uninteresting to one's audience back home; it has been overdetermined for them. But "authentic" experience is experience of the banal, and therefore of the undistinctive. There is a filling station in "Brazil," but as the table of contents reminds us, it is a lot like the "Filling Station" "Elsewhere."

And that filling station is a construct of the class prejudices that prevail in one's home culture, prejudices that these texts and their collation allow us to perceive as global.

But against the glimmers of critical self-consciousness in these texts of cultural context must be set the overwhelming counterweight of their patronizing curiosity. In fact, Bishop's Brazil poems work far better before Bishop goes "to the interior" (90); before that point they are full of disorienting strangeness, and after that they are full of the confirmation of prejudice. A few examples are enough. The savage children of "Manuelzinho": "—Impossible to make friends, / though each will grab at once / for an orange or a piece of candy" (98). "How they deal with beggars" in "Pink Dog": "They take and throw them in the tidal rivers" (190). The undisciplined nature of everyday life in Brazil: "people / all apparently changing their minds, embarking, / disembarking, rowing clumsy dories" ("Santarém," 186). The dehumanizing, racist image in "Under the Window: Ouro Prêto": "Here comes some laundry tied up in a sheet, / all on its own, three feet above the ground. / Oh, no—a small black boy is underneath" (153). Such observations are the ground bass of the Brazil poetry.[70]

Attempts to read Bishop's portrayal of her Brazilian experience must take Weiner's critique into account by recognizing that the nature of Bishop's developing ideal biography, however it ought to have situated her as an insightful outsider in Brazil, simply does not rescue the textual moves that make South America quaintly inferior and helplessly deficient in comparison to North America. Bracketing those textual moves out of an internal canon for Bishop is tempting but unfair. The Brazil poems have their uses as a site for observing how even the best-intentioned expatriates end up importing a cultural bias that one cannot easily imagine one's way out of—or, in the classroom, a way of holding our liberal self-confidence in check, of asking what prejudices we share with the poet that we so admire. Such texts should no more be suppressed in the study of Bishop than "Visits to St. Elizabeths"; in fact, they suggest a rationale for studying texts like Pound's Cantos that remain permanently objectionable. The lesson of the Cantos is that the aesthetics of high modernism slip easily into the politics of fascism. The lesson of "Brazil" is that one set of marginal experiences (lesbian) does not automatically give one membership in another (South American). The common elements of marginal experience are analogous, but not always in ways transparent to the experiencer.

While Bishop's work offers an opportunity to break from and to critique the projects of presence, ideal biography, and literary Americanism, it would be naïve to think that readers at any level beyond abso-

lute innocence of history could break out of all the implications of biographical reference. The poem that is quickly becoming Bishop's most
memorable anthology piece, "One Art," is a test case for the limits of
the avoidance of presence.

> —Even losing you (the joking voice, a gesture
> I love) I shan't have lied. It's evident
> the art of losing's not too hard to master
> though it may look like (*Write* it!) like disaster. (178)

The text of the poem is gender-neutral; even its speaker is only identified as a woman because she has lost her "mother's watch." The lover is
not identified at all. But the poem's rhetoric, in talking around its subject, in almost getting through the whole structure of the villanelle without *writing* it, subtly enacts the feeling of not daring to tell one's love's
name that still lies heavily on gay love poetry in the classroom or in
general reviews.

When reading and teaching this poem (written in 1975), I have always assumed that it was about Lota de Macedo Soares, the poet's lover
from the early 1950s until her 1967 suicide.[71] But Brett C. Millier suggests that the poem, while hardly unconnected to Soares (who figures
metonymically in the "continent" and the "loved houses"), was actually written during a period when Bishop feared she was going to lose the
love of Alice Methfessel.[72] And this single suggestion from the poet's
"actual biography" makes every difference to reading the poem; it becomes a factor one cannot ignore. If "One Art" is only about Soares, it
is a poem that puts a brave face on tragedy but lets the tragedy through
at the end. If it is a poem to Methfessel, it has a happy ending because
its brave face is almost a seductive bluff, and the ending is an admission of need rather than an irruption of despair.

The way to teach (and to "read," in the sense of teaching oneself)
"One Art" in a manner that employs reception, the inescapability of
biographical narrative, and a sense of the potential "textuality" of the
poem (in Roland Barthes's sense of openness to possibility) is therefore
not to enclose the poem as icon or shut it off from life but to try every
approach. Connect it with a lost lover; connect it with one potentially
regained. Detach it momentarily from its author, reverse its gender signs
and permutations, return it to its setting. Imagine different situations
for its writing (because all that matter now are the many possible situations for its reading).

I may seem to be saying "deconstruct" the poem, but deconstruction
carries the connotation of an absolute denial of the reader's personality,
a denial I would as absolutely object to. The first close deconstructive

reading of the poem by David Shapiro talks about everything *but* the poem's personal sexual appeal: "A reading of this poem shows it as a *grammatology* in Derrida's sense, a scene of writing given to us as an analysis of writing itself, with all the whims of an almost absolute negativity. . . . The poem has not at its coda but at its very non-Aristotelian heart the art of losing oneself, the art of losing a self, the art of almost losing a text, the art of losing the shifty shifter 'you.' . . . This is a poem that is not tied down to things nor morbidly dependent upon the earth."[73] There could be no clearer practical example than Shapiro's reading of "One Art" that deconstructive readings in American critical practice are as totalizing as those of the poetics of presence. Shapiro's reading is the extreme of a negation of readerly presence, seeing the text unavoidably as a site for the analysis of writing, which, like *any* text, it logically *must* be. Such assertions are nonstatements, but their danger is not merely in their nonsense but in their foreclosure of any moral response. Readings like Shapiro's thereby explain the attractions of presence for feminist criticism and the manifold objections (which are hardly ubiquitous or total) that feminist critics have made to poststructuralist theory. One cannot read texts as sites for a discourse of gender if texts cannot be anything but analyses of a neuter textuality.

Must feminist criticism then return to intentionality, to the old historicism, to ideal biography, in order to preserve a sense of the importance of gender to reading? Reception study should show that the answer is "no," precisely because the poem's affect *is* the poem. The poem is from a woman to her lost lover, and the dynamic played out in the poem modifies ("is modified in," W. H. Auden would say) the poem's readers, whether they are men or women, gay or straight. In a sense, the "formative" role of a poem like "One Art" scarcely exists in Jauss's realm of public and political events; it is subliminal in terms of universal history broadly conceived. It is all the more crucial to the role of literature in creating future histories. People read this poem, and people say, That is not how I love; or, That is how I have loved but could never tell anyone. If poetry means anything, that is how it means it.

Conclusion: The Continuing Presence of Dickinson

Texts and their readings work in the present, and work best in the present when the play of interpretation is given as much range as the texts will allow. In the first chapter of this study, I theorized that texts (or the communities that surround them) *do* act to constrain readings—but not always in the direction of univocality. The power of a text like "One Art" may reside in the fact that its referents stay just out of the reader's grasp, so that the text remains "open" in Umberto Eco's sense. It may seem tempting to nail such a text once and for all to a definite referent. But just as Eco demonstrates with respect to closed texts like the Superman comic book cycle, the closed text has a way of producing multiple antithetical readings—or, rather, interpretive communities in the face of a closed text are free to build mutually uncommunicative, and ultimately incomprehensible, dialects of interpretive discourse around the text.

It may be that the final result of any interpretive strategy that seeks to freeze a text in the moment of its historical production functions to close that text. In this way, a biographically oriented feminism is akin not just to old historicisms like Robertsonianism but also to the enabling closures effected by conspiracy theories of one kind or another (whether fictional, as in Eco's novels, or all too real, as in the Kennedy assassination). To conclude that the texts that a woman writes must be anchored in the solution to her actual biography is to submit to the desire to escape from reception by returning to the actual fixed presence of the woman writer. One's own readings will then be cleansed by a fidelity to the actual circumstances of that author's life.

But the escape from reception brings the present reader back with present preconceptions to the figure of the woman behind the texts—a figure no less deferred and displaced by feminist readings than by any other kinds of interpretation. That woman author becomes a site for enlistment into the theoretical battles of the present, the kind of enlistment that often obscures her real conservatism. Dickinson, Moore, and Bishop wrote many conservative texts and lived conservative lives in their respective cultures. If they had been radicals—as many of their contemporaries were—we could not read them so easily today. If they had been radicals their voices would not have found early reception in male-dominated literary and academic communities. That is the paradox of the reception that makes women's writing available as it mutes those women's voices.

Feminist interpretation of Emily Dickinson is hardly limited to those readings based on the desire to escape from reception that I will critique here. One should not make generalizations about "feminist criticism of Emily Dickinson"; it would take another study the length of this one even to begin to write its history. Feminist criticism of Dickinson begins with Susan Gilbert. It moves into print with Ellen Battelle Dietrick in the 1890s and Ella Gilbert Ives in the 1900s, and it begins to establish a sense of its own tradition with the work of Amy Lowell. Rebecca Patterson and Ruth Miller were among the most perceptive and serious Dickinson critics of the 1950s and 1960s, and Sandra Gilbert and Susan Gubar made Dickinson a focal point in their enormously influential *The Madwoman in the Attic* (1979). In the last two decades the tradition becomes increasingly rich and diverse, mixing feminist approaches with other critical paradigms to produce a range of interpretations that represent most of the academic ways of reading now available and create some new ones. Barbara Mossberg has studied Dickinson family dynamics; Joanne Dobson has studied the context of Dickinson's work that the writing of other American women provides; Mary Loeffelholz has studied the implications of psychoanalysis and its feminist critiques; Cynthia Griffin Wolff has written a feminist-informed biography of the poet; and Joanne Feit Diehl has explored Dickinson's complex relation to her male precursors—and there are many others who could be mentioned. I name these specific studies to illustrate the strength and diversity of the field.[1]

All of these critics share some common ground and have disagreements with one another. By choosing to look at two of the sharpest and most distinctive feminist reimaginings of Dickinson's presence in recent years, by Paula Bennett and Martha Nell Smith, I am emphatically *not* claiming that these are the only, or the typical, current feminist approaches to Dickinson. They are far from catalyzing a new orthodoxy of thought about Dickinson; but Bennett and Smith, in their own different ways, have established principles for reading Dickinson that no critic can ignore—and these principles deserve treatment here, to see how the poetics of presence continues to work its way into contemporary discourse.

Paula Bennett's *Emily Dickinson: Woman Poet*, particularly the chapter "Of Genre, Gender, and Sex," and Martha Nell Smith's *Rowing in Eden: Rereading Emily Dickinson* take quite different approaches to reestablishing a presence for Dickinson behind her poems—so different, it might be fair to say, that what one critic brings into focus requires a blurring of the other's central concern.[2] Bennett reads Dickinson's texts as encoding a physical, genital sexuality that informs nearly every image of poems that are both auto- and homoerotic. But Bennett is deliberately inconclusive about the addressees of these poems, staying outside the tradition of guessing the identity of Dickinson's lover(s). Smith, by contrast, does not have to guess who Dickinson's lover was; the extant correspondence between Emily Dickinson and Susan Gilbert Dickinson speaks for itself of a love relationship between the two women. But Smith is far less certain than Bennett about the need to establish this love affair as one of primarily genital sexuality, and she suggests that the dimensions of desire, especially for women without a social framework to serve as a context for their love, are not easily reducible to physical facts.

But love is the focus of both readings of Dickinson. As we have seen in chapter 3, the potential that Dickinson's texts offered for eroticizing readings by male critics early in this century was an important component of her early acceptance into the canon. A potential for feminist eroticizing seems to be an important component of some current work in maintaining Dickinson's canonical status. Both Bennett and Smith make the strongest possible arguments for Dickinson's strength as a major poet; and both do so by perpetuating the attachment of the Dickinson texts to an authorial presence beyond.

Bennett's argument is less theoretically geared than Smith's (Bennett specifically states that hers "is not a theoretically-oriented study" [22]). It is also more tendentious and more provocative. Bennett starts by quoting one of the more outrageous expressions of male Victorian organicism, Charles D. Meigs's 1851 assertion that "strong" poetic ideas are "not woman's province, power, nor mission" (151). The well-diffused cultural idea that the gender of a writer's body determines the strength of that writer's expression was clearly as salient a problem for Dickinson as it had been for Anne Bradstreet or would be for Gilbert and Gubar. As Bennett proceeds to demonstrate, the salience of that cultural construction of gender can serve as the point of departure for reading Dickinson's coded resistance to it—a resistance that tends to come in the form of an exaggeration of women's assigned roles of littleness, hiddenness, and innerness.

Dickinson assures her unnamed "Master" that she "bends her smaller life to his" (L-248, *SL* p. 167)—and this is exactly where Bennett locates her poetic power. Instead of challenging the power that the male feels is rooted in the phallus only he possesses, Dickinson asserts herself through a hidden, diminutive, clitorocentric power. Bennett reads the assertion of this clitorocentric power through Dickinson's many invocations of "small, round objects" (172), such as bees, crumbs, pellets, peas, pebbles. "Like phallic images . . . such images have a sexual base, and so does the power women so paradoxically attribute to them. In identifying their 'little hard nut[s]'—or their little flowers—with 'something precious,' women are expressing through the paradoxes of their symbolism their body's subjective consciousness of itself. That is, they are expressing their conscious or unconscious awareness of the organic foundation of their (oxymoronic) sexual power" (172). Bennett herself characterizes this argument "fearfully" as "treading close to essentialism" (212), but that is not quite the problem that I sense there—or, rather, the problem is in a different register. The psychological essentialism of female subjectivity is one issue; the more general poetics of presence is another. What I am concerned with in Bennett's analysis is not where Dickinson's subjective consciousness resided, nor whether one cedes ground to gender essentialists by locating it, but how much it matters to reading the texts.

Bennett's readings finally center on an organicist notion of poetic expression: "this concept of female sexuality validated the poet's view of herself and of her poetry: unknown yet great, a "Child" yet still a "Queen," a rosebud that could speak with power" (180). Organicism implies originality ("few women poets take their commitment to the small as far as Dickinson did" [212]); organicism and originality together entail a reading of the monologic, clitorocentric voice in the texts. So in poem after poem Bennett identifies and names the refractions of image after image as clitorally centered, and, borrowing Naomi Schor's "definition of the clitoral as 'detail'," she speculates in a footnote that "Dickinson's poetry, in so far as it privileges both smallness and detail, is clitoral throughout" (212).

My critique of Bennett is ultimately not one of content at all but of the framing of content. It is a critique of the way that scholarly arguments are produced and validated. The brilliance of Bennett's readings is that she identifies, quite fearlessly, the resonances that sexual imagery in Dickinson's texts can have for a reader attuned to their patterns and contexts. After Bennett, one cannot read certain Dickinson poems in old ways ever again—as we have seen already when encountering "Forbidden fruit a flavor has" (P-1377) in its Victorian printing. But to validate her own readings, Bennett depends not on the license of textuality or on her own rhetorical power but on the devices of presence, constructing an ad hoc narrative of the sexuality of the historical Emily Dickinson, tracing its contextual affiliations to other nineteenth-century texts, and in short positing a woman who apparently lived for autoerotic experience that included homoerotic fantasies.

The distinction between content and frame in scholarly argument is not, one hopes, over-subtle. In fact, in both classroom and scholarship, it is a distinction with widely divergent ramifications. It is one thing to say (content) that poems by Emily Dickinson provoke thought about autoeroticism and include homoerotic imagery that her contemporaries could elide but that we can no longer ignore. It is another thing altogether to say (frame) that Emily Dickinson, spinster of Amherst, sat around masturbating and thinking of other women—and although this is *not* what Bennett says, it is what is both implied by presence-based arguments and heard by audiences who read about "her homoerotic and autoerotic commitment to women" (180). The image of Emily Dickinson masturbating is not itself a problem. The image of her desiring, or still more achieving, an articulation of autoeroticism that would have been audible in her own culture or even *to herself* is the problem, because it dehistoricizes the poet absolutely in one grand gesture of feminist enlistment. Reading Dickinson in Bennett's terms becomes an enlistment of a feminist representation of the woman poet in the service of a late twentieth-century discourse of female sexuality. Bennett, as it were, presses the mute button to get the sound of Dickinson's voice back; but her own argument has been that Dickinson's voice is muted as a condition of its rhetorical strategy. Bennett proceeds to recuperate the poet's voice through an interpretive process that remasters that voice as if the constraints that were its precondition had never existed. By framing that recuperation as homo- and autoerotic, Bennett places Dickinson squarely in the tradition of Walt Whitman, as the American Homer has come to be reinterpreted in the 1990s as the great gay precursor. The power of Bennett's Dickinson is still a power very much in line with the Whitman template, obscuring still further the sexual differences that made the situation of Victorian women historically unique.

In Bennett's chapter, we can see the limits that a presence-based eroticization of texts continues to impose even upon interpretations that have great potential impact on the poet's reception. In Smith's *Rowing in Eden*, the theoretical problems are more far-reaching and more totalizing. It

would be fair to say of Smith's book that it is the fullest and most serious intentionalist, testamentary recuperation of Dickinson yet attempted, and that it finally accords Dickinson unreservedly the level of creative seriousness usually represented in American literary studies by
Melville, Twain, or Faulkner. Any scholar who has devoted years to the
study of the poet must thank Smith for taking that study to this new
level. Smith completes the textual recuperation of Dickinson's true intentions that began with Bianchi's publication of the manuscripts held
by Susan Dickinson and is carried out in increasingly diplomatic textual criticism by Bingham, Johnson, Franklin, and Susan Howe. At the
same time, Smith argues for the holistic aesthetic value of this true intention in a way that has never quite been dared in past scholarship.
And she maintains, in a far more thoroughgoing way than Sewall or
Wolff or Judith Farr, that the center of Emily Dickinson's emotional
life—in the realm of "actual" biography—was in her relationship with
Susan.[3] Even those readers who cannot accept the whole of Smith's
claims on these issues will find their thinking about them to be affected
by her persuasive arguments well into the twenty-first century.

Smith's theoretical method might be described as a poststructuralist
intentionalism—and why not, for the ne plus ultra of anti-intentional-
ism was certainly reached in the structuralist concept of the crystalline
text. Having swung so far, Foucault's pendulum begins to come back toward authorial intention even in that theorist's own "What Is an Author?" Feminist critics have a powerful incentive to exploit intentionalism, because, as Smith points out, "for women to forswear or play with
the idea of relinquishing authorial power they have traditionally been
denied is a quite different matter than for men to do so" (56). Smith
describes her slant on intentionalism in this way:

> Speculating about Dickinson's intentions, we need not be regulatory and
> draw inflexible conclusions circumscribing her desires or literary experi-
> mentations, but, aware that our horizons of expectations are predeter-
> mined by standard histories and literary traditions, should consciously
> cultivate horizonal change. More than a century ago, Dickinson produced
> works that call all our modes of textual regulation into question and re-
> mind us, as do the tenets of contemporary literary theory, that a control
> which proposes to fix and finish literary or biographical texts, even if pred-
> icated on an author's plainly stated intention, is in fact illusory. (57)

Authorial power, intention, critical power (and the energy it draws from
authorial power), and textuality run somewhat together in this analysis, but it is admirably balanced. The test of Smith's theoretical balance
between intention and textuality must of course be her actual specula-

tion on Dickinson's work, and it therefore makes sense to proceed directly to her most tendentious speculation on intention and reception—the reading of the poem that gives her book its title, "Wild Nights—Wild Nights!" (P-249).

Smith prints the 1891 edition of this poem, which reads:

> Wild nights! Wild nights!
>   Were I with thee,
> Wild nights should be
> Our luxury!
>
> Futile the winds
> To a heart in port,—
> Done with the compass,
> Done with the chart.
>
> Rowing in Eden!
> Ah! the sea!
> Might I but moor
> To-night in thee! (Smith 65)

She then says of this publication, "Though he says that they should change her word 'as little as possible,' Higginson gave his nod to this sanitized version of 'Wild Nights'" (65). Sanitized because, as an untrammeled erotic lyric, the poem could not appear in its manuscript form in front of a Victorian reading audience.

One anticipates something pretty shocking in that manuscript. When Smith prints it in facsimile (66), the shock amounts to this: Todd and Higginson mislineated the final stanza of the poem. In print transcription ("translation" is Smith's much more evocative term), that stanza reads:

> Rowing in Eden—
> Ah! the Sea!
> Might I but moor—
> Tonight—
> In thee!

Apart from this change (and changes in punctuation and, of course, the transition from calligraphy to typeface), the 1891 Todd-Higginson version of the poem is verbally identical to the manuscript. But the poem was "sanitized" in this first edition "since Higginson and Loomis Todd most likely did not imagine that Dickinson meant for the last stanza to be five lines" (67). Thomas H. Johnson repeated their sanitizing. "The idea of a regular four-line stanza dictates the perception of these editors" (67).

If this is one of Dickinson's "radical experimentations" (67), it is perhaps the feeblest radical experiment ever made in verse. It would be fair to ask what possible difference there could be between verbally identical four-line and five-line stanzas. Smith's answer is that the five-line version employs "unconventional lineation, encouraging readers to passionate pause, consonant with the poem's sensual suggestions" (65). In other words, it resists performability in a slightly different way. Smith's intentionalism urges her to bear witness to this resistance. At the same time, her poststructuralism urges her to characterize Dickinson's textual practice as one that "spotlights the meaning-producing processes of give and take between author and text, text and reader, reader and author, inevitable in reading" (52).

The implication of Smith's reading is that the fusion between intentionalism and poststructuralism breaks down at the scale of translating manuscript to print. Smith has clearly chosen this minimal-distinction example to be as provocative as possible, to test that fusion to its limits. But if the point of the texts is the latitude they offer for the performability of freeplay (especially oral/aural freeplay), then the difference between a four- and a five-line stanza is nil. If the point of the texts is to convey absolute intentionalist control, the choice of a four-line translation indeed "sanitizes" the poem, because only the five-line version can adequately convey the very determinate "passionate pause."

But "sanitizing" is only a meaningful term to apply to what Todd and Higginson did to this poem if one assumes a horizon of expectations that is intentionalist at a virtually scriptural level—and this is where reception falls decisively out of Smith's critical suspension. It is simply inconceivable that any reader could read the 1891 printing of the poem and then, turning to the manuscript version, have felt that the print version sanitized the other. One might indeed be shocked by either version, and one might indeed prefer the calligraphic manuscript to the print version, but it is hard to see any sort of bowdlerizing impulse to the editorial act performed here. Nor would a nineteenth-century reader—I daresay not even the ghost of Edgar Allan Poe—have been able to perceive a radically original formal experiment in the five-line stanza. Yet to ascribe such originality to Dickinson is an imperative of Smith's use of the poetics of presence.

Unless, of course, one *is* at the level of scriptural exegesis—and then, as any student of the New Testament knows, there are no accidental accidentals, only inspired ones. But to seek inspiration on this scale—rather than on the far rougher and more tolerant scale of historically possible reception—is to make the author into God, and Smith's criticism into a kind of ritual curse on the defacer of the Book.

To return for the implications of this case for other feminist critics: such scriptural reverence for Dickinson's intentions is only fair play. For generations now, American literary scholars have devoted exactly such reverential treatment to accidentals and substantives in James Fenimore Cooper, in Stephen Crane, in Harold Frederic—and in virtually no woman writer other than Dickinson. One can hardly request that feminist critics forgo the institutional prestige conferred on women writers (and therefore on women critics) by such textual scholarship; and Dickinson scholars, female or male, are in debt to Smith for her continual deepening of textual questions about this woman writer in particular.

Far more troubling than the implications of Smith's justifiable seriousness in textual matters is her overall interpretive framework, which returns, in an unqualified way, both to the projects of presence and to some of the corollary projects of American literary nationalism that do not even seem to be in her way but find themselves included in the package. Smith is concerned with the very real impact of theoretical issues of reception on current readings and disseminations of Dickinson and critiques the persistence of the myth of the "poetess" in images of Dickinson (45–46). She expects her own readings of Dickinson "to adduce ways in which the cycle of reception can be illuminatingly broken" (49). I suspect that the cycle of reception is no more breakable than the hermeneutic circle, but I will concede Smith at least that metaphor. What is harder to concede is what remains after she does, metaphorically, break it. The project of breaking out of reception leads one back to the validating presence of the author, and that presence has the effect of vitiating Smith's analyses.

The main conclusion of *Rowing in Eden* is that we have been reading the wrong text all along—that Dickinson's work should not be read in the sequences of theme, chronology, or even those of her own fascicles, which have served as the organizing principles of the successive editions. Instead, Smith proposes reading Emily Dickinson (and not just Dickinson but both women, who were equals) through her correspondence with Susan Huntington Gilbert Dickinson, her lover, neighbor, and sister-in-law. That correspondence is the natural textual unit for her work, which is further distorted by the current division of it into "poems" and "letters," with the consequent scattering of this central correspondence over six volumes and two genres. Smith instead argues for the essentially poetic genre of the "letter-poem."[4]

The idea is compelling. We are faced with an author who had no "public" ideal biography but who created her authorial biography more in her correspondence with her sister-in-law than anywhere else. In recuperating this biography, Smith asks us and shows us how to imagine our way back into the circumstances of a love relationship between Dickinson and Sue (as she continues to call them despite their status as equals; the canonical author keeps the privilege of a last-name basis). To read these texts, we must continuously rehearse the biographical events that enabled the texts to be produced, because "through all the anger, disappointments, exultations, emotional distance, and intense spiritual, intellectual, and erotic unions that inevitably accompany a deep and lasting love relationship, Dickinson equated Sue with Eden, the land of imagination" (205). The two were collaborators in a "poetry workshop" (evidence of which survives in the drafts of "Safe in Their Alabaster Chambers") and were lesbian lovers somewhere along Adrienne Rich's continuum from emotional friendship to genital sexuality.

Smith insists that "what these characterizations tell about biography will ever be open to question" (158), but just as in the attempt to read "Wild Nights" in an indeterminate way, the attempt to read the Dickinson-Sue correspondence in an indeterminate way shades into determinism. Their intimate correspondence is unique and private, reaching the limits of a shared duolect (which is drawn still further in the direction of monologism by the fact that virtually none of Sue's half of the correspondence survives). The correspondence bears the traces of great emotional pain—especially because someone (Austin Dickinson has been blamed) tried to mutilate so much of it. It is the organic record of years of lived female experience.

And what of its status as text? Smith implies that to read the correspondence faithfully is to relive it, to summon up the presence of its authors and reenact their love affair in an almost ritualistic way. To attempt to play with the text of the correspondence would be to violate the extremely personal and specific terms of its commitment to paper. The further we move toward a sense of correspondence rather than "poems" or "letters," the further our generic confidence breaks down and the more we must submit ourselves to the uniquely informing presence of the correspondents' lives—since the traces authorize no other approach. In Smith's readings, this leads to an emotional reidentification with Sue and her struggles in particular—and disdain for Mabel Loomis Todd, who becomes the "other woman," "who edited her texts posthumously but never met her face to face" (131), who must be driven out of her tainted relationship to the Dickinson texts, where she is "mutilator" (286), tamperer, creator of gaps and errors, producer of malicious gossip, and generally more of a wrecker of the lesbian hearth than she ever was of Sue's heterosexual marriage.[5]

The ultimate cultural value at stake in the invocation of the poetics of presence for reading this correspondence is nothing less than the project of Americanism. Smith explains the political significance of Dickinson's mixing of poetry and letters in her correspondence with Sue:

> Such moves constitute the ultimate democratization of poetry, integrating it into quotidian production. In an age when Emerson, declaring "We have listened too long to the courtly muses of Europe" (see "The American Scholar"), called for America's literary independence and yearned for a truly American poet while Whitman worked hard to fulfill such a dream, these "letter-poems" were, as Sue Dickinson seemed to realize, part of that same cultural and artistic project. (111)

We have come back, in this story, to Rupert Hughes's 1896 connection of Dickinson to Whitman because both were "bigly democratic." The ultimate value and purpose of literature, even in such an uncompromisingly feminist and poststructuralist analysis, is to advance the Americanist project of a kind of tautologically defined "democracy."

How can criticism become free of the inherited values of presence and the projects of literary nationalism? I will step aside at this point and allow a transnational lesbian critic to suggest one way. (The conclusion of this book will be as much as possible hers and not mine.) Elizabeth Bishop's reading of Rebecca Patterson's reading of Emily Dickinson was determined in its production, certainly, by the ethics of the closet that surrounded all of her texts. The review was distinctly transnational in its production, too: Bishop wrote it aboard the ship that was taking her to Brazil for the first time.[6] But these circumstances of production are merely neat coincidences. The usefulness of Bishop's reading of Patterson today is that it retains a critical potential well beyond its production, in its own sense of a dialogic basis for the reception of texts.

In 1952, Bishop reviewed Rebecca Patterson's *The Riddle of Emily Dickinson* for *The New Republic*. Patterson's book was the first thorough attempt to identify Dickinson's lover as a specific woman, Kate Scott Anthon. Bishop found that specific identification no more convincing than the next forty years of Dickinson scholarship have found it. What is especially interesting is Bishop's discomfort with the way Patterson reads a dialogic set of texts—the Dickinson poems and letters—as clues to a unitary narrative. "For 400 pages Mrs. Patterson tracks down the until now unknown person (she believes it to have been a person, not persons) for whom Emily Dickinson is supposed to have cherished a hopeless passion and to whom she is supposed to have written every one of her love poems. . . . That her thesis is partially true might have occurred to any reader of Emily Dickinson's poetry—occurred on one page to be contradicted on the next."[7] Bishop denies that Patterson has proved her thesis, but she does not attempt to debunk or disprove the basic idea that Dickinson could have been in love with another woman; nor does she reject the idea that Kate Scott might have been briefly one of the poet's love interests. The deduction that Bishop finds unseemly is not sexual but narrative; the conclusion that she is intent on resisting is not that of lesbian attachments but that of a totalizing reading that would locate all of Dickinson's poetic motivation in a single love affair.

Bishop suggests that Patterson failed to take into account "the possibility that a poet may write from sources other than autobiographical, the perfectly real enjoyment in living expressed in many of the poems, the satisfaction that Emily Dickinson must have felt in her work, no matter what, and, quite simply, the more demonstrative manners of another period. When the poems are quoted they are used or misused merely as bits of 'evidence,' and poor Mrs. Anthon's exuberant underlinings in the books of poetry she carried with her are subjected to the same treatment."[8]

That poetry can be about life but at the same time proceed from sources "other than autobiographical" is a concept diametrically opposed to the assumptions of the poetics of presence. Abandoning those assumptions, Bishop frees herself to read a corpus of poetry in a dialogic way, untroubled by the nature of Dickinson's writing, where every page is "contradicted by the next."

Notes

Preface

1. Jane Tompkins writes: "A literary classic is a product of all those circumstances of which it has traditionally been supposed to be independent" (*Sensational Designs: The Cultural Work of American Fiction, 1790–1860* [New York: Oxford University Press, 1986], 4). According to Paul Lauter, "the literary canon is, in short, a means by which culture validates social power" (*Canons and Contexts* [New York: Oxford University Press, 1991], 23).

2. Denis Donoghue argues that "the question of literary merit, as distinct from sociological interest, is rarely raised by feminist critics. When it is, the argument is desperate" ("A Criticism of One's Own," in *Men in Feminism*, ed. Alice Jardine and Paul Smith [New York: Methuen, 1987], 149). For a good overview of the struggle between power and intrinsic value in thought about the canon of nineteenth-century American literature, see Frederick Crews, "Whose American Renaissance?" *New York Review of Books* (27 Oct. 1988): 68–81.

3. See Barbara Herrnstein Smith, *Contingencies of Value: Alternative Perspectives for Critical Theory* (Cambridge, Mass.: Harvard University Press, 1988), esp. pp. 17–27.

4. Ibid., 17, 28.

5. In an important sense, David Reynolds's *Beneath the American Renaissance: The Subversive Imagination in the Age of Emerson and Melville* (New York: Knopf, 1988) can be seen as the most wide-ranging and comprehensive attempt at an enlistment of "major" "literary" authors (Reynolds's terms) in the cause of pluralism. Reynolds traces the roots of the literary accomplishments of the major figures of the American Renaissance to the popular culture that is usually neglected as "beneath" the canon. Far from being emblems for elitism, the major authors, in Reynolds's argument, participate as the best representatives of the wider literary world.

6. See Peter Carafiol, *The American Ideal: Literary History as a Worldly Activity* (New York: Oxford University Press, 1991); Carafiol, "Commentary: After American Literature," *American Literary History* 4 (1992): 539–49.

7. See Roman Jakobson, "Linguistics and Poetics," reprinted in *Modern Criticism and Theory*, ed. David Lodge (London: Longman, 1988), 33–34.

8. For "universal" themes in particularized works, see the backs of paperback classics. There is possibly no better (or more widely read) formulation of the value of universality than this often-derided set of *seuils* to the received canon. Some random examples: Chekhov's "ability to explore simple situations for the fullest, most universal meanings [is] unsurpassed" (Anton Chekhov, *Four Great Plays* [New York: Bantam, 1958], back cover); "The stories of Sarah Orne Jewett and Mary Wilkins Freeman offer the modern reader . . . insight into human dilemmas still pertinent today" (*Short Fiction of Sarah Orne Jewett and Mary Wilkins Freeman* [New York: Signet, 1979], back cover); Melville's *White-Jacket* is "both a fascinating documentary of Navy life in the 1840s and an unforgettable exploration of human ethics, justice needs, and the depths of the human soul" ([New York: Signet, 1979], back cover).

9. See Lauter, "Race and Gender in the Shaping of the American Literary Canon: A Case Study from the Twenties," *Canons and Contexts*, 22–47; Harold H. Kolb, Jr., "Defining the Canon," in *Redefining American Literary History*, ed. LaVonne Brown Ruoff and Jerry W. Ward, Jr. (New York: Modern Language Association, 1990), 35–51.

10. See Anna Mary Wells, "Early Criticism of Emily Dickinson," *American Literature* 1 (1929): 243–59. See further James Woodress, ed., *Eight American Authors* (New York: Norton, 1971); Jackson R. Bryer, ed., *16 Modern American Authors* (Durham: Duke University Press, 1990); Earl N. Harbert and Robert A. Rees, eds., *15 American Authors before 1900* (Madison: University of Wisconsin Press, 1984). For an insightful discussion of Willa Cather's literary fame, see Sharon O'Brien, "Becoming Noncanonical: The Case against Willa Cather," *American Quarterly* 40 (1988): 110–26.

11. See Margaret Holley, *The Poetry of Marianne Moore: A Study in Voice and Value* (Cambridge: Cambridge University Press, 1987).

12. *Complete Poetry and Selected Prose of Walt Whitman*, ed. James E. Miller, Jr. (Boston: Houghton, 1959), 456.

13. Ibid.; *Poems by Emily Dickinson*, ed. Martha Dickinson Bianchi and Alfred Leete Hampson (Boston: Little, 1937); Marianne Moore, *Selected Poems* (New York: Macmillan, 1935); Elizabeth Bishop, *The Complete Poems 1927–1979* (New York: Farrar, 1983). All references to these books will be by parenthetical page number in the text.

Chapter 1: The Poetics of Presence in Literary Reception

1. A very lack of rigorous formulation distinguishes "presence" in my sense from the more technical sense employed by Jacques Derrida, "Structure, Sign and Play in the Discourse of the Human Sciences," in *The Structuralist Controversy: The Languages of Criticism and the Sciences of Man*, ed. Richard Macksey and Eugenio Donato, trans. Alan Bass (Baltimore: Johns Hopkins University Press, 1972), 247–65. Here, "presence" is for Derrida the sense of an authority at the center of a structure of meanings that can ultimately connect signifier to

referent and therefore ground the system rather than laying it open to endless deferral and substitution. Derrida's concept of presence is perhaps the central insight of poststructuralist thought, but for much of the prestructuralist criticism that I discuss here, this insight would simply not have registered—for the excellent reason that these critics (from E. P. Whipple through Stuart Sherman to John Hollander) conceive of textuality not just in terms of hermeneutic authority but in terms of the actual living image of the writer.

2. Michel Foucault, "What Is an Author?" reprinted in *Modern Criticism and Theory*, 204.

3. A. C. Goodson, "Structuralism and Critical History in the Moment of Bakhtin," in *Tracing Literary Theory*, ed. Joseph Natoli (Urbana: University of Illinois Press, 1987), 42.

4. Joseph Natoli, "Tracing a Beginning through Past Theory Voices," in *Tracing Literary Theory*, 23.

5. Recent studies of dialogic poetry include David B. Morris, "Burns and Heteroglossia," *The Eighteenth Century: Theory and Interpretation* 28.1 (1987): 3–27; David H. Richter, "Dialogism and Poetry," *Studies in the Literary Imagination* 23.1 (1990): 9–27.

6. Lennard J. Davis, "The Monologic Imagination: M. M. Bakhtin and the Nature of Assertion," *Studies in the Literary Imagination* 23.1 (1990): 34.

7. M. M. Bakhtin, "Discourse in the Novel," *The Dialogic Imagination*, trans. Caryl Emerson and Michael Holquist (Austin: University of Texas Press, 1981), 278.

8. Studies of the unary dialogic artist include Morris's "Burns and Heteroglossia"; R. B. Kershner, *Joyce, Bakhtin, and Popular Literature: Chronicles of Disorder* (Chapel Hill: University of North Carolina Press, 1989); and Ian Marshall, "Heteroglossia in Lydia Maria Child's *Hobomok*," LEGACY 10.1 (1993): 1–16.

9. Tenney Nathanson, *Whitman's Presence: Body, Voice, and Writing in Leaves of Grass* (New York: New York University Press, 1992), 2.

10. Hans Robert Jauss, "Literary History as a Challenge to Literary Theory," *Toward an Aesthetic of Reception*, trans. Timothy Bahti (Minneapolis: University of Minnesota Press, 1982), 5.

11. John Macy, *The Spirit of American Literature* (New York: Boni, 1913), 210.

12. Levin L. Schücking, *The Sociology of Literary Taste*, trans. E. W. Dickes (1931; reprint, New York: Oxford University Press, 1944), 35.

13. See Ezra Greenspan, *Walt Whitman and the American Reader* (Cambridge: Cambridge University Press, 1990), chap. 7.

14. Thomas Kuhn, *The Structure of Scientific Revolutions* (Chicago: University of Chicago Press, 1970), explains the theory of paradigm shifts that has itself become a paradigm in the intellectual history of so many disciplines other than science.

15. See Carl L. Becker, *The Heavenly City of the Eighteenth-Century Philosophers* (New Haven: Yale University Press, 1932).

16. See Wolfgang Iser, *The Act of Reading: A Theory of Aesthetic Response*

(Baltimore: Johns Hopkins University Press, 1978); Michael Riffaterre, *Semiotics of Poetry* (Bloomington: Indiana University Press, 1978).

17. The fullest and most original version of the argument against idealized reader-response criticism is made in Stanley Fish's "Interpreting the *Variorum*," *Is There a Text in This Class?: The Authority of Interpretive Communities* (Cambridge, Mass.: Harvard University Press, 1980), 147–73.

18. See Janice A. Radway, *Reading the Romance: Women, Patriarchy, and Popular Literature* (Chapel Hill: University of North Carolina Press, 1984).

19. For an overview in Whitman studies one must go back to Charles B. Willard, *Whitman's American Fame: The Growth of His Reputation in America after 1892* (Providence: Brown University Press, 1950), which is still an intensely interesting and valuable book. Its counterpart in Dickinson studies is Klaus Lubbers, *Emily Dickinson: The Critical Revolution* (Ann Arbor: University of Michigan Press, 1968), which has never been superseded. For excellent specialized essays dealing with aspects of Whitman's reception, see Ed Folsom, "'Affording the Rising Generation an Adequate Notion': Walt Whitman in Nineteenth-Century Textbooks, Handbooks, and Anthologies," *Studies in the American Renaissance,* 15th ed., ed. Joel Myerson (Charlottesville: University Press of Virginia, 1991); Eric Savoy, "Reading Gay America: Walt Whitman, Henry James, and the Politics of Reception," in *The Continuing Presence of Walt Whitman: The Life after the Life,* ed. Robert K. Martin (Iowa City: University of Iowa Press, 1992), 3–15. No standard reception histories exist for either Moore or Bishop, probably because both became canonical after such studies fell out of fashion.

20. See O'Brien, "Becoming Noncanonical"; Jo-Ann Wallace, "Laura Riding and the Politics of Decanonization," *American Literature* 64 (1992): 111–26.

21. Northrop Frye, seen by Barbara Herrnstein Smith as one of the principal exilers of evaluation, actually tended to see value as self-evident, ridiculing attempts to establish "a theory explaining *why* some writer is of the first rank, and another only of the tenth," for instance ("On Value Judgments," in *Criticism,* ed. L. S. Dembo [Madison: University of Wisconsin Press, 1968], 41–42). But that same essay is also Frye's implicit admission that any author, any text, is as worthy of study as another; in achieving an impossible theory of value, Frye says, "we should also be proving that it was less important to study the smaller man" (42). For Frye—a problematic but very influential and enabling theorist—the very devotion of study to "the smaller man" is a self-confirming value judgment, because "when a critic interprets, he is talking about his poet; when he evaluates, he is talking about himself, or, at most, about himself as a representative of his age" (39).

22. Hershel Parker suggests that such writers *were* read by graduate students of the 1950s but relegated to a "specialist" canon deemed unworthy of major professional research. When feminist critics trained only in the general canon first encountered these writers, they only apparently "rediscovered" what their supposedly better-trained elders had known about all along. Sounds like an institutional force to me. See *Flawed Texts and Verbal Icons: Literary Authority in American Fiction* (Evanston: Northwestern University Press, 1984), 235.

23. John Guillory sees current moves to bring women writers into the can-

on as "modernizing" moves, not rightings of gender biases. In Guillory's analysis "the existence of canonical women authors, even before the revisionary movement of the last decade, invalidates in strictly logical terms the category of gender as a *general* criterion of exclusion; which is to say that in the case of an excluded woman author, it will not be sufficient merely to invoke the category of gender in order to explain the lack of canonical status. The principle that explains the exclusion of Harriet Beecher Stowe from the canon on the basis of gender cannot really account for the complexity of the historical circumstances governing the reception of Stowe's work, for the same reason that it cannot account for the counterexample of Jane Austen's canonical status" (*Cultural Capital: The Problem of Literary Canon Formation* [Chicago: University of Chicago Press, 1993], 17). But I would see Austen (in American literary scholarship, Dickinson) not as a counter*example* but as the well-known exception that proves the rule. In the study of British literature Austen has always been the great miniaturist who proves by her mastery of an excessively constricted milieu that women should attempt nothing beyond that milieu. The general exclusion of so many women who *did* attempt much beyond it is precisely the problem.

24. Betsy Erkkila, *The Wicked Sisters: Women Poets, Literary History, and Discord* (New York: Oxford University Press, 1992), 16.

25. Ibid.

26. Margaret Mead writes: "Men owe their manhood to a theft and a theatrical mime, which would fall to the ground in a moment as mere dust and ashes if its true constituents were known. A shaky structure, protected by endless taboos and precautions, . . . it survives only as long as every one keeps the rules. Iatmul men who see their whole social order threatened by the coming of the European threaten in tearful rage to complete the ruin by showing the flutes to the women, and the missionary who shows the flutes to the women has broken the culture successfully" (*Male and Female: A Study of the Sexes in a Changing World* [New York: William Morrow, 1949], 103). I quote this remarkable passage with some consciousness of the ironies possible in its application to male involvement in feminist theory.

27. Martha Nell Smith, *Rowing in Eden: Rereading Emily Dickinson* (Austin: University of Texas Press, 1992).

28. E. D. Hirsch's formulation of the interplay between determinate meaning and open-ended significance can both frame and illuminate reception-based studies. Hirsch states that "quite aside from the context in which the utterance occurs, the details of meaning that an interpreter understands are powerfully determined and constituted by his meaning expectations. And these expectations arise from the interpreter's conception of the type of meaning that is being expressed" (*Validity in Interpretation* [New Haven: Yale University Press, 1967], 72).

29. For the concept of "interpretive community," see Fish, *Is There a Text in This Class?*

30. See Susan K. Harris, *19th-Century American Women's Novels: Interpretative Strategies* (Cambridge: Cambridge University Press, 1990); Cathy N. David-

son, *Revolution and the Word: The Rise of the Novel in America* (New York: Oxford University Press, 1986); Nina Baym, *Novels, Readers and Reviewers: Responses to Fiction in Antebellum America* (Ithaca: Cornell University Press, 1984).

31. See Stanley Fish, *Doing What Comes Naturally: Change, Rhetoric and the Practice of Theory in Literary and Legal Studies* (Durham: Duke University Press, 1989).

32. For an analogy in sociological thought, see David Layzer, "On the Evolution of Intelligence and Social Behavior," in *Sociobiology Examined,* ed. Ashley Montagu (New York: Oxford University Press, 1980), 220–53. Layzer treats human nature in general as an emergent rather than a deterministic phenomenon.

33. See Umberto Eco, "Introduction: The Role of the Reader," *The Role of the Reader* (Bloomington: Indiana University Press, 1979), 3–43.

34. Walter M. Miller, Jr., *A Canticle for Leibowitz* (1959; reprint, New York: Bantam, 1976).

35. See Harold Bloom, *A Map of Misreading* (1975; reprint, Oxford: Oxford University Press, 1980).

36. Eco writes: "Those texts that obsessively aim at arousing a precise response on the part of more or less precise empirical readers . . . are in fact open to any possible 'aberrant' decoding" ("Introduction: The Role of the Reader," 8).

37. *An American in Paris,* dir. Vincente Minnelli, M-G-M, 1951.

38. Gérard Genette, *Palimpsestes: La littérature au second degré* (Paris: Seuil, 1982), 263.

39. See Gérard Genette, *Seuils* (Paris: Seuil, 1987).

40. See Roy Harvey Pearce, *The Continuity of American Poetry* (1961; reprint, Princeton: Princeton University Press, 1977).

41. See Harold Bloom, *Wallace Stevens: The Poems of Our Climate* (Ithaca: Cornell University Press, 1977).

42. Harold Bloom, "Introduction," *Eugene O'Neill* (*Modern Critical Views*) (New York: Chelsea House, 1987), 2. The irony here is that O'Neill is practically the only writer that Bloom would place outside of the transcendentally defined American tradition; in order to place O'Neill, Bloom sums up that entire tradition at some length.

43. Terence Diggory, *Yeats and American Poetry: The Tradition of the Self* (Princeton: Princeton University Press, 1983).

44. Mutlu Konuk Blasing, *American Poetry: The Rhetoric of Its Forms* (New Haven: Yale University Press, 1987).

45. Jeffrey Walker, *Bardic Ethos and the American Epic Poem: Whitman, Pound, Crane, Williams, Olson* (Baton Rouge: Louisiana State University Press, 1989); Thomas Gardner, *Discovering Ourselves in Whitman: The Contemporary American Long Poem* (Urbana: University of Illinois Press, 1989), 1.

46. See *Voices and Visions: The Poet in America,* ed. Helen Vendler (New York: Random House, 1987).

47. David Bromwich, *Politics by Other Means: Higher Education and Group Thinking* (New Haven: Yale University Press, 1992), 101.

48. F. O. Matthiessen, "Introduction," *The Oxford Book of American Verse* (New York: Oxford University Press, 1950), xxvii.

49. See Sanford Pinsker, "Philip Rahv's 'Paleface and Redskin'—Fifty Years Later," *Georgia Review* 43 (1989): 477–89.

50. Philip Rahv, "Paleface and Redskin," *Kenyon Review* 1.3 (1939): 251–52.

51. Ibid., 254.

52. Ibid., 255.

53. Ibid., 256.

54. See Lewis Mumford, *The Golden Day: A Study in American Experience and Culture* (New York: Horace Liveright, 1926).

55. See Daniel Hoffman, *Poe Poe Poe Poe Poe Poe Poe* (1972; reprint, New York: Vintage, 1985).

56. Joanne Feit Diehl, *Women Poets and the American Sublime* (Bloomington: Indiana University Press, 1990), 3.

57. See Annette Kolodny, *The Lay of the Land: Metaphor as Experience and History in American Life and Letters* (Chapel Hill: University of North Carolina Press, 1975); Kolodny, "Letting Go Our Grand Obsessions: Notes toward a New Literary History of the American Frontiers," *American Literature* 64 (1992): 1–18.

58. See Judith Fetterley, *The Resisting Reader: A Feminist Approach to American Fiction* (Bloomington: Indiana University Press, 1978).

59. Nina Baym, "Melodramas of Beset Manhood: How Theories of American Fiction Exclude Women Authors," reprinted in *Feminism and American Literary History: Essays* (New Brunswick: Rutgers University Press, 1992), 10.

60. Baym, "Melodramas of Beset Manhood," 18.

61. For the concept of fossilized poetic genres, see M. M. Bakhtin, "From the Prehistory of Novelistic Discourse," *The Dialogic Imagination*, 41–83.

62. Willis J. Buckingham comments on this change in the context and assumptions of American poetry criticism from the 1860s to the 1890s. See "Poetry Readers and Reading in the 1890s: Emily Dickinson's First Reception," in *Readers in History*, ed. James L. Machor (Baltimore: Johns Hopkins University Press, 1993), 164–79.

63. See Charles Molesworth, *Marianne Moore: A Literary Life* (New York: Atheneum, 1990).

64. Henry David Thoreau, *Walden* (New York: Collier, 1962), 151.

Chapter 2: Whitman as the American Homer

1. Chauncey C. Starkweather, "Special Introduction," *Essays of American Essayists*, rev. ed. (New York: Co-operative Publication Society, 1900), vi.

2. Van Wyck Brooks, *America's Coming-of-Age* (New York: Huebsch, 1915), 119–20. Kenneth M. Price, *Whitman and Tradition: The Poet in His Century* (New Haven: Yale University Press, 1990), 114, emphasizes the crucial role played by Brooks in early twentieth-century reception of Walt Whitman.

3. John Knapp, "National Poetry," *North American Review* 8 (1818): 169–76.

4. Stuart P. Sherman, "Walt Whitman," *Americans* (1922; reprint, New York: Scribner's, 1923), 155.

5. The frontispiece to the 1852 edition of Rufus Wilmot Griswold's *The Po-ets and Poetry of America, to the Middle of the Nineteenth Century* (Philadelphia: A. Hart) gives one schematic picture of the canon a few years before *Leaves of Grass*. The engraving features five poets. Alone at the top center is a naked bust of Dana in marble. Side by side below him are Bryant and Halleck in their street clothes; side by side below them are Sprague and Longfellow (who is the youngest and has the most hair).

6. Edward Tyrrel Channing, "On Models in Literature," *North American Review* 3 (July 1816): 207.

7. Park Benjamin, "Recent American Poetry," *United States Magazine and Democratic Review* 5 (June 1839): 541.

8. Margaret Fuller, "American Literature," reprinted in *The Writings of Margaret Fuller*, ed. Mason Wade (New York: Viking, 1941), 358.

9. "The Poet," in *The Collected Works of Ralph Waldo Emerson, Volume III: Essays: Second Series*, ed. Joseph Slater, Alfred R. Ferguson, and Jean Ferguson Carr (Cambridge, Mass.: Harvard University Press, 1983), 21.

10. Channing, "On Models in Literature," 208.

11. Fuller, "American Literature," 360.

12. George Edward Woodberry, *America in Literature* (London: Harper, 1903), 38.

13. William Cullen Bryant, review of Solyman Brown's *An Essay on American Poetry*, in *North American Review* 7 (July 1818): 200.

14. Fuller, "American Literature," 385.

15. Ibid., 365.

16. Richard H. Fogle, "Organic Form in American Criticism, 1840–1870," in *The Development of American Literary Criticism*, ed. Floyd Stovall (Chapel Hill: University of North Carolina Press, 1955), 90–91, 93.

17. Barrett Wendell, *A Literary History of America* (New York: Scribner's, 1901), 476.

18. Ibid., 466.

19. Brooks, *America's Coming-of-Age*, 164–65.

20. Ibid., 112.

21. Ibid., 125.

22. Bernard Smith, "Van Wyck Brooks," reprinted in *After the Genteel Tradition*, ed. Malcolm Cowley (Carbondale: Southern Illinois University Press, 1964), 58, 57.

23. Fuller, "American Literature," 381–82.

24. Ibid., 359.

25. Ibid.

26. Bliss Perry, *Walt Whitman: His Life and His Work* (Boston: Houghton, 1906), 6.

27. See Ngũgĩ wa Thiong'o, *Decolonising the Mind: The Politics of Language in African Literature* (London: James Currey, 1986). For an Americanist's analysis, see Lawrence Buell, "American Literary Emergence as a Postcolonial Phenomenon," *American Literary History* 4 (1992): 411–42.

28. See Darwin Shrell, "Nationalism and Aesthetics in the *North American*

Review: 1815–1850," *Studies in American Literature,* ed. Waldo McNeir and Leo B. Levy (Baton Rouge: Louisiana State University Press, 1960), 11–21.

29. E. P. Whipple, review of Rufus Griswold's *The Poets and Poetry of America,* in *North American Review* 58 (Jan. 1844): 37–39.

30. Ralph Waldo Emerson, "The American Scholar," *The Collected Works of Ralph Waldo Emerson Volume I: Nature, Addresses, and Lectures,* ed. Robert E. Spiller and Alfred R. Ferguson (Cambridge, Mass.: Harvard University Press, 1971).

31. Fuller, "American Literature," 359.

32. Channing, "On Models," 207.

33. Ngũgĩ, *Decolonising the Mind,* 17.

34. See especially Eric Cheyfitz, *The Poetics of Imperialism: Translation and Colonization from the Tempest to Tarzan* (New York: Oxford University Press, 1991).

35. Knapp, "National Poetry," 176.

36. Edgar Allan Poe, "Griswold's American Poetry," *Boston Miscellany of Literature* 2 (1842): 218.

37. Robert Walsh, review of Samuel Kettell's *Specimens of American Poetry,* in *American Quarterly Review* 6 (Sept. 1829): 262.

38. Bryant, review of Brown, 200.

39. Woodberry, *America in Literature,* 183–84.

40. Ibid., 38.

41. Ibid., 243.

42. Brooks, *America's Coming-of-Age,* 15.

43. Whipple, review of Griswold, 13.

44. A. H. Everett, "American Poets," *North American Review* 33 (Oct. 1831): 297–324.

45. See Thomas McFarland, *Originality & Imagination* (Baltimore: Johns Hopkins University Press, 1985).

46. Samuel Taylor Coleridge, *Biographia Literaria* (London: R. Fenner, 1817), chap. 20.

47. Jauss, "Literary History as a Challenge to Literary Theory," 12.

48. Fuller, "American Literature," 365.

49. Ibid., 360.

50. Angus Fletcher, "Style and the Extreme Situation," in *Textual Analysis,* ed. Mary Ann Caws (New York: Modern Language Association, 1986), 301.

51. For the concept of "scale-dependence" in literary study, see N. Katherine Hayles, "Chaos as Orderly Disorder: Shifting Ground in Contemporary Literature and Science," *New Literary History* 20 (1989): 305–22.

52. Edgar Allan Poe, review of Lydia Sigourney's *Southern Literary Messenger,* reprinted in *Essays and Reviews* (New York: Library of America, 1984), 882–83.

53. Edgar Allan Poe, review of Elizabeth Oakes Smith's *Godey's Lady's Book,* reprinted in *Essays and Reviews,* 915–16.

54. Edward Everett Hale, review of Walt Whitman's *Leaves of Grass,* in *North American Review* 42 (Jan. 1856): 275.

55. For a schematic discussion of these different imitative genres, see Genette, *Palimpsestes*.

56. William Cullen Bryant, "On Originality and Imitation," reprinted in *Prose Writings of William Cullen Bryant*, vol. 1, ed. Parke Godwin (New York: Appleton, 1884), 35.

57. Ibid., 39–40.

58. For the intense contradictions between solipsism and communal address in Whitman's poetics, see Greenspan, *Walt Whitman and the American Reader*, chap. 11.

59. Macy, *The Spirit of American Literature*, 212.

60. Ibid., 234.

61. Compare Carafiol's discussion of the dichotomy between thought and expression in the formulations of Transcendentalist scholarship (*The American Ideal*, 94–95).

62. George Santayana, "The Genteel Tradition in American Philosophy," reprinted in *Selected Critical Writings of George Santayana*, vol. 2, ed. Norman Henfrey (Cambridge: Cambridge University Press, 1968), 97.

63. R. W. B. Lewis, *The American Adam: Innocence, Tragedy and Tradition in the Nineteenth Century* (Chicago: University of Chicago Press, 1955), 44.

64. Emerson, "Literary Ethics," *The Collected Works*, 1:105–6.

65. Emerson, "The Poet," *The Collected Works*, 1:20.

66. Benjamin T. Spencer, *The Quest for Nationality: An American Literary Campaign* (Syracuse: Syracuse University Press, 1957), 150.

67. Emerson, *Nature*, 7.

68. Ibid., 36.

69. Emerson, "The Poet," 5–6.

70. See Susan Howe, "Encloser," in *The Politics of Poetic Form*, ed. Charles Bernstein (New York: ROOF, 1990), 175–96.

71. Bakhtin, "Discourse in the Novel," 270.

72. Sherman, "Walt Whitman," 165.

73. Betsy Erkkila, *Whitman the Political Poet* (New York: Oxford University Press, 1989), 282.

74. Sherman, "Walt Whitman," 155.

75. Fogle, "Organic Form in American Criticism," 90–91.

76. Knapp, "National Poetry," 172.

77. Fogle, "Organic Form in American Criticism," 75.

78. For the concept of *kulturragende Schicht*, see Robert C. Holub's discussion of Levin Schücking's work in *Reception Theory: A Critical Introduction* (London: Methuen, 1984).

79. For more on Whipple see Denham Sutcliffe, "'Our Young American Macaulay,' Edwin Percy Whipple, 1819–1886," *New England Quarterly* 19 (1946): 3–18.

80. See Gail Hamilton, *A Battle of the Books* (Cambridge, Mass.: Riverside Press, 1870).

81. See Greenspan, *Walt Whitman and the American Reader*, 154.

82. Edwin P. Whipple, "Intellectual Health and Disease," in *Literature and Life* (1849; reprint, Boston: Osgood, 1871), 191.

83. Whipple, "Bryant," in *Literature and Life*, 304–5.
84. Perry, *Walt Whitman*, 56.
85. Brooks, *America's Coming-of-Age*, 119.
86. J. G. Holland, "Is It Poetry?" *Scribner's Monthly* 12 (May 1876): 123.
87. J. G. Holland, "Our Garnered Names," ibid. 16 (Oct. 1878): 896.
88. J. G. Holland, "Literary Eccentricity," ibid. 22 (Oct. 1881): 945–46.
89. Holland, "Our Garnered Names," 896.
90. Jauss, "Literary History as a Challenge to Literary Theory," 36.
91. Ibid.
92. T. W. Higginson, "Recent Poetry," *Nation* 33 (15 Dec. 1881): 476.
93. Robert Underwood Johnson, "Walt Whitman," *Remembered Yesterdays* (Boston: Little, 1923), 337.
94. T. W. Higginson, *Contemporaries* (Boston: Houghton, 1900), 84.
95. Higginson, "Recent Poetry," 476.
96. Arthur Gilman, *Poets' Homes: Pen and Pencil Sketches of American Poets and Their Homes* (Boston: Lothrop, 1879), 53–54.
97. For all these divergent Whitmans, see Willard, *Whitman's American Fame*.
98. See Mark Van Doren, "Walt Whitman, Stranger," *American Mercury* 35 (1935): 277–85.
99. See Henry Seidel Canby, *Walt Whitman: An American* (Boston: Houghton, 1943).
100. See Gay Wilson Allen, *The Solitary Singer: A Critical Biography of Walt Whitman* (New York: Macmillan, 1955); Roger Asselineau, *The Evolution of Walt Whitman* (Cambridge, Mass.: Harvard University Press, 1960, 1962).
101. Boris Tomasevskij, "Literature and Biography," reprinted in *Readings in Russian Poetics*, ed. Ladislav Matejka and Krystyna Pomorska, trans. Herbert Eagle (Cambridge, Mass.: MIT Press, 1971), 51–52.
102. See Greenspan, *Walt Whitman and the American Reader*; Price, *Whitman and Tradition*; and Mark Delancey, "Texts, Interpretations, and Whitman's 'Song of Myself,'" *American Literature* 61 (1989): 359–81.
103. For the concept, see J. Hillis Miller, "The Critic as Host," in *Deconstruction and Criticism* (New York: Seabury Press, 1979), 217–53.

Chapter 3: Dickinson: Reading the "Supposed Person"

1. *Emily Dickinson: Selected Letters*, ed. Thomas H. Johnson (Cambridge, Mass.: Harvard University Press, 1986), 173.
2. For a critique of "book-centered" approaches to literary tradition, see Marilyn Butler, "Against Tradition: The Case for a Particularized Historical Method," in *Historical Studies and Literary Criticism*, ed. Jerome J. McGann (Madison: University of Wisconsin Press, 1985), 25–47.
3. *Dickinson: Selected Letters*, 179.
4. Dickinson writes: "'What do I think of *Middlemarch*?' What do I think of glory—except that in a few instances this 'mortal has already put on immortality.' George Eliot is one" (letter of late April 1873 to Louise and Frances Norcross, *Dickinson: Selected Letters*, 217).
5. For the best historical situation of Dickinson within the demands the role

of a woman writer placed upon her, see Joanne Dobson, *Dickinson and the Strategies of Reticence: The Woman Writer in Nineteenth-Century America* (Bloomington: Indiana University Press, 1989).

6. For the discontinuities of the Dickinson texts, see especially Sharon Cameron, *Choosing Not Choosing: Dickinson's Fascicles* (Chicago: University of Chicago Press, 1992).

7. Letter of July 1862, *Dickinson: Selected Letters*, 176.

8. George F. Whicher, "A Centennial Appraisal," reprinted in *The Recognition of Emily Dickinson: Selected Criticism since 1890*, ed. Caesar R. Blake and Carlton F. Wells (Ann Arbor: University of Michigan Press, 1964), 139.

9. Margaret Dickie, "Dickinson's Discontinuous Lyric Self," *American Literature* 60 (1988): 537.

10. Ibid., 539.

11. See John White Chadwick, "Poems by Emily Dickenson [*sic*]" and "Emily Dickinson," reprinted in *Emily Dickinson's Reception in the 1890s: A Documentary History*, ed. Willis J. Buckingham (Pittsburgh: University of Pittsburgh Press, 1989), 62–64, 102–5.

12. "Recent Books of Verse," reprinted in *Emily Dickinson's Reception in the 1890s*, 317.

13. The complicated situation of Dickinson's publication history makes it necessary to cite the poems several different ways. I have always used the text from *Poems by Emily Dickinson* (1937). But I have also always included the poem number used by Thomas H. Johnson in *The Poems of Emily Dickinson* (Cambridge, Mass.: Harvard University Press, 1955).

14. Mabel Loomis Todd, "Introductory" to *Letters of Emily Dickinson*, reprinted in *Emily Dickinson's Reception in the 1890s*, 342.

15. Ibid.

16. Todd's "*no*" can be seen in the facsimile (*The Manuscript Books of Emily Dickinson*, ed. R. W. Franklin [Cambridge, Mass.: Harvard University Press, 1981], 981). The 1929 text of this poem is an excellent example of a hymn-stanza relineated as free verse.

17. See Chadwick's reference to this poem's "pretty blasphemies" ("Emily Dickinson," 102).

18. Arlo Bates, "Miss Dickinson's Poems," reprinted in *Emily Dickinson's Reception in the 1890s*, 32.

19. See Paula Bennett, "The Pea That Duty Locks: Lesbian and Feminist-Heterosexual Readings of Emily Dickinson's Poetry," in *Lesbian Texts and Contexts*, ed. Karla Jay and Joanne Glasgow (New York: New York University Press, 1990), 104–25.

20. Allen Tate, "Emily Dickinson," reprinted in *The Recognition of Emily Dickinson*, 164.

21. See Philip J. Klass, *UFO Abductions: A Dangerous Game*, updated edition (Buffalo: Prometheus, 1989), for a deconstruction of the typical abduction story and a fine analysis of the culture of the occultist interpretive community.

22. See Timothy Morris, "The Development of Dickinson's Style," *American Literature* 60 (1988): 27.

23. See Timothy Morris, "The Free-rhyming Poetry of Emerson and Dickinson," *Essays in Literature* 12 (1985): 225–40. For much fuller treatments of Dickinson's style and its relation to that of her contemporaries, see Cristanne Miller, *Emily Dickinson: A Poet's Grammar* (Cambridge, Mass.: Harvard University Press, 1987), and Judy Jo Small, *Positive as Sound: Emily Dickinson's Rhyme* (Athens: University of Georgia Press, 1990).

24. Maurice Thompson, "Miss Dickinson's Poems," reprinted in *Emily Dickinson's Reception in the 1890s*, 95.

25. Arlo Bates, "Literary Affairs in Boston," reprinted in *Emily Dickinson's Reception in the 1890s*, 190.

26. Anonymous, "Form and Substance," reprinted in *Emily Dickinson's Reception in the 1890s*, 120.

27. Thomas Bailey Aldrich, "In Re Emily Dickinson," reprinted in *Emily Dickinson's Reception in the 1890s*, 283, 284.

28. Louise Chandler Moulton, "With the Poets," reprinted in *Emily Dickinson's Reception in the 1890s*, 244.

29. T. W. Higginson, "Emily Dickinson's Letters," reprinted in *Emily Dickinson's Reception in the 1890s*, 190.

30. See Chadwick, "Emily Dickinson," 104.

31. Carrie Blake, "Emily Dickinson," reprinted in *Emily Dickinson's Reception in the 1890s*, 111. Blake's article is a report of a talk on the poet given by Heloise Edwina Hersey.

32. Rupert Hughes, "The Ideas of Emily Dickinson," reprinted in *Emily Dickinson's Reception in the 1890s*, 501.

33. In terms just of Dickinson's own composition of the poems, "A sloop of amber slips away" is probably a very late reworking of "Where ships of purple gently toss." Johnson dates the manuscripts respectively as 1861 and 1884.

34. Andrew Lang, "Some American Poets," reprinted in *Emily Dickinson's Reception in the 1890s*, 82.

35. Martha Dickinson Bianchi, *The Life and Letters of Emily Dickinson* (Boston: Houghton, 1924), 52–53.

36. See Genevieve Taggard, *The Life and Mind of Emily Dickinson* (New York: Knopf, 1930); George Frisbie Whicher, *This Was a Poet: A Critical Biography of Emily Dickinson* (New York: Scribner's, 1938).

37. Percy Lubbock, "Determined Little Anchoress," reprinted in *The Recognition of Emily Dickinson*, 119–20.

38. Theodore Spencer, "Concentration and Intensity," reprinted in *The Recognition of Emily Dickinson*, 132.

39. Bliss Carman, "A Note on Emily Dickinson," reprinted in *Emily Dickinson's Reception in the 1890s*, 505, 506, 507. One should note that Carman is here reading "This world is not conclusion " (P-501), of which the Todd edition provides only the first three stanzas, thereby making the poem appear to close on a note of Christian affirmation.

40. Bates, "Miss Dickinson's Poems," 29.

41. Hughes, "The Ideas of Emily Dickinson," 500, 502.

42. Ibid., 499.

43. Ellen Battelle Dietrick, "One-Sided Criticism," reprinted in *Emily Dickinson's Reception in the 1890s*, 291.

44. Harry Lyman Koopman, "Emily Dickinson," reprinted in *Emily Dickinson's Reception in the 1890s*, 512.

45. Ibid.

46. "A New England Nun" is the title story of an 1891 collection by Mary E. Wilkins (later Freeman) and was first connected explicitly to Dickinson's work by Louis J. Block, who used the phrase as the title of his *Dial* essay (reprinted in *Emily Dickinson's Reception in the 1890s*, 419–21.) See also Aliki Barnstone's "Houses within Houses: Emily Dickinson and Mary Wilkins Freeman's 'A New England Nun,'" *Centennial Review* 28 (1984): 129–45. Freeman's "A Poetess" may be even more relevant to the study of Dickinson in capturing the stereotypical role of a small-town woman writer. See "A New England Nun" (1–17) and "A Poetess" (140–59) in *A New England Nun* (New York: Harper, 1891).

47. Lubbock, "Determined Little Anchoress," 120.

48. Koopman, "Emily Dickinson," 510.

49. Ella Gilbert Ives, "Emily Dickinson: Her Poetry, Prose and Personality," reprinted in *The Recognition of Emily Dickinson*, 76.

50. William Dean Howells, "Editor's Study," reprinted in *Emily Dickinson's Reception in the 1890s*, 78.

51. Elizabeth Shepley Sergeant, "An Early Imagist," reprinted in *The Recognition of Emily Dickinson*, 89.

52. Whicher, *This Was a Poet*, 153, 165.

53. See Yvor Winters, "Emily Dickinson and the Limits of Judgment," in *The Recognition of Emily Dickinson*, 187–200; R. P. Blackmur, "Emily Dickinson: Notes on Prejudice and Fact," in *The Recognition of Emily Dickinson*, 323–47; "Emily Dickinson," *The Complete Prose of Marianne Moore* (New York: Viking, 1986), 290–93.

54. See Susan Miles, "The Irregularities of Emily Dickinson," *The London Mercury* 13 (Dec. 1925): 145–58; T. Walter Herbert, "Near-Rimes and Paraphones," *Sewanee Review* 45 (1937): 433–52.

55. Whicher, *This Was a Poet*, 167.

56. Conrad Aiken, "Emily Dickinson," reprinted in *The Recognition of Emily Dickinson*, 114.

57. Ibid., 114.

58. Ibid., 117.

59. Ibid., 115.

60. Ibid., 116.

61. Norman Foerster, "Emily Dickinson," in *The Recognition of Emily Dickinson*, 95.

62. Ibid., 96–97. One might as well point out that for all his sense of region, Foerster places the poet several miles west of where she actually lived.

63. Ibid., 96.

64. Ibid., 97.

65. Bianchi, *The Life and Letters of Emily Dickinson*, 47.

66. There is active in the 1990s a considerable minority of Dickinson schol-

ars devoted to proving the existence of her love affair with Charles Wadsworth. See William H. Shurr, *The Marriage of Emily Dickinson: A Study of the Fascicles* (Lexington: University Press of Kentucky, 1983). There is, however, a breathtaking absence of evidence for any of Dickinson's supposed love affairs, except for her fierce lifelong attachment to Susan Gilbert Dickinson and her restrained courtship late in life with Otis Lord.

67. Taggard, *The Life and Mind of Emily Dickinson*, 121.

68. Ibid., 121–22.

69. Whicher, *This Was a Poet*, 97, 99.

70. Allen Tate, "New England Culture and Emily Dickinson," reprinted in *The Recognition of Emily Dickinson*, 157.

71. For Matthiessen's refusal to read his sexuality into his scholarship, see Michael Cadden, "Engendering F.O.M.: The Private Life of *American Renaissance*," in *Engendering Men*, ed. Joseph A. Boone and Michael Cadden (New York: Routledge, 1990), 26–35.

72. Granville Hicks, "Emily Dickinson and the Gilded Age," in *The Recognition of Emily Dickinson*, 171.

73. T. O. Matthiessen, "The Private Poet: Emily Dickinson," reprinted in *The Recognition of Emily Dickinson*, 224.

74. Robert Hillyer, "Emily Dickinson," reprinted in *The Recognition of Emily Dickinson*, 103–4.

75. See Mary Loeffelholz, *Dickinson and the Boundaries of Feminist Theory* (Urbana: University of Illinois Press, 1991).

76. Edward Sapir, "Emily Dickinson, a Primitive," *Poetry* 26 (1925): 105.

77. See "The Metaphysical Poets" (1921), in *Selected Prose of T. S. Eliot*, ed. Frank Kermode (London: Faber, 1975), 63.

78. Tate, "New England Culture and Emily Dickinson," 156.

79. Ibid., 157.

80. Ibid.

81. Ibid., 161–62.

82. Ibid., 167.

83. Ibid.

84. Ibid., 159.

85. Ibid., 163.

86. Blackmur, "Emily Dickinson," 217–18.

87. Ibid., 201.

88. Ibid., 218.

89. See Eco, "Introduction: The Role of the Reader."

90. Blackmur, "Emily Dickinson," 219.

91. Ibid., 218.

92. Ibid., 219.

93. Ibid., 220.

94. Ibid., 223.

95. Eunice Glenn, "Emily Dickinson's Poetry: A Revaluation," *Sewanee Review* 51 (1943): 574–75.

96. Moore, "Emily Dickinson," 292.

Chapter 4: Marianne Moore: The Porcelain Garden

1. The best example of Moore criticism dealing with her and with the male poets of her generation is John Updike's "Notes" in the *New Yorker* (26 Jan. 1957): 28–29. The essay is a humor piece that pokes fun at Eliot, Pound, and Moore for what Updike perceives as the pedantry of high modernism.

2. See Celeste Goodridge, *Hints and Disguises: Marianne Moore and Her Contemporaries* (Iowa City: University of Iowa Press, 1989).

3. See Louise Bogan, review of Marianne Moore's *Nevertheless*, *New Yorker* (11 Nov. 1944): 88–89; Wallace Fowlie, "Marianne Moore," *Sewanee Review* 60 (1952): 537–47; Delmore Schwartz, "The Art of Marianne Moore," *New Republic* (4 Jan. 1960): 19; Hugh Kenner, "Meditation and Enactment," *Poetry* 102 (1963): 109–15.

4. *The Complete Poems of Marianne Moore* (1967; reprint, New York: Penguin, 1982), back cover.

5. Winthrop Sargeant, "Humility, Concentration, and Gusto," *New Yorker* (16 Feb. 1957): 39.

6. William Carlos Williams, "Marianne Moore" (1925), reprinted in *Marianne Moore: A Collection of Critical Essays*, ed. Charles Tomlinson (Englewood Cliffs, N.J.: Prentice-Hall, 1969), 54.

7. T. S. Eliot, "Marianne Moore" (1923), reprinted in ibid., 49.

8. Ibid.

9. T. S. Eliot, "Introduction," in Marianne Moore, *Selected Poems* (New York: Macmillan, 1935), viii.

10. Kenner, "Meditation and Enactment," 115.

11. Eliot, "Introduction," xi.

12. Williams, "Marianne Moore," 52.

13. Fuller, "American Literature," 385.

14. Williams, "Marianne Moore," 54.

15. Ibid., 55.

16. Fuller, "American Literature," 365.

17. Williams, "Marianne Moore," 57.

18. Bakhtin, "Discourse in the Novel," 297.

19. Ibid., 279. For more on the dialogic potential of poetry, see Richter, "Dialogism and Poetry."

20. According to Viktor Shklovskii, "The technique of art is to make objects 'unfamiliar,' to make forms difficult, to increase the difficulty and length of perception because the process of perception is an end in itself and must be prolonged" ("Art as Technique" [1917], *Russian Formalist Criticism: Four Essays*, trans. Lee. T. Lemon and Marion J. Reis [Lincoln: University of Nebraska Press, 1965], 12).

21. Hicks, "Emily Dickinson and the Gilded Age," 171–72.

22. Williams, "Marianne Moore," 58.

23. Ibid., 54.

24. Ibid.

25. See Harold Bloom, "Introduction," *Marianne Moore* (New York: Chelsea House, 1987), 1–9.

26. See, for instance, "Wish for a Young Wife," *The Collected Poems of Theodore Roethke* (Garden City, N.Y.: Doubleday, 1966), 217; Denise Levertov, "Who He Was," *Collected Earlier Poems 1940–1968* (New York: New Directions, 1979), 11.

27. Charles Tomlinson, "Abundance, Not Too Much," in *Marianne Moore*, ed. Tomlinson, 10.

28. Ibid. 11.

29. Kenneth Burke, "Motives and Motifs in the Poetry of Marianne Moore" (1942), reprinted in ibid., 96.

30. The ne plus ultra of such totalizing readings of *The Waste Land* is surely Everett Gillis, *The Waste Land as Grail Romance: Eliot's Use of the Medieval Grail Legends* (Lubbock: Texas Tech Press, 1974).

31. David Bergman, "Marianne Moore and the Problem of 'Marriage,'" *American Literature* 60 (1988): 241–54.

32. Tate, "New England Culture and Emily Dickinson," 157.

33. R. P. Blackmur, "The Method of Marianne Moore," in *Marianne Moore*, ed. Tomlinson, 84–85.

34. Ibid., 85.

35. Ibid., 85–86.

36. Louis Simpson, "Poetry Chronicle," *Hudson Review* 16 (1963): 131–32.

37. Harriet Monroe, "A Symposium on Marianne Moore," *Poetry* 19 (1922): 210.

38. See Morton Dauwen Zabel, "A Literalist of the Imagination," *Poetry* 47 (1936): 326–36.

39. See, for instance, Robert Cantwell, "The Poet, the Bums, and the Legendary Red Men," *Sports Illustrated* (15 Feb. 1960): 74–84.

40. Ezra Pound, "Marianne Moore and Mina Loy," in *Marianne Moore*, ed. Tomlinson, 46.

41. Williams, "Marianne Moore," 52.

42. Rebecca Price Parkin, "Certain Difficulties in Reading Marianne Moore: Exemplified in Her 'Apparition of Splendor,'" *PMLA* 81 (1966): 167–72.

43. Eliot, "Introduction," xi.

44. Charles Tomlinson, "Introduction," in *Marianne Moore*, ed. Tomlinson, 4–5.

45. See Philip Ferguson Legler, "Marianne Moore and the Idea of Freedom," *Poetry* 83 (1953): 158–65.

46. Howard Nemerov, "A Few Bricks from Babel," *Sewanee Review* 62 (1954): 655.

47. On suggestions that Moore may be a moralist, Oliver Evans says simply: "Fortunately this is not true of her best work." See "Poetry: 1930 to the Present," in *American Literary Scholarship: An Annual 1964*, ed. James Woodress (Durham: Duke University Press, 1966), 208.

48. Randall Jarrell, "Her Shield" (1953), reprinted in *Marianne Moore*, ed. Tomlinson, 117.

49. Ibid., 116–17.

50. Ibid., 122.

51. See Randall Jarrell, "Fifty Years of American Poetry," *Prairie Schooner* 37 (1963): 1–27.

52. "Best Living Poet," *Newsweek* (24 Dec. 1951): 69–71. See also *Esquire* (June 1966).

53. See Charles Molesworth, *Marianne Moore: A Literary Life* (New York: Atheneum, 1990); George Plimpton, "The World Series with Marianne Moore," *Harper's* 229 (Oct. 1964): 50–58.

54. Lloyd Frankenberg, "Marianne Moore's Imaginary Garden," *Pleasure Dome: On Reading Modern Poetry* (1949; New York: Gordian Press, 1968), 151.

55. Fowlie, "Marianne Moore," 539, 541.

56. Ibid., 547.

57. Stanley J. Kunitz, "The Pangolin of Poets," *Poetry* 59 (1941): 98.

58. Updike, "Notes," 28.

59. Robert Bly, "A Wrong Turning in American Poetry" (1963), reprinted in *American Poetry: Wildness and Domesticity* (New York: Harper, 1990), 11. The title of this very recent edition of Bly's collected essays perpetuates the paleface and redskin dichotomy.

60. M. L. Rosenthal, "Ladies' Day on Parnassus," *Nation* 184 (16 Mar. 1957): 239–40.

61. Louise Bogan, "Verse," *New Yorker* 30 (4 Sept. 1954): 75–76; Hugh Kenner, "Supreme in Her Abnormality," *Poetry* 84 (1954): 356–63.

62. Nemerov, "A Few Bricks from Babel," 655.

63. Simpson, "Poetry Chronicle."

64. Howe, "The Greenest Land She's Almost Seen," *New Republic* 132 (23 May 1955): 20.

65. See Alfred Kreymborg, *Troubadour: An Autobiography* (New York: Boni, 1925), 245.

66. Kenneth Burke, "Likings of an Observationist," *Poetry* 87 (1956): 239–47.

67. Kenner, "Meditation and Enactment," 114–15.

68. *The Complete Prose of Marianne Moore,* 441.

69. Elizabeth Bishop, "Efforts of Affection: A Memoir of Marianne Moore," *The Collected Prose* (New York: Farrar, 1984), 143.

70. Erkkila, *The Wicked Sisters,* 101.

71. Ibid., 108.

72. See Lois Bar-Yaacov, "Marianne Moore, Ezra Pound: In Distrust of Whose Merits?" *American Literature* 63 (1991): 1–25.

Chapter 5: Constraint and Recuperation in the Early Reception of Elizabeth Bishop

1. See Baym, "Melodramas of Beset Manhood."

2. See Norma Procopiow, "Survival Kit: The Poetry of Elizabeth Bishop," *The Centennial Review* 25.1 (1981): 1–19.

3. Stephen Stepanchev, *American Poetry since 1945: A Critical Survey* (New York: Harper, 1965), 70, 79.

4. Ibid., 74.

5. Louise Bogan, "Verse," *New Yorker* (5 Oct. 1946): 113–14.

6. Robert Lowell, "Thomas, Bishop, and Williams," *Sewanee Review* 55 (1947): 497.

7. Randall Jarrell, "The Poet and His Public," *Partisan Review* 13 (1946): 499.

8. Jarrell, "Fifty Years of American Poetry," 21.

9. Irvin Ehrenpreis, "Solitude and Isolation," *Virginia Quarterly Review* 42 (1966): 332–33.

10. William Jay Smith, "New Books of Poems," *Harper's* 233 (Aug. 1966): 90.

11. H. T. Kirby-Smith, Jr., "Miss Bishop and Others," *Sewanee Review* 80 (1972): 484.

12. Frankenberg, *Pleasure Dome*, 332, 333.

13. Ibid., 337.

14. Oscar Williams, "North but South," *New Republic* (21 Oct. 1946): 525.

15. Marianne Moore, "A Modest Expert," *The Nation* (28 Sept. 1946): 354.

16. James G. Southworth, "The Poetry of Elizabeth Bishop," *College English* 20 (1959): 213.

17. Donald Hall, review of Elizabeth Bishop's *Poems*, in *New England Quarterly* 29 (1956): 251, 252.

18. Howard Nemerov, "The Poems of Elizabeth Bishop," *Poetry* 87 (1955): 182.

19. Edwin Honig, "Poetry Chronicle," *Partisan Review* 23 (1956): 115.

20. Ibid., 116.

21. Ibid., 116–17.

22. Ibid., 117.

23. See Bly, "A Wrong Turning in American Poetry," 26.

24. Nemerov, "The Poems of Elizabeth Bishop," 180; Honig, "Poetry Chronicle," 117.

25. Smith, "New Books of Poems," 90.

26. Louis L. Martz, "Recent Poetry: Looking for a Home," *Yale Review* 55 (1966): 459.

27. Ibid., 459–60.

28. Howard Moss, "All Praise," *Kenyon Review* 28 (1966): 256.

29. Peter Michelson, "Sentiment and Artifice: Elizabeth Bishop and Isabella Gardner," *Chicago Review* 18.3–4 (1966): 189.

30. Ibid., 193.

31. Martz, "Recent Poetry," 460.

32. Frank J. Warnke, "The Voyages of Elizabeth Bishop," *New Republic* (9 Apr. 1966): 21.

33. Daniel Hughes, "American Poetry 1969: From B to Z," *Massachusetts Review* 11 (1970): 682.

34. Jan B. Gordon, "Days and Distances: The Cartographic Imagination of Elizabeth Bishop," *Salamgundi* 22–23 (1973): 300.

35. Ibid., 302.

36. Ruth Quebe, "Water, Windows and Birds: Image-Theme Patterns in Elizabeth Bishop's *Questions of Travel*," *Modern Poetry Studies* 10.1 (1980): 68–82.

37. David Kalstone, "Questions of Memory—New Poems by Elizabeth Bishop," *Ploughshares* 2.4 (1975): 173–81.

38. Calvin Bedient, "Desultorily Yours," *Sewanee Review* 86 (1978): 292, 293.

39. Harold Bloom, "Geography III by Elizabeth Bishop," *New Republic* (5 Feb. 1977): 29.

40. Ibid., 30.

41. John Hollander, "Questions of Geography," *Parnassus* 5 (1977): 363.

42. David Bromwich, "Verse Chronicle," *Hudson Review* 30 (1977): 280.

43. Tomasevskij, "Literature and Biography," 53.

44. Compare also Thomas J. Travisano, *Elizabeth Bishop: Her Artistic Development* (Charlottesville: University of Virginia Press, 1988), which takes a similar developmental approach to Bishop's career. Travisano is less biographical and more abstract, however, saying of Bishop finally that "she simply wrote poems" (6).

45. Procopiow, "Survival Kit," 2.

46. Ibid., 17.

47. Robert Dale Parker, *The Unbeliever: The Poetry of Elizabeth Bishop* (Urbana: University of Illinois Press, 1988), 30.

48. See Patricia Storace, "Visits to St. Elizabeth's," *Parnassus* 12.2/13.1 (1985): 163–78; Victoria Harrison, "The Dailiness of Her Center: Elizabeth Bishop's Late Poetry," *Twentieth Century Literature* 37 (1991): 253–72; Renée R. Curry, "Augury and Autobiography: Bishop's 'Crusoe in England,'" *Arizona Quarterly* 47.3 (1991): 71–91; Jeredith Merrin, *An Enabling Humility: Marianne Moore, Elizabeth Bishop, and the Uses of Tradition* (New Brunswick: Rutgers University Press, 1990); Jacqueline Vaught Brogan, "Elizabeth Bishop: Perversity as Voice," *American Poetry* 7.2 (1990): 31–49; Lois Cucullu, "Trompe l'Oeil: Elizabeth Bishop's Radical 'I,'" *Texas Studies in Literature and Language* 30 (1988): 246–71.

49. See Marilyn May Lombardi, "The Closet of Breath: Elizabeth Bishop, Her Body and Her Art," *Twentieth Century Literature* 38 (1992): 152–75.

50. See Jane Shore, "Elizabeth Bishop: The Art of Changing Your Mind," *Ploughshares* 5.1 (1979): 178–91.

51. Bonnie Costello, *Elizabeth Bishop: Questions of Mastery* (Cambridge, Mass.: Harvard University Press, 1991).

52. Ibid., 3.

53. Ibid., 11.

54. Susan Schultz's essay "Marianne Moore and Elizabeth Bishop," *Wilson Quarterly* 13.3 (1989): 128–38, was a kind of watershed in open scholarly discussion of Bishop's lesbian sexuality.

55. One can read the critical collections edited by Harold Bloom or by Schwartz and Estess without ever becoming aware of the poet's sexuality. For a critique of sexual silences in Bishop studies, see Sue Russell, "A Slight Transvestite Twist: Elizabeth Bishop's Lifetime 'Impersonation' of an Ordinary Woman," *Lambda Book Report* 3.10 (May/June 1993): 8–10.

56. Jonathan Raban, "The Idea of Elsewhere," *New Republic* 209 (19/26 July 1993): 36.

57. Lorrie Goldensohn, *Elizabeth Bishop: The Biography of a Poetry* (New York: Columbia University Press, 1992), 29.

58. Ibid., 64.

59. See C. Jan Swearingen, *Rhetoric and Irony: Western Literacy and Western Lies* (New York: Oxford University Press, 1991).

60. Curry, "Augury and Autobiography," 72.

61. See Michaelangelo Signorile, *Queer in America* (New York: Random House, 1993).

62. Goldensohn, *Elizabeth Bishop*, 233.

63. The most thorough interrogation of the concepts and ideologies of American literary studies is William C. Spengemann's *A Mirror for Americanists: Reflections on the Idea of American Literature* (Hanover, N.H.: University Press of New England, 1989).

64. An interesting example in recent Bishop criticism is Robert Boschman, "Anne Bradstreet and Elizabeth Bishop: Nature, Culture and Gender in 'Contemplations' and 'At the Fishhouses,'" *Journal of American Studies* 26 (1992): 247–60. Boschman makes a fine synthetic comparison of the two poems. But what is particularly interesting is the rhetorical framework of the essay, which assumes that there is no need to defend a comparison of these two poets who are remote in time and culture from each other. In the Americanist project, there *is* no need to defend comparing Bradstreet with anyone, however little her poetry may, on the face of it, have to do with theirs.

65. Goldensohn, *Elizabeth Bishop*, 210.

66. Erkkila, *The Wicked Sisters*, 144.

67. Lynn Keller, *Re-making It New: Contemporary American Poetry and the Modernist Tradition* (Cambridge: Cambridge University Press, 1987).

68. Bishop comments on Brazilian people in her letters: "They haven't the faintest idea how to treat pets, and imported them at I hate to think what expense"; "the general level of looks is rather low, I'm afraid—and the ugliness of the 'poor people'—I don't know what to call them—is *appalling—nobody* seems 'well-made', except some of the Negroes" (Brett C. Millier, *Elizabeth Bishop: Life and the Memory of It* [Berkeley: University of California Press, 1993], 261, 264).

69. Deborah Weiner, "'Difference That Kills'/Difference That Heals: Representing Latin America in the Poetry of Elizabeth Bishop and Margaret Atwood," in *Comparative Literature East and West: Traditions and Trends*, ed. Cornelia N. Moore and Raymond A. Moody (Honolulu: College of Languages, Linguistics and Literature, University of Hawaii, 1989), 208.

70. David Bromwich writes: "Poems about squatters and other half-cherished neighbors—efforts of self-conscious whimsy (like 'Manuelzinho') or of awkward condescension (like 'Filling Station') . . . are the only poems Bishop ever wrote that dwindle as one comes to see them more clearly" ("Elizabeth Bishop's Dream-Houses," *Raritan* 4.1 [1984]: 77–94).

71. Other critics have made this assumption; see Goldensohn, *Elizabeth Bishop*, 261.

72. Millier, *Elizabeth Bishop*, 513–14.

73. David Shapiro, "On a Villanelle by Elizabeth Bishop," *Iowa Review* 10 (1979): 79–80.

Conclusion

1. See Barbara Antonina Clarke Mossberg, *When a Writer Is a Daughter* (Bloomington: Indiana University Press, 1982); Joanne Dobson, *Dickinson and the Strategies of Reticence* (Bloomington: Indiana University Press, 1989); Loeffelholz, *Dickinson and the Boundaries of Feminist Theory;* Cynthia Griffin Wolff, *Emily Dickinson* (New York: Knopf, 1986).

2. Paula Bennett, *Emily Dickinson: Woman Poet* (Iowa City: University of Iowa Press, 1990); Martha Nell Smith, *Rowing in Eden: Rereading Emily Dickinson* (Austin: University of Texas Press, 1992). References will be parenthetical in the text.

3. See Judith Farr's analysis of Emily and Susan in *The Passion of Emily Dickinson* (Cambridge, Mass.: Harvard University Press, 1992). Betsy Erkkila also reconsiders this relationship in *The Wicked Sisters*.

4. Technically, the sharp distinction between letters and poems is a flaw in the Johnson editions of both. It should be noted, however, that Johnson erred on the side of printing texts twice if they occurred in letters but seemed to be poems as well. Logically, one can only identify a letter, not a poem. If a text is sent to a recipient or drafted as though it were to be sent, it's a letter; whether it's prose or poetry after that point is undecidable. That a text is by rhetorical frame or documentary provenance a letter is a more valuable piece of information than whether a critic thinks that text is poetic. Johnson's generic assignments have caused confusion, a confusion severely but judiciously critiqued by Smith; by Bennett in " 'By a Mouth That Cannot Speak': Spectral Presence in Emily Dickinson's Letters," *Emily Dickinson Journal* 1.2 (1992): 76–99; and by Jo-Anne Cappeluti in "Fading Ratios: Johnson's Variorum Edition of Emily Dickinson's Poetry," *Emily Dickinson Journal* 1.2 (1992): 100–120. Yet in the light of Bennett's claim that "Johnson . . . was re-writing her texts" ("By a Mouth," 84), one should insist on a basic fact: Johnson reproduced every known Dickinson text to a standard of faithfulness rarely matched in textual scholarship, and he did not change, alter, or suppress anything in those texts. These critiques of Johnson boil down to dissatisfaction because he chose to adopt print conventions.

5. When trying to confront Betsy Erkkila's powerful discussion of Dickinson's class situation in "Emily Dickinson and Class," *American Literary History* 4 (1992), Smith falls back on disparaging Erkkila by claiming that she got most of her data on Dickinson's class attitudes from sources contaminated by Todd (232–33). At times when reading *Rowing in Eden* one gets the impression that what Richard B. Sewall calls "The War between the Houses," in which the Todd and Dickinson camps fought over Emily's literary legacy, has never ceased. It is a feud still being carried on by academic proxies many years after the deaths of the last descendants of those who started it.

6. Millier, *Elizabeth Bishop*, 237.

7. Elizabeth Bishop, "Unseemly Deductions," *New Republic* (18 Aug. 1952): 20.

8. Ibid.

Index

Aiken, Conrad, 71
Alcott, Bronson, 123
Aldrich, Thomas Bailey, 62, 68, 115–16
Allen, Gay Wilson, 51
American Indians: in critical discourse, 2, 18, 31, 34, 67
An American in Paris, 13
American literary nationalism, 27, 31–35, 44, 96, 126–27, 129, 141, 143
Animal House, 100
Anthon, Kate Scott, 143–44
Asselineau, Roger, 51
Assimilation, 25
Auden, W. H., 104, 131
Austen, Jane, 149*n*

Bakhtin, M. M., 3–4, 44, 86–87, 89
Barbarism: as critical value, 28, 67
Barnstone, Aliki, 158*n*
Barthes, Roland, 130
Bar-Yaacov, Lois, 102
Bates, Arlo, 59, 61–62, 67
Baym, Nina, 20, 104, 126
Beatles, 3
Becker, Carl L., 7
Bedient, Calvin, 117
Benjamin, Park, 28
Bennett, Paula, 60, 134–37
Bergman, David, 90
Bianchi, Martha Dickinson, 66, 72, 91, 138
Bible, 12, 140–41
Bishop, Elizabeth, 8, 17, 52, 103; biographical image, 23; on Marianne Moore, 84, 92, 101–2; reception, 104–31, "At the Fishhouses," 111–12; *Questions of Travel*, 112–15; "Visits to St. Elizabeths," 114; on Emily Dickinson, 143–44
Blackmur, R. P.: on Emily Dickinson, 66, 70, 75, 77–79; on Marianne Moore, 90, 92, 96
Blasing, Mutlu Konuk, 16–17
Bloom, Harold, 12, 16–17, 81; on Marianne Moore, 88; on Elizabeth Bishop, 117–18
Bly, Robert, 98
Bogan, Louise, 99, 103; on Marianne Moore, 82; on Elizabeth Bishop, 107
Boschman, Robert, 165*n*
Bradstreet, Anne, 2, 135, 165*n*
Brogan, Jacqueline Vaught, 121
Bromwich, David, 17, 117–18, 165*n*
Brooklyn Dodgers, 93, 100–101
Brooks, Gwendolyn, 103
Brooks, Van Wyck, 27, 31, 36, 47, 76
Bryant, William Cullen, 37, 42, 45–48, 79, 86, 152*n*; as candidate for the American Homer, 28; and organicism, 30; on nationalism, 35; on originality, 41
Burke, Kenneth, 88–89, 100
Butler, Marilyn, 155*n*
Byron, George Gordon, 74

Cameron, Sharon, 156*n*
Canby, Henry Seidel, 51
Cappeluti, Jo-Anne, 166*n*

TIMOTHY MORRIS is assistant professor of English at the University of Texas at Arlington. He teaches American poetry, American women writers, and sport literature; his articles on these subjects have appeared in *American Literature*, *ATQ*, *English in Texas*, *Essays in Literature*, *Studies in American Fiction*, and *Studies in the Novel*. He lives in Dallas with his wife, Margaret, and his son, Fran.